3 1134 00293 238

D1164033

E   Eisenhower Public Library
4613 N. Oketo Avenue
Harwood Heights, Il. 60706

708-867-7828

Hayek's Journey

Also by Alan Ebenstein

The Greatest Happiness Principle:
An Examination of Utilitarianism

Great Political Thinkers: Plato to the Present

Introduction to Political Thinkers

Today's Isms: Socialism, Capitalism,
Fascism, Communism, Libertarianism

Edwin Cannan: Liberal Doyen

Friedrich Hayek: A Biography

Hayek's Journey

The Mind of Friedrich Hayek

Alan Ebenstein

HAYEK'S JOURNEY
Copyright © Alan Ebenstein, 2003.
All rights reserved. No part of this book may be used or reproduced in any
manner whatsoever without written permission except in the case of brief
quotations embodied in critical articles or reviews.

First published in 2003 by PALGRAVE MACMILLAN™
175 Fifth Avenue, New York, N.Y. 10010 and
Houndmills, Basingstoke, Hampshire, England RG21 6XS.
Companies and representatives throughout the world.

PALGRAVE MACMILLAN IS THE GLOBAL ACADEMIC IMPRINT OF THE
PALGRAVE MACMILLAN division of St. Martin's Press, LLC and of Palgrave
Macmillan Ltd. Macmillan® is a registered trademark in the United States,
United Kingdom and other countries. Palgrave is a registered trademark in the
European Union and other countries.

1-4039-6038-0 hardback

Library of Congress Cataloging-in-Publication Data
is available from the Library of Congress

A catalogue record for this book is available from the British Library.

First Palgrave Macmillan edition: August 2003
10 9 8 7 6 5 4 3 2 1
Printed in the United States of America.

Contents

It is only by extending the rules of just conduct to the relations with all other men, and at the same time depriving of their obligatory character those rules which cannot be universally applied, that we can approach a universal order of peace which might integrate all mankind into a single society.

—Friedrich Hayek, *Law, Legislation and Liberty*

Preface and Acknowledgments

IN ANOTHER BOOK, *FRIEDRICH HAYEK: A BIOGRAPHY* (Palgrave, 2001), I presented aspects of Hayek's life and an overview of his thought. This book is different from the first, and readers of both will notice little overlap. While the first work was mostly biographical and historical, this one focuses on Hayek's thought and intellectual evolution.

Many good people assisted in the preparation of this book. I thank my editor at Palgrave, Michael Flamini, and others with Palgrave, particularly Alan Bradshaw and William Berry, first. A number of individuals read drafts of the manuscript or draft chapters, providing extensive and helpful comments and suggestions. I thank Lee Gientke, Nik Schiffmann, Jim Waddingham, Joe Atwill, Fiona Maclachlan, Bettina Bien Greaves, Sudha Shenoy, Tom Schrock, Gerald Steele, Hans Jörg Hennecke, David Theroux, Art Rupe, John DeLoreto, Rob Ebenstein, and Greg Ransom. The Hayek e-mail list moderated by Greg through the Friedrich Hayek Scholars' Page is a significant resource, and I thank those who participate in it.

A number of individuals assisted by providing recollections of Hayek. I thank Larry Hayek for graciously answering questions about his father on several occasions, Arthur Seldon for his continued interest in this project, and Charlotte Cubitt for sharing her recollections and materials. I thank Milton Friedman for his advice on several chapters. Others who assisted by providing information or in some other way include Ross Emmet, Leonard Liggio, Gordon Lloyd, Jim Powell, Peter Digeser, Malachi Haim Hacohen, Pete Boettke, Richard Ebeling, Eric McDaniel, and Walter Mead. Needless to say, none of the above is responsible for the accuracy of any of the information or interpretations here.

The Max Planck Institute funded my participation at a conference in Germany that was very helpful, as did the Liberty Fund for a conference on Frank Knight. I also should like to thank the Independent Institute and Cato Institute.

I hope that these books on Hayek will assist in understanding his life and thought. The first is more expressionistic and historical. This one is more impressionistic and philosophical. The first primarily concerns Hayek's life—what he experienced. This one is on his mind—the receptacle and driving force of his experience.

Alan Ebenstein
Santa Barbara, California
May 14, 2003

Introduction

We must make the building of a free society once more an intellectual adventure, a deed of courage. What we lack is a liberal Utopia, . . . a truly liberal radicalism. . . . The main lesson which the true liberal must learn from the success of the socialists is that it was their courage to be Utopian . . . which is daily making possible what only recently seemed utterly remote.

—Friedrich Hayek, *Studies in Philosophy, Politics, and Economics*

THIS BOOK IS INTENDED TO PRESENT THE EVOLUTION of the complete life work of Friedrich Hayek, the great Austrian political and pure philosopher. Hayek was the greatest philosopher of liberty in the twentieth century. Starting in 1944 with *The Road to Serfdom,* he enunciated a comprehensive philosophy of liberty that inspires the heart and mind. His great works in political philosophy after *The Road to Serfdom* were, in 1960, *The Constitution of Liberty;* from 1973 to 1979, the three volumes of *Law, Legislation and Liberty* (mostly written during the 1960s); and his late, unfinished "The Fatal Conceit."

Hayek's contributions are so protean in so many areas that there is now disagreement as to where he will be remembered most. Paradoxically, he may be unlikely to be remembered most as a technical economist. Hayek, indeed, emphasized that to be a good economist, one must be much more than an economist. For most of his professional career, from the 1940s through 1980s, he really became a social philosopher rather than an economist.

Hayek had his greatest impact in the area of the division of knowledge. He first put forward his concept of the division of knowledge in his November 10, 1936, presidential address to the London Economic Club, "Economics and Knowledge." Here he drew attention to the fact that knowledge is divided among the minds of all humanity.

Economic systems that build on divided knowledge prosper. Those that attempt to centralize decision-making, on the assumption of centralized knowledge, falter. Decentralized knowledge implies decentralized decision-making.

Hayek's argument, following his predecessor and teacher Ludwig von Mises, was empirical: Free market orders are more productive than central government control of economies, which certainly appears to have been proven to be the case. Moreover—and this is where Hayek's greatest fame lay—Hayek advanced Mises's argument one step further to the political realm. It is inevitable in the political realm, Hayek argued, that collective government control of an economy will lead to totalitarianism because every aspect of economic life becomes politicized. The free market, though based on state laws and their enforcement, keeps discretionary government intervention to a minimum.

Hayek's thought did not emerge in a vacuum, and part of the goal here, particularly in the early chapters, is to trace the intellectual background of his work. The dominating idea in Hayek's early life was Darwinian evolutionary theory, stemming from his father's and grandfather's work in botany and biology. Hayek ended his career with an evolutionary account of the growth of civilization.

Hayek's background in German and Viennese intellectual thought is another source of his work. While the account here can only be brief, the Germanic idealist and romantic philosophical tradition exemplified by such figures as Leibniz, Kant, Hegel, Marx, and Nietzsche was very different from the philosophical and literary heritage of the Anglo-American world. In addition, while the focus here is on German and Austrian similarities of identity, the influence of the Viennese philosopher and physicist Ernst Mach on the intellectual milieu in which Hayek grew to maturity was significant.

The Austrian school of economics exerted a more substantial influence on the emerging international academic economics profession during the last decades of the nineteenth century and first decades of the twentieth than is now often recognized. Especially through the work of Carl Menger, but also through that of his first teacher in economics, Friedrich von Wieser, Hayek was vitally influenced by the founding Austrian economists. The influence of Wieser on Hayek has almost always not been adequately emphasized.

Ludwig von Mises played the crucial role in converting Hayek from his early mild Fabian socialism to a more free market perspective. The work of Mises that most influenced the young Hayek was *Social-*

ism. The question of the relationship between Hayek's and Mises's conceptions of business cycle theory has often been discussed, and the perspective here is more in accord with those writers who argue for de-homogenization of the two men's views in technical economic theory.

Hayek's early academic work was in theories of money and capital and the influences of money and capital on economic activity. He thought the primary cause of the Great Depression was a worldwide misstructuring of capital production in country after country. He thought that the U.S. Federal Reserve Board practiced an expansionary monetary policy between 1927 and 1931. He considered capital to be heterogeneous rather than homogeneous in typical quality.

The work of Hayek's friend John Maynard Keynes dominated academic economic theory around the world from the 1930s through 1970s. Keynes worked to develop new models of understanding economic activity as financial, economic, social, and government institutions changed during the later nineteenth century and first decades of the twentieth. His theories were a rival to and shed light on Hayek's.

Hayek moved from economic theory to political philosophy during the 1940s for, really, the rest of his career. This move was led by his focus on prices as guides to economic production. In time, he was led to explore the concept of prices providing information more generally and the related concept of prices transmitting information that is not known to any one person. This, in turn, led Hayek to the idea of tacit, unarticulated, and nonverbal knowledge and the role of institutions in transmitting such knowledge.

He conceived a great treatise during the later 1930s, "The Abuse and Decline of Knowledge," which would follow from his earlier work in knowledge and on which he worked during the early 1940s. He thought that the hubris of reason—an overestimation of what individual human reason can accomplish—results in the nemesis of the planned society through the attempt to implement this conception of reason through government.

The Road to Serfdom was an advance sketch of the intended second part of "The Abuse and Decline of Reason." As a result of this book, Hayek became famous worldwide as the greatest champion of traditional classical liberalism and the most exciting proponent of new libertarian ideas. In chapter 9 here, on *The Road to Serfdom,* an appendix discusses Hayek's divorce and remarriage. Though these were personal events, rather than having to do with the evolution of his thought and work, they were central to his life.

Generally, my approach is to trace the evolution of Hayek's thought through different interests and stages, but I also present some biographical and historical information to provide insight on the times and circumstances in which he worked. I quote extensively from Hayek and others to provide context and the meaning of his and others' words, and to ensure reliability in the reader's mind. In addition, Hayek's thoughts are often complex, and require space for their enunciation.

His work in epistemology (theory of knowledge), psychology, and methodology (scientific or philosophical method) was among the most difficult in his corpus for the nonspecialist to appreciate. These were, however, core areas in Hayek's canon. In particular, the ideas of tacit knowledge, unarticulated knowledge, nonverbal knowledge, spontaneous formation of social and societal institutions, spontaneous order, and prices and profits as information and knowledge communicators and indicators are vital to consider in evaluating Hayek's work and contribution.

Hayek's idea was that an erroneous conception of what is possible for the individual mind to create regarding societal institutions leads to the decline of the reason that is possible in social life. He called the idea that humanity can design whatever institutions it wishes "constructivism." Hayek was in many respects a philosophical idealist, in that he believed that ideas rule the world. It was the idea of constructivism, he thought, that has such destructive consequences. If he could combat this idea, then much good would result.

But if constructivism will not do, then what should replace it? This was the basic question that Hayek sought to answer during the remainder of his career as the leading political philosopher of the twentieth century. Hayek's approach was largely Burkean. He saw much good in inherited institutions, and yet, at the same time, he also saw the desirability and necessity of change. He adopted an evolutionary interpretation of the progress of human society wherein the most economically productive laws, rules, morals, and practices come to prevail in the end through a Darwinian struggle of the greatest economic productivity among societies.

He thought that much knowledge is not verbally or explicitly known to the individual. This idea—of tacit (as opposed to explicit) knowledge—is difficult but important. It underlies to a considerable extent the idea of the entrepreneur—the individual who can make a profit but who cannot necessarily say how he does it.

The idea of unarticulated, nonverbal, or tacit knowledge led, in Hayek's mind, to the further idea that legal and moral institutions store, embed, and convey tacit knowledge. Hayek considered the most important of these institutional practices to be the rule of law. The rule of law allows individuals to lead rational lives. It is because we know what others are allowed and not allowed to do that we are able to plan our lives. Where not rules but dictatorship reigns, then Hayek, following the British political philosopher Thomas Hobbes, held that the life of man in society is "solitary, poor, nasty, brutish, and short."

Ideally, the rule of law should guarantee to each person a protected sphere within which he could plan his life, to a considerable extent, as he pleased. Private property, Hayek held, is essential to each person's private sphere. Unless an individual knows what is surely his and what is surely not, much societal discord results.

Hayek perhaps best expressed the tie between his theories of knowledge and political order when he received an honorary doctorate from Rikkyo University in Tokyo in 1964. In his acceptance speech he discussed the development of his work, saying that the task of economic theory is

> to explain how an overall order of economic activity was achieved which utilized a large amount of knowledge which was not concentrated in any one mind but existed only as the separate knowledge of different individuals. But it was still a long way from this to an adequate insight into the relations between the abstract rules which the individual follows in his actions and the abstract overall order which is [thereby] formed. . . . It was only through a reexamination of the age-old concept of freedom under the law, the basic conception of traditional liberalism, and of the problems of the philosophy of the law which this raises, that I have reached a tolerably clear picture of the nature of the spontaneous order of which liberal economists have so long been talking.

In other words, spontaneous order rests on law.

Hayek thought that his psychological and philosophical studies underlay his work in optimal societal order—utopia. He believed it is necessary to understand how knowledge is generated and transmitted in order to consider optimal societal institutions. He considered the idea and practice of private property to be essential to maximal economic productivity.

In *The Constitution of Liberty* he put forward most forcefully his idea of the protected sphere that is necessary for private property and the private domains that private property creates. Hayek followed the great classical liberal and libertarian tradition of John Stuart Mill, who argued during the nineteenth century for the desirability of political liberty and individual freedom. According to Mill, there can be no advance for society as a whole unless the individual is at liberty and free to live his life largely as he wishes and to try new things and experiences that are not necessarily sanctioned by the majority of a society at a particular point in time.

Hayek's discussion of the appropriate role of government was never really adequate, at least from a libertarian perspective. He sanctioned in principle much government activity that any democratic welfare statist could support, and he did not really consider the libertarian test for interference with the lives of others—to prevent harm to others.

Classical liberalism and libertarianism are ultimately radical creeds. They foresee worlds that have never been rather than must necessarily be (dogmatic leftists) or never were (dogmatic rightists). Hayek closed *The Constitution of Liberty* with the thought that he was not a conservative and that his position, that of the true or classical liberal or libertarian, was as far from conservatism as from socialism.

Hayek's views of and relationship with Karl Marx, John Stuart Mill, the Chicago school of economics, and Milton Friedman are not always fully understood. Though Hayek decried the practical outcomes of Marx's work and his political philosophy, he had high regard for Marx as a technical economist whose work preceded his own business cycle theory. Hayek's views of Mill fluctuated over his lifetime, from a position of relative support to one of relative opposition, though Hayek's later opposition to Mill was largely based on misinterpretation of Mill. Hayek ultimately adopted Mill's standard of "affect" on or "concern" for others as the right criterion to justify government action. This is a substantially more general criterion than the true libertarian one of to prevent harm to others.

Hayek was at the University of Chicago from 1950 to 1962, and this was truly a decisive phase in his career. Whether he would have otherwise achieved the renown he has in the United States without his residence here or done the work he did in *The Constitution of Liberty* is an open question. Hayek was not close academically to the Chicago school of economics while he was at Chicago or at other times. Friedman and Hayek were close primarily through extracurricular activities, such as the Mont Pelerin Society and as advisers to students involved with the Intercollegiate Society of Individualists, and philosophically regarding the practical reform of government, rather than through academic affairs or in technical economic theory.

Hayek's work in pure philosophy was truncated. He did not follow this chord in his thought as much as he pursued other areas. His most impressive exposition of his views was in his 1967 collection of essays, *Studies in Philosophy, Politics and Economics.* In the first article republished in this volume, "Degrees of Explanation," he put forward the view that prediction, whether in the natural or the social realm, is the true mark of science. He did not think, though, that the same degree of prediction that is possible in the natural sciences is possible in the social. He also thought that facts in the social sciences are perceived from the inside while knowledge of the natural sciences is perceived from the outside. Only pattern prediction, he thought, or prediction of the principle is possible in the social sciences.

Hayek's most influential work to date has been in political and economic philosophy. He crucially explored the vital connection between rules and human orders that are formed by them in *Law, Legislation and Liberty,* especially its first volume, *Rules and Order.*

His idea was essentially that societies are distinguished by their rules, morals, norms, customs, and laws. These create a stable pattern of interaction that allows individuals to lead their lives rationally. In *Law, Legislation and Liberty,* he reached the summit of his career as a political philosopher. Without law, there can be no order. The state is not inimical to liberty. Rather the state creates human freedom and liberty.

Law, Legislation and Liberty has been unduly neglected among Hayek's canon. He considered it a more original work than *The Constitution of Liberty,* and also more difficult. He remarked of his intellectual progress that he frequently made his best formulations of ideas as he completed a project. That he wrote *Rules and Order* soon after completing *The Constitution of Liberty* indicates that the former's ideas may in some sense be considered to be the philosophical reflections stirred up by writing the latter.

In *Law, Legislation and Liberty* he distinguished between "order" and "organization," stating that in the former, government is conceived as providing fixed rules within which individuals can make choices, and in the latter, all members of a society are conceived as together moving toward a set or known goal. He thought that far more economic productivity is likely to characterize societies that are orders rather than organizations.

Hayek's ultimate social goal—his utopia—was the unification of all humankind in one society. He wrote in *Law, Legislation and Liberty* that it is "only by extending the rules of just conduct to the relations with all other men, and at the same time depriving of their obligatory character those rules which cannot be universally applied, that we can approach a universal order of peace which might integrate all mankind into a single society." One of the paradoxes of Hayek is that he wrote better than he thought. That is, there are at least two ways to interpret the quoted sentence. What he meant was that in order to reach the universal order of peace in a single society, all rules would have to be applied to everyone. But the other, and potentially better, way to read this sentence is that in order to reach a universal order of peace in a single society, all rules would have to be able to be applied by everyone.

To understand Hayek's thought best, it is perhaps best to provide some definitions. By "society," he meant the largest communitarian organization of which individuals are a part, which includes but is broader than the state and government. The "state" is the ongoing apparatus of organized coercive relationships in a society, and "government" is the empowered directors of the state—legislative, executive, and judicial. While Hayek used "liberty" and "freedom" interchangeably, this author tends to use "liberty" for state order and "freedom" in the context of the highest human standard of living. "Social" is typically used in this book to indicate smaller-scale societal relationships, and "societal" is used to indicate larger institutions. "Information" is interpersonal data; "knowledge" is the information and understanding that an individual may possess, whether he can express it in words or not.

Hayek emphasized prediction in his work. It is important in theoretical work to make predictions about the future, because it is so easy to rationalize or justify the past. It is also important in scientific work to make predictions in numbers, because numbers are subject to verification. As Hayek emphasized, numerical predictions can be made in ranges.

Though Hayek chose his words very carefully, he did not emphasize the philosophy of words, if he considered it all. An idea stemming from the Vienna circle of logical positivists, a group from which Hayek dissented, is that it should be possible to achieve a pure language of communication. As Wittgenstein indicated in much of his early work, that which can be said should be able to be said clearly and precisely.

A pure language of communication would reduce all communication to statements that can be verified or corroborated by the senses.

The truth surely includes what one is experiencing sensorily at the moment. Therefore, even if a pure language of communication, an idea also expressed by the term "physicalism," were not descriptive of the entire truth, it would describe a portion of it.

Humanity's ability to communicate is becoming vastly greater. Knowledge and information are exploding. The greater shared understanding of the world that humanity is coming to possess should result, as the contemporary Austrian economist Israel Kirzner has emphasized theoretically, in circumstances in which an individual's predictions of the future become more and more accurate. From an Austrian perspective, this should lead to greater economic prosperity.

Hayek's later monetary work constitutes some of his most creative practical policy suggestions. His ideas of competing and private currencies may come into existence during coming years for technological reasons.

Hayek saw the development of world civilization in the direction of greater material wealth as largely evolutionary. He explored this concept in his final published work, *The Fatal Conceit: The Errors of Socialism,* of which a corrected and revised version that is as close as possible to Hayek's final work on the manuscript should be prepared. Hayek's intellectual legacy is too important for anything other than the highest academic standards to be applied to his work.

Yet no really good analysis of "The Fatal Conceit" has been possible, because the published version was fatally flawed. Further consideration of Hayek's final work would have to await preparation of a scholarly edition of "The Fatal Conceit" that would be true to the author's final writing and remove the accretions of William Bartley, the published version's editor. ("The Fatal Conceit" is typically used here to refer to Hayek's work; *The Fatal Conceit: The Errors of Socialism* is used to refer to the published version.)

Hayek started from an evolutionary perspective in the natural sciences. He ended his career with an evolutionary account of the development of human civilization, wherein the societies with the most materially productive rules, laws, morals, customs, and traditions will reproduce most in the end. Societal selection operates both within and among societies, and is driven not by the selection of genetically influenced attributes but by the selection of the societal practices most conducive to economic productivity, prosperity, and peace. Hayek saw life as a competition to extend itself most, whether in the biological or the social realm.

1

Darwinian Evolutionary Theory

HAYEK REMARKED IN A PAPER READ BEFORE THE CAMBRIDGE University Moral Science Club on November 14, 1942, that he originally came to economics "thoroughly imbued with a belief in the universal validity of the methods of the natural sciences." A way to understand Hayek's mature thought is to recognize the extent to which he stemmed from a scientific—and, in particular, biological—background.

The idea of Darwinian natural evolution was paramount in Hayek's early development. His family background was primarily in the natural sciences. While his maternal grandfather, Franz von Juraschek, was an economist and friend of some of the original members of the Austrian school of economics, Juraschek died in 1910, when Hayek was ten or eleven. Despite Hayek's precociousness, he could not have been much influenced by this grandfather. A far greater intellectual influence on Friedrich was his father, August, who was a medical doctor for the City of Vienna and a part-time professor of botany at the University of Vienna. Hayek mentioned the intellectual influence of his father on him in a late interview: "We have talked . . . about my contemporaries and to some extent about the influence of my father, which was of some importance."

August von Hayek's practical influence was as great as his intellectual influence. Wherever the Hayeks lived, their home was filled to overflowing with August's botanical collections. August wrote profusely on botanical subjects, with nearly a publication a year during some stretches early in his career. His later work in the 1920s was republished over forty years later. In the 1970 republication of his *Prodomus Florae Peninsulae Balcanicae* (Introduction to Flora of the

Balkan Peninsula), William Stearn wrote: "When August von Hayek died . . . he had seen through the press only one volume of his monumental flora of the Balkan peninsula, a work descriptive of about 6,700 species as well as numerous varieties and forms." Friedrich recalled that his father had an excellent memory.

August's own father, Gustav—Friedrich's paternal grandfather, who lived longer than Hayek's maternal grandfather—was also a biologist. Gustav wrote a number of monographs during the latter decades of the nineteenth century on Darwinian topics and was a science teacher at a leading Viennese *Gymnasium* (secondary school). Hayek remarked many times that his family background was in the natural sciences—the direction his brothers and children would follow—and that he was the only one in his family in the social sciences.

The intellectual milieu of Hayek's youth was Darwinian. Hayek remarked that both his father and paternal grandfather were Darwinians and that everyone with whom his family associated through his father's university connections was secular. He recalled that, when he was about fourteen, his father gave him a substantial treatise on the theory of evolution. If he had received the work a year later, he noted, "I probably would have stuck with biology. The things did interest me immensely."

Hayek was extremely interested in botany until he was fifteen or so. It is easy to imagine that conversations regarding his father's botanical work were a frequent topic around the Hayek family dinner table. August traveled extensively on plant expeditions and had a small business selling and exchanging plant specimens with which young Fritz (Hayek's nickname, which he disliked) assisted him. The two also went to meetings of the Vienna Zoologic and Botanical Society together. It is possible that three generations of von Hayeks sometimes attended these meetings—Gustav, August, and Friedrich.

Hayek was the oldest of three brothers, with Heinz one and a half and Erich five years younger than he. He wrote in unpublished autobiographical notes that although his siblings, particularly Heinz, were relatively close in age to him, Hayek somehow felt a division between him and them, and that he was older and of another generation. While growing up, he typically preferred to associate with adults and others older than himself.

The exact extent of Hayek's precociousness is unknown, though an interviewer once stated that he read as an infant. Hayek himself observed that he read fluently and frequently before he enrolled in school.

He also said that writing and particularly spelling only came later and more slowly, indicating that he might have had a greater ability as a young child to assimilate information than to organize and express it. This natural inclination may shed light on his characterization of himself intellectually as a "puzzler" rather than a "master of his subject."

Hayek did not always absorb as much light as he could have from other minds. He remarked of his mature intellectual cast: "It's very curious. I am hardly capable of restating the ideas of another person because I read and embody what I like to my own thoughts. I cannot read a book and give an account of its arguments. I can perhaps say what I have learnt from it. But that part of the argument which is not sympathetic to me, I pass over." Indeed, he said in a 1942 lecture that this was almost philosophically his position: "If we can understand only what is similar to our own mind, it necessarily follows that we must be able to find all that we can understand in our own mind."

Hayek recalled his study habits at the University of Vienna, which also give insight into the natural cast of his mind. He never kept notes of the lectures he attended, nor did he read prescribed textbooks in detail or attempt to memorize them. Instead, he read three or four textbooks rapidly to obtain more general information on the subject area. Then he pursued particular areas of interest in greater depth in the more specialized literature. His composite, broader, and deeper knowledge often gave him, he thought, greater knowledge than his peers even in their areas of specialty, because he had a more comprehensive view. He pursued a general course of study as a student at Vienna rather than focusing exclusively in any one field.

～

The influence of Charles Darwin and the theory of evolution on contemporary thought during the latter decades of the nineteenth century and first decades of the twentieth century was second to none. A religious view of the world in which it was literally created as described in Genesis gave way to the scientific conception of the world in which the earth came into existence billions of years ago and life on it gradually evolved over hundreds of millions and billions of years. That this represented a fundamental change in the outlook of the common person is an understatement. And, of course, this new view of the world—or paradigm, or *Weltanschauung*—did not take root overnight.

Moreover, a very crude understanding of evolutionary selection came into being. "Survival of the fittest" became the general idea of Darwinian evolutionary selection that filtered through to the majority of people. Hayek always insisted that the idea of undirected, natural evolution occurred first in the study of society and was then applied by Darwin to biological life. There is little question that Hayek's view here was largely correct. Intellectual historian Pat Shipman writes that "since well before the publication of *The Origin of Species,* the philosopher Herbert Spencer had been developing concepts of society and government that were closely congruent with Darwin's evolutionary ideas as he eventually articulated them. Indeed, one phrase now almost wholly identified with evolutionary theory—'survival of the fittest'—was Spencer's, not Darwin's. . . . There is no question but that Darwin was heavily influenced by Spencer."

Hayek himself wrote in his later works in political philosophy that Darwin was influenced by ideas of spontaneous evolution that were first developed in the realm of society. He wrote in *The Constitution of Liberty* that there can be "little doubt" that it was from "the theories of social evolution that Darwin and his contemporaries derived the suggestion for their theories. . . . It is unfortunate that at a later date the social sciences, instead of building on these beginnings in their own field, re-imported some of these ideas from biology and with them brought in such conceptions as 'natural selection,' 'struggle for existence,' and 'survival of the fittest,' which are not appropriate in their field; for in social evolution, the decisive factor is not the selection of the physical and inheritable properties of the individuals but the selection by imitation of successful institutions and habits. . . . [W]hat emerges is . . . ideas and skills." In *The Fatal Conceit: The Errors of Socialism,* he noted that "Darwin was reading Adam Smith just when, in 1838, he was formulating his own theory."

The beauty of evolution is that it is into the unknown. The detrimental aspect of planning is that it is limited to what individuals can conceive at a point in time. It is precisely the virtue of natural and spontaneous evolution that its outcomes are not known to individuals before they occur. Who could have planned or foreseen, for example, the Internet and its myriad effects on society and the economy? Natural evolution, whether physiologically or institutionally, is, Hayek argued, the best and indeed the only way forward.

"Probably the best illustration of a theory of complex phenomena which is of great value . . . is the Darwinian theory of evolution by natural selection," he wrote in a 1961 paper. He added in a lecture two years later on the legal and political philosophy of David Hume, whom he considered the greatest political philosopher and his chief inspirer, and who is usually considered the greatest original writer in the English language in pure philosophy, that "Hume may be called a precursor to Darwin in the field of ethics. In effect, he proclaimed a doctrine of the survival of the fittest among human conventions—fittest not in terms of good teeth but in terms of maximum social utility." He also noted here that "the transmission of ideas from Hume to Darwin is continuous and can be traced in detail." The "most direct channel seems to have been Erasmus Darwin, who was clearly influenced by Hume and whose influence on his grandson is unquestioned." In addition, Hume and Adam Smith were close friends and intellectual interlocutors. In short, the tie between natural and societal evolution was great. The difference between them is what is passed down: in the former, biologically inheritable traits; in the latter, human institutions, practices, outlooks, and attitudes, among many other social conventions, including, more generally, laws and morals.

In *Law, Legislation and Liberty,* Hayek continued with this theme when he remarked that it was in the "discussion of such social formations as language and morals, law and money, that in the eighteenth century the twin conceptions of evolution and the spontaneous formation of an order were at last clearly formulated, and provided the intellectual tools which Darwin and his contemporaries were able to apply to biological evolution." He also clarified here that the "error of 'Social Darwinism' was that it concentrated on the selection of individuals rather than on that of institutions and practices," and that the "other great misunderstanding which has led to a discrediting of the theory of social evolution, is the belief that the theory of evolution consists of 'laws of evolution.'"

Much of Hayek's work in the essays that became *The Counter-Revolution of Science* (which was originally conceived as the first half and historical part of an intended two-part treatise, "The Abuse and Decline of Reason"; a preliminary and popular sketch of the second half of this work became *The Road to Serfdom*) was devoted to criticism of the idea that societal evolution follows laws of development that allow prediction of the future in detail. Hayek believed this idea to be misconceived and held that the mind cannot foresee its own advance.

He noted in *The Counter-Revolution of Science* that the French Enlightenment was "characterized by a general enthusiasm for the natural sciences as never yet known before." As a result, "both the two great intellectual forces which in the course of the nineteenth century transformed social thought—modern socialism and that species of modern positivism, which we prefer to call scientism—spring directly from this body of professional scientists and engineers which grew up in Paris." Hayek did not believe that the same sort of prediction—and therefore control—that is possible in the natural sciences is attainable in the realm of society. At best, he thought, only a "pattern" of the future can be predicted in social life. He thought that to attempt to formulate laws of societal development akin to the laws of the physical sciences, as Marx attempted, is doomed to failure.

Karl Marx, too, was highly influenced by Darwin. He sent Darwin a copy of *Capital* (though he did not, as is occasionally reported, ask if he could dedicate the work to Darwin). According to one commentator, Marx considered himself to be the "Darwin of society." After reading the *Origin of Species,* Marx thought, in the words of another, that it provided "the foundation in natural history for the theory of class struggle." In his eulogy at Marx's grave, Friedrich Engels said that "just as Darwin discovered the law of the development of organic nature, so Marx discovered the law of development of human history." In *The Communist Manifesto* (written before the *Origin of Species*), Marx said of the relation between Communists and proletarians that Communists "have over the great mass of the proletariat the advantage of clearly understanding the line of march, the conditions, and the ultimate general results of the proletarian movement." Hayek thought this type of societal prediction impossible.

Hayek perhaps best indicated what he had in mind by order that is possible without an orderer and of Darwin's influence on the popular mind when he remarked, of the period before Darwin: "It is difficult to remember now, perhaps most difficult for those who hold religious views in their now prevailing form, how closely religion was not long ago still associated with the 'argument from design.' The discovery of an astounding order which no man had designed was for most men the chief evidence for the existence of a personal creator." In the same way that the universe and life itself can possess great orderliness with no direction, Hayek held that it is possible for societies to evolve without direction. His work was in large part an attempt to apply the truths of natural physical evolution to society.

While humanity cannot control or even know the outcomes of societal evolution, Hayek thought that they can control the conditions in which societal evolution takes place. The optimal environment, because it will lead to the greatest diversity and material progress, is one of maximum individual freedom for people to do as they wish without the coercive interposition of others. This will result in the greatest happiness and social harmony. Hayek concluded *The Constitution of Liberty* with the words of the great German liberal Wilhelm von Humboldt with which John Stuart Mill had prefaced *On Liberty* a century before: "The grand, the leading principle towards which every argument unfolded in these pages directly converges, is the absolute and essential importance of human development in its richest diversity."

2

German and Viennese Intellectual Thought

IN THE PREFACE TO *THE CONSTITUTION OF LIBERTY* HAYEK GAVE the following background on himself. Given the place in which he published this—the beginning of what he intended as his great positive work—it deserves added attention. "Perhaps the reader should ... know," he wrote on his sixtieth birthday, that "[m]y mind has been shaped by a youth spent in my native Austria and by two decades of middle life in Great Britain. ... [T]he book is to a great extent the product of this background." Hayek's childhood, youth, and early adulthood in Austria were vital in shaping his thought.

The German-speaking countries have, of course, a different history from the English-speaking world, and this background greatly influenced Hayek's thought. There is a tendency in the English-speaking world (as there was, and perhaps to some extent still is, a tendency among the French) to see their civilization as the societal conduit through which all human communities will eventually pass. The German-speaking countries also possessed this conception.

For centuries, the Germans considered themselves the successors of the Roman Empire. Though Rome conquered the west bank of the Rhine, which separates Germany and France, it never subdued the tribes residing in what is today Germany. Charlemagne, originally king of the Franks, founded and became emperor of the Holy Roman Empire in 800. In this year he was crowned by Pope Leo III head of the Christian dominions in what had been the west of the ancient Roman Empire and Germany. At its height, during the tenth and eleventh centuries, the Holy Roman Empire included most of what is now Germany, Austria, Switzerland, Belgium, the Netherlands, eastern France, western Poland, the Czech Republic, and northern and central Italy.

Germany's greatest European prominence, before the twentieth century, came during the Middle Ages. Germany was the most populous nation in central and western Europe by 1600, with 20 million people, compared to 12 million in France and 4 million in England.

Then came the disastrous Thirty Years' War, from 1618 to 1648, during which the German population was reduced by perhaps as much as one-third. Towns, villages, and whole territories were reduced to ashes, flourishing centers of trade and industry were wiped out, churches were burned, women and children were victimized. Cannibalism and polygamy were practiced in some regions. It took Germany over two centuries to recover. By 1800 its population was only 22 million, compared with 27 million in France and 10 million in England.

During the eighteenth and nineteenth centuries, German-speaking countries produced great musicians, poets, and philosophers. This was the German era of Bach, Mozart, Beethoven, and Brahms; of Goethe, Schiller, Novalis, and Lessing; of Kant, von Humboldt, Burkhardt, and Menger; among many others.

During the twentieth century, Germany moved in its incomprehensible direction. In a saying from the years after Adolf Hitler and the Nazi Party took over, Germany moved from a nation of "poets and thinkers" (*Dichter und Denker*) to a nation of "judges and hangmen" (*Richter und Henker*). Germany threw the world into turmoil and global conflict, murdered 6 million Jews in gas chambers and concentration camps, enslaved entire nations, and prepared to abolish Christianity. The Germany of Hitler, Himmler, Goering, and Goebbels was a deliberate attempt to destroy all of the main elements of Western civilization—Greek rationalism, Hebrew monotheism, and Christian love. Rationalism was to be replaced by feeling based on the irrational forces of "blood and soil"; monotheism by the cult of Wotan and other Germanic deities; love by ruthlessness and militarism.

So devastating was the blow that Nazi Germany attempted to inflict on the world that Germany will never recover its former position. It is permanently discredited.

It is not held here that there was intellectually the distinction between Germany and Austria from the mid-nineteenth through mid-twentieth centuries that some perceive, though during this period separate political identities did arise. The relationship between Germany and Austria was closer than that between the United States and Canada, but not as close as between two states in the United States. It is appropriate to consider the larger Germanic idealist and philosophical heritage from which Hayek emerged before considering issues of Austro/Germanic differences and Vienna.

The British intellectual tradition is empirical and liberal, the French is rationalist and aristocratic, and the German is idealist and conservative. In the words of historian of philosophy Barry Smith: "German philosophy is determined primarily by its orientation around epistemology: attention is directed not to the world, but to our knowledge of the world." In the great ontological debate between mind and matter, German philosophy comes down solidly on the side of mind. Its emphasis is intuition as opposed to reason, ideas as opposed to facts.

The German idealist philosophical tradition from which Hayek emerged is usually held to begin with Gottfried Leibniz, who wrote mostly during the second half of the seventeenth century. Leibniz put forward the idea of "monads," a starkly idealist conception. Essentially, "each monad is a soul," in the words of Bertrand Russell. Leibniz reversed the traditional conception of mind and matter by applying attributes of matter (in terms of sensory experience) to mind. Mind is what it experiences. Every mind or soul becomes an independent attribute of the universe, divinely ordered or arranged. Leibniz's focus truly was mind.

Leibniz was born at the end of the Thirty Years' War. Religious struggles, such as the Thirty Years' War, are often protracted and intense because they concern fundamental individual beliefs and values to which compromise is not always applicable. Chaos and disorder reigned in the larger society from which Leibniz emerged. It is not surprising that his philosophy moved in the direction of mind from a strictly sociological perspective, for the world was too hard to bear.

Even more relevant to Leibniz's philosophy was, perhaps, the structure of the German language compared to other languages. German emphasizes nouns more than English and French do, which may lead to more conceptual and holistic approaches in the thought of German speakers—just as the English and French focus on verbs may result in more action-oriented and empirical thought in their speakers. Whatever the source, however, German thought tends to be deep rather than clear, and directs its attention not to the world but to what individuals can know of the world. Along these lines, it is interesting to observe that, in his reformation of Christianity, the German Martin Luther was in the idealist and spiritual tradition of Plato and St. Augustine rather than in the more empirical and rational tradition of Aristotle and St. Thomas Aquinas.

Immanuel Kant is often considered the greatest philosopher since the classical age, although this was not the view of some of the greatest post-Kant philosophers in the British empirical tradition, including John Stuart Mill and Bertrand Russell. Nor did Hayek have an unqualifiedly high opinion of Kant, though he considered him to have been a significant and important thinker.

Hayek was not primarily influenced by Kant in the area of political philosophy. He could, indeed, have hardly been more explicit than he was in *The Constitution of Liberty* that, from the perspective of political philosophy, "philosophers"—most prominently, Kant— "have sometimes defined freedom as action in conformity with moral rules. But this definition of freedom is a denial of the freedom with which we are here concerned."

Where Kant primarily influenced Hayek was in ontology and metaphysics—Hayek's comprehensive and total view of the world and of life experience—as a number of writers and philosophers, including Tibor Machan, maintain. Machan remarks that Hayek's "conception of how we are aware of reality manifests his basically Kantian framework." Hayek, following in a long line of Germanic and idealist philosophers, adopted a view of reality as "the relation between the physical and the sensory world," in the tradition of Kant, a tradition that, Hayek held, "goes back to Galileo Galilei, who in 1623 had written: 'I think that these tastes, odors, colors, etc. are nothing else than mere names, but hold their residence solely in the sensitive body, so that, if the animal were removed, any such quality would be abolished and annihilated.'"

Hayek emphasized his debt to Kant in ontology. He remarked in a 1974 interview, shortly before receiving word that he had won the Nobel Prize, that "on the issue of the theory of knowledge, I am probably a Kantian more than anything else." In his work in psychology, *The Sensory Order,* he remarked that "the fact that the world which we know seems wholly an orderly world may . . . be merely a result of the method by which we perceive it," similar to Kant's position. According to British political philosopher John Gray, in *The Sensory Order* "the British empiricist view that our knowledge of the world comes from information we receive via the senses is rejected in favor of a modified

Kantian view in which order is imposed on our sensations by innate (but for Hayek alterable by evolution) mental categories."

Germanic philosophical idealism is also reflected in the work of Johann Goethe, whom Hayek often read as a young man. In introducing Hayek's *The Sensory Order,* Heinrich Klüver wrote that Hayek's theory, "from a broad point of view . . . may be said to substantiate Goethe's famous maxim 'all that is factual is already theory.'" Hayek used this line of Goethe's as the epigraph to the first part of his 1967 *Studies in Philosophy, Politics and Economics.* What Goethe apparently meant is that mind must first have a way of interpreting experience; next, experience is interpreted by mind. Thus, "all that is factual is already theory," because the way that facts (experience) are interpreted is mentally constructed. There are no atomistic facts in this perspective, because all experience is interpreted. As student of the philosophy of science and Hayek e-mail list moderator Greg Ransom observes: "'Empirical Data' even in economics is heavily theory laden. . . . [T]heory is unavoidably used to construct the 'data.'"

Following Kant, the most significant German philosopher was Georg Wilhelm Friedrich Hegel, whose emphasis on mind and idealism was, if anything, even greater than Kant's, as his practical influence also may have been during the nineteenth century. Hayek abhorred Hegel, considering his work virtually without value. At the same time, Hegel's emphasis on mind and idealism indicate the philosophical heritage from which Hayek sprang.

Karl Marx was strongly influenced by Hegel. At first glance, the placement of Marx in the German idealist tradition would appear mistaken, for Marx was explicitly a materialist. But historian of political thought William Ebenstein writes:

> Although Marx very early criticized Hegel, he never abandoned the basic categories of Hegel's thought. Like Hegel, Marx felt that history had meaning, and that it moved in a set pattern toward a known goal. In a rationalized version of the religious conception of history, in which history derives meaning from God and moves toward the kingdom of God, Hegel replaced God with the concept of Spirit or Reason, and history was seen by Hegel as the progressive unfolding of Reason. Marx held that history had both a meaning and a goal, and the historical process was dominated by the struggles between social classes; each phase of the struggle, as in Hegel, represented a higher phase of human evolution than the preceding one. The goal of history was predetermined for Marx. . . .

Philosophers in the idealist tradition may be more likely to put forward a determined end to history, for the tradition does not emphasize action in the real world as the empirical tradition does. Experience is the great relativizer and compromiser. Thus, Marx believed he had turned Hegel on his head by emphasizing matter rather than spirit. Marx did not hold that he had abandoned the form of Hegel's thought, which, in turn, Hegel received in considerable part from Kant.

In a fuller survey of the Germanic philosophical heritage during the eighteenth and nineteenth centuries, particularly one paying special attention to idealism, attention would be paid to a host of other figures, including, for example, Christian Wolff, Johann Gottlieb Fichte, Friedrich Shelling, and particularly Arthur Schopenhauer. For now, though, we shall focus on just one other Germanic writer during the nineteenth century who is not considered an idealist, but neither was he a rationalist, liberal, or empiricist: Friedrich Nietzsche. Nietzsche represents the romantic strand in Germanic thought (although he would have disputed this description), and his ideas were current when Hayek was growing up.

Romanticism finds fertile soil in idealism (to the extent that romanticism was not a reaction to the Enlightenment) in that emphasis on mind rather than on matter leads to generally less empirical and more emotional ways of thought than empiricism, and perhaps to greater emphasis on natural beauty than empiricism—though empiricism also concentrates preeminently on nature. The irrational strain in idealism is also found in romanticism. Irrationalism, as romanticism, tends to lead to the celebration of nature rather than the attempt to tame and control it that is characteristic of empiricism. Romanticism in part also sprang from the first reaction to industrialization.

There are considerable affinities between idealism and romanticism, indicated in part by Kant's admiration for Jean-Jacques Rousseau. For both idealism and romanticism, the focus is not on rational control and scientific observation of the real world of experience, but on internal mental conceptions and, in the case of romanticism, feelings. Romanticism is individualistic, in the sense that all that matters to the individual is his or her experience; in a political sense, however, crucially, romanticism is conservative and even reactionary in its tendencies to oppose material progress and the advance of knowledge.

Nietzsche's thought is best unraveled starting from his famous statement: "God is dead." Nietzsche saw Western society as at a full stop and sought the "revaluation of all values"—a new moral order. What had been was worthless, in part because of Darwinian theories that showed human descent from animals. What Nietzsche believed was required were new moral concepts to fill the place left by the departure of the old.

Nietzsche sought a new sort of aristocracy of super- or above-men, which would be the ultimate goal of civilized existence. The sources of this Nietzschean idea were several. Darwin's theory of evolution suggested to Nietzsche the notion of humanity as an evolving species, although Nietzsche emphatically rejected the concept of the superman or above-man as the outcome of a biological process; in a sense, the superman or above-man is a spiritualized form of Darwinism.

Hayek referred to Nietzsche perhaps only once, in *The Road to Serfdom,* when he noted that it was

> entirely in the spirit of collectivism when Nietzsche makes his Zarathustra say:
> A thousand goals have existed hitherto, for a thousand people existed. But the fetters for the thousand necks is still lacking, the one goal is still lacking. Humanity has no goal yet.
> But tell me, I pray, my brethren: if the goal be lacking to humanity, is not humanity itself lacking?

It is not known to what extent, if at all, Hayek read Nietzsche as a youth or young man. Nietzsche's thought is representative, however, of sentiments that raged through the Germanic world during the first half of the twentieth century.

∾

Among the Germanic idealist philosophical tradition's most significant contributions to broader thought are the concepts of "understanding" (*Verstehen*) and "worldview" (*Weltanschauung*), the latter of which has become especially popular through Thomas Kuhn's work on paradigms. The essence of any of these concepts—understanding or worldview (or paradigm)—is that individuals possess a view of life or experience, a view that is not necessarily verbal. Rather, it is an understanding of the way that the world is. One does not necessarily like the way that the world is, but one accepts that this is the way that it is.

Kuhn emphasized the collective nature of paradigms, which he "take[s] to be universally recognized scientific achievements that for a

time provide model problems and solutions to a community of practitioners." However, notwithstanding this aspect of paradigms from
Kuhn's perspective, the idea of common recognition is an unnecessary
addition to the core concept. The original paradigm is merely the view
of the world, or understanding, held by potentially one person.
Whether or how this view spreads is secondary, derivative, and separate. The essential idea is that individuals have understandings, world-
views, or paradigms. This is the basic element.

Hayek, who was fifteen when the Great War started, recalled
in his unpublished autobiographical notes that the world before the
war was what he considered the normal world of his youth to be. He
was always aristocratic personally. Pulitzer Prize–winning historian
Barbara Tuchmann provided this optimistic glimpse of the world before the Great War: "The proud tower built up through the great age
of European civilization was an edifice of grandeur and passion, of
riches and beauty and dark cellars. Its inhabitants lived, as compared
to a later time, with more self-reliance, more confidence, more hope;
greater magnificence, extravagance and elegance; more careless
ease, more gaiety, more pleasure in each other's company and conversation, more injustice and hypocrisy, more misery and want, more
sentiment including false sentiment, less sufferance of mediocrity,
more dignity in work, more delight in nature, more zest. The Old
World had much that has since been lost, whatever may have been
gained."

Before World War II, there was not the effort that has since
sometimes been made to differentiate Austria from Germany. Historically, Austria and Germany were in the same political system of the
Holy Roman Empire of the German Nation for a thousand years.
While during the last centuries of this agglomeration, political divi-
sions rendered the empire increasingly irrelevant, and although Austria was predominantly Catholic while the rest of Germany was
predominantly Protestant, the similarities between the two far exceeded their differences, or the similarities between either and any
other country. There was a great deal of cultural and personal movement throughout the German-speaking countries. Clemens Metter-
nich, Austria's longtime conservative premier during the nineteenth
century, was from the Rhineland. Hitler was from Vienna.

Hayek noted the association between Germany and Austria in
a remark he made on Friedrich von Wieser, his main economics professor at the University of Vienna, on Wieser's death in 1926: "He was

wholeheartedly a German and perhaps even more wholeheartedly an Austrian of the best sort." The great philosopher from Vienna Ludwig Wittgenstein, who was Jewish and Hayek's distant cousin (although Hayek was Catholic), remarked in his diary during service in World War I that Austria was, with Germany, "the German race," and: "I am German through and through." Henry Seager, a young American economist, treated Berlin and Vienna as synonymously German in an article he wrote on economics at the universities in the two cities in 1893.

A distinct though not separate intellectual tradition developed at the University of Vienna during the second half of the nineteenth century that was more empirical than elsewhere in the German-speaking countries. The dominant figure at Vienna through whom this tradition largely emerged was Ernst Mach. According to historians of Vienna Allan Janik and Stephen Toulmin: "Seldom has a scientist exerted such an influence upon his culture as Ernst Mach." Hayek recalled that when he was a student at the university: "Mach's ideas were the main focus of philosophical discussions." According to Hilde Spiel, another historian of Vienna: "No account of the influence exercised by thinkers on creators in . . . Vienna can fail to begin with Ernst Mach. Even before this great . . . physicist and epistemologist came to the Austrian capital . . . in 1895, his ideas had spread among its young intelligentsia."

To a contemporary reader, nonetheless, Mach's *Analysis of Sensations* (1886) disappoints. There is a loud echo of Hume in the work, for Mach, like Hume, emphasized the tangibility of all knowledge—ultimately, all knowledge is based in the senses. In *The Analysis of Sensations*, he wrote: "My table is now brightly, now dimly lighted. Its temperature varies." Hume's parallel statement in *A Treatise of Human Nature* (1739) was: "The table before me is alone sufficient by its view to give me the idea of extension. This idea, then, is borrowed from, and represents some impression, which this moment appears to the senses." Mach emphasized the internal nature of all knowledge, as knowledge is experienced in the mind. Finally, he emphasized the importance of quantitative and mathematical methods and models to understand sensory experience.

Hayek, highly influenced by Mach as a young man, began reading him immediately following his return from service in World War I. He remarked about four decades later that he was "stimulated by Mach's work to study psychology and the physiology of the senses," though his interest in these areas derived as much from disagreement as agreement with Mach's work. Of his own relationship with the contemporaneous Vienna circle of logical positivists, Hayek said that "these two apparently absolutely contrary trends come from a common initial viewpoint"—in Mach.

3

The Austrian School of Economics

THE AUSTRIAN SCHOOL OF ECONOMICS, FROM WHICH HAYEK EMERGED and to which he contributed, has shown remarkable perseverance, consistency, and development for over 130 years. One of the surprising aspects about the Austrian school is that no adequate history of it, even of its classical phase for the six decades or so after 1871, has been written. Of the first four most significant early figures who were associated with the Austrian school—Carl Menger, Eugen von Böhm-Bawerk, Friedrich von Wieser, and Ludwig von Mises—no adequate biography of any has been published. Though economic historian Karen Vaughn has written of the development of contemporary Austrian economics, there is as yet no full, encompassing history of Austrian approaches in economics from Menger to the present.

Carl Menger was born in 1840 and died in 1921. Hayek saw him only once, when Menger strode by in an academic procession at the University of Vienna when Hayek was a student. Menger was originally from Galicia, then a province of Austria and now a part of Poland and the Ukraine. Hayek wrote in a biographical essay on Menger that Menger, as a child, "still saw the conditions of semi-servitude of the peasants, which in this part of Austria had persisted longer than in any part of Europe outside Russia."

Menger is one of those rare figures in intellectual thought whose work becomes more valuable as time progresses; the same can be said of Hayek. Menger's successors in the Austrian school of economics considered his work supreme. Hayek wrote in 1934 of the Austrian school that "its fundamental ideas belong fully and wholly to Carl Menger." Hayek also said then that there "can be no doubt among historians that if, during the last sixty years, the Austrian school has occupied an almost unique position in the development of economic science, this is entirely due to the foundations laid by this one man. . . . [W]hat is common to the members of the Austrian school, what constitutes their peculiarity and provided the foundations for their later contributions, is their acceptance of the teaching of Carl Menger." Ludwig von Mises praised Menger five years earlier, saying that "every economic thought today is connected with what Menger and his school demonstrated. 1871, the date of the publication of Menger's *Principles of Economics,* is usually considered the opening of a new epoch in the history of our science." On Menger's death, the Swedish economist Knut Wicksell wrote: "His fame rests on this work [*Principles of Economics*] and through it his name will go down to posterity, for one can safely say that since Ricardo's *Principles* there has been no book . . . which has exercised such great influence on the development of economics." Among Austrians, Wieser, Mises, and Hayek all said that *Principles of Economics* was Menger's most important work.

Hayek emphasized Menger's *Principles* and *Investigations into the Method of the Social Sciences with Special Reference to Economics* (1883) in his personal development as an economist. He remarked in 1978: "I was a direct student of Wieser, and he originally had the greatest influence on me. I only met Mises really after I had taken my degree. But I now realize—I wouldn't have known it at the time—that the decisive influence was from just reading Menger's [*Principles*]. I probably derived more from not only the [*Principles*] but also the [*Investigations*], not for what it says on methodology but for what it says on general sociology. This conception of the spontaneous generation of institutions is worked out more beautifully there than in any other book I know." Hayek also said that he "really got hooked" on economics when he "found Menger's [*Principles*] such a fascinating book—so satisfying."

During the 1860s, Menger worked as a financial journalist in Vienna for the Austrian civil service. He was especially struck by the divergence between academic theories of price and what businessmen considered the decisive determinants of price to be. Menger studied academic economic theory for only a few years before he wrote *Principles of Economics.*

The *Principles* was a masterful work, extraordinarily clear and precise in presentation. Menger began the book with a chapter on the nature of goods. "All things are subject to the law of cause and effect," he stated. "This great principle knows no exception, and we would search in vain in the realm of experience for an example to the contrary." Menger thus grounded his economic theories in experience, despite attempts made sometimes—by both foes and allies—to portray him otherwise. He was not Kantian in his approach, though some followers of his were, including Mises and, in his ontology, Hayek.

For an item to be a human good, it must fulfill a human need. "If a thing is to become a good," Menger wrote, all four of the following prerequisites must be simultaneously present:

1. A human need.
2. Such properties as render the thing capable of being brought into a causal connection with the satisfaction of this need.
3. Human knowledge of this causal connection.
4. Command of the things sufficient to direct it to the satisfaction of the need.

Menger's theory of economic activity is therefore located in the external world of experience and, perhaps even more fundamentally, is based on knowledge. Human knowledge of causal connections in the external world of sensory experience unlocks the door of economic wealth. As John Locke, one of the greatest English philosophers of economics as well as of the state, wrote in his fundamental *Second Treatise of Civil Government* (1689), matter does not itself provide one-hundredth of the value of goods—no, he clarifies himself a few pages later, matter itself does not provide one-thousandth of the value of goods. Rather, knowledge—knowledge of how to use matter—is the great source of economic progress and development.

Menger was a philosopher, accordingly, of the external world of experience, appropriate enough for someone identified as an economist. He was not concerned with Kantian "things-in-themselves," but with real goods in the real world of experience. Kant's name does not appear in Menger's *Principles*.

Indeed, Menger emphasized the extent to which his work was different from previous works in economics because of his emphasis on the world of sensory experience. He criticized the contemporaneous disregard in which economics was held because of "the sterility of all past endeavors to find its [economics'] empirical foundations." In prepositivist fashion, he "endeavored to reduce the complex phenomena of human economic activity to the simplest elements that can still be subjected to accurate observation."

Menger added to his realist conception of the human condition, and his emphasis on knowledge as the means to better this condition, the further postulate that goods are produced in stages, or are of different "orders": "In addition to goods that serve our needs directly (and which will, for sake of brevity . . . be called 'goods of first order') we find a large number of other things in our economy that cannot be put in any direct causal connection with the satisfaction of our needs, but which possess goods—character no less certainly than goods of first order. In our markets, next to bread and other goods capable of satisfying human needs directly, we also see quantities of flour, fuel, and salt. . . . That these things are . . . treated as goods in human economy, just like goods of first order, is due to the fact that they serve to produce goods of first order."

This conception of the different orders of goods underlies much of subsequent Austrian developments in economic theory, particularly relating to a trade or business cycle. Contemporary Austrian economic theorist Roger Garrison writes of the "time-consuming, multi-stage capital structure envisioned by Carl Menger."

Principles of Economics was originally conceived by Menger as the first and more general part of a larger treatise. The title could also be translated as "Foundations of Economics." It is largely concerned with basic issues of goods, value, and price. Menger's goal, like that of Hayek and other Austrians, was the highest standard of living possible for the most people. The Austrian school of economics, similar to the great British utilitarian tradition, emphasizes human welfare above all else.

Menger truly emphasized the importance of knowledge in economic life. He quoted Adam Smith to the effect that the division of labor is the greatest source of wealth, but then Menger said, no, this is not really right: "The quantities of consumption goods at human disposal are limited only by the extent of human knowledge. . . . Nothing is more certain than that the degree of economic progress of mankind will still, in future epochs, be commensurate with the degree of progress of human knowledge." Knowledge is the ultimate source of wealth and ultimate form of power.

Menger emphasized foreknowledge, furthermore, as Hayek did, writing: "Knowledge of requirements for goods in future time periods is the first prerequisite for the planning of all human activity directed to the satisfaction of needs. Whatever may be the external conditions . . . under which this activity of men develops, its success will be dependent principally upon correct foresight." Hayek, too, in a passage in "Economics and Knowledge," said that, in the market economy, "all knowledge is capacity to predict." He added: "To him [Menger] economic activity is essentially planning for the future." If knowledge is the ultimate form of wealth, then correct foreknowledge is its supreme substance. Knowledge is power. Foreknowledge is command.

It is sometimes maintained that Menger was predominantly influenced by German historical economists, but based on the available information, this does not appear to have been the case. While some of Menger's first introduction to economics was through German textbook writers (in substantial part influenced by Smith), he cited British and French authorities as often as German historical authors in *Principles of Economics,* and Adam Smith received special attention. Moreover, as Erich Streissler, a leading contemporary historian of Austrian economics, has come to realize after doing work on the notebooks (which only became available in 1986) of Crown Prince Rudolf of Austria, whom Menger tutored, Menger was a "classical liberal of the purest water, an economist, furthermore, who worked from an intimate knowledge of Adam Smith. . . . The whole framework of the lectures and most of the arguments are taken from Adam Smith's *An Inquiry into the Nature and Causes of the Wealth of Nations* (1776), by then exactly 100 years old! . . . Menger . . . [had] a much smaller agenda for the state in mind than even Adam Smith."

Menger first enunciated the Austrian theory of subjective value in *Principles of Economics:* "Value is . . . nothing inherent in goods, no property of them." Value, he declared, is "a judgement economizing men make about the importance of the goods at their disposal for the maintenance of their lives and well-being. Hence value does not exist outside the consciousness of men." According to Hayek: "The concept which [Menger] gave the new school [which is] its special character . . . [is] value in its subjective, personal sense."

The theory of subjective value was a major departure from previous economic theories based on objective cost variables—for example, the labor that goes into producing goods and services. Menger disagreed with the labor theory of value. Rather, for him and for subsequent

Austrians, goods are worth only what they are worth to individuals. Goods have no value apart from the value people place on them.

Menger made a splash in the world of the Austrian intelligentsia. In 1873, at the age of thirty-three, he became an associate professor at the University of Vienna. It was in 1876 that he became one of the tutors to the eighteen-year-old Crown Prince Rudolf von Habsburg. However, as the crown prince committed suicide in 1889, in sensational circumstances with his mistress, Menger's opportunity for direct influence on the throne was limited. According to Austrian economic historian Mark Skousen, Menger may have been being "groomed to become the prime minister" prior to the suicide.

In 1883, Menger began the well-known *Methodenstreit* (battle of methods) with the publication of his *Investigations into the Method of the Social Sciences with Special Reference to Economics*. Many articles and papers have been written on the *Methodenstreit,* but not much light has been shed by this literature. The following is only one, of many, interpretations.

While Menger dedicated *Principles of Economics* to the leader of the German historical school of economics, Wilhelm Roscher, too much has been made of the very laudatory comments at the conclusion of the volume's preface on German historical economics. The work was written in the years immediately following the Austro-Prussian War of 1866, and Austrian authors were likely to be conciliatory toward Germany.

Twelve years after the 1871 publication of the *Principles,* the necessity to be laudatory toward German economics no longer existed, and Menger was anything but. Moreover, the German historical school was passing to a second generation that was farther from classical English economics than the original German historical school was. Menger was more critical of the second generation of German historical economists.

Menger sought "exact laws." By this, he meant correlations between words and sensory experience that are always true—valid theory. This was the great dispute in the *Methodenstreit,* for the second generation of German historical economists, led by Gustav Schmoller, rejected the idea of prediction as the criterion of theory. Instead, their emphasis was, as their name suggests, on the historical development of economic institutions.

Mises provided this brutal description of the German historical economists: "Economics in the second German Reich, as represented by the Government-appointed university professors, degenerated into an unsystematic, poorly assorted collection of various scraps of knowledge borrowed from history, geography, technology, jurisprudence, and party politics, larded with depreciatory remarks about the errors in the 'abstractions' of the Classical schools. Most of the professors more or less eagerly made propaganda in their writings and in their courses for the policies of the Imperial Government: authoritarian conservatism, *Sozialpolitik*, protectionism, huge armaments, and aggressive nationalism." "Austrian" was originally a dismissive label given by German historical economists to Menger and his followers, but the name took on a positive connotation.

Henry Seager, a young American economist who attended Menger's 1892–93 lectures, remarked that Menger began his lecture course on economics with a "vivid sketch of the characteristic features of modern industrial society, emphasizing especially its dependence upon ... institutions." The third book of Menger's *Investigations,* "The Organic Understanding of Social Phenomena," is perhaps the part that retains most interest, providing as it does Menger's most detailed description of the spontaneous development of societal institutions.

Menger began the third book's first chapter, "The Analogy Between Social Phenomena and Natural Organisms," with the statement that there

> exists a certain similarity between natural organisms and a series of structures of social life, both in respect to their function and to their origin. . . . In natural organisms we can observe a complexity almost incalculable in detail, and especially a great variety of the parts. . . . All this variety, however, is helpful in the preservation, development, and the propagation of the organisms as *units*. . . . Natural organisms almost without exception exhibit, when closely observed, a really admirable functionality of all parts with respect to the whole, a functionality which is not, however, the result of human *calculation,* but of a *natural* process. Similarly we can observe in numerous social institutions a strikingly apparent functionality with respect to the whole. But with closer consideration they still do not prove to be the result of an *intention aimed at this purpose,* i.e., the result of an agreement of members of society or of positive legislation. They, too, present themselves to us rather as "natural" products (in a certain sense), as *unintended results of historical development.*

It is vital to observe in Menger's presentation here that he refers to societal institutions. He did not argue that there is no planning or direction in human society, but that institutions most often evolve unintentionally. He continued this theme in the second chapter of the third book discussing "social phenomena which are not a product of agreement or of positive legislation, but are unintended results of historical development." It was in this chapter that Menger asked: "How can it be that institutions which serve the common welfare and are extremely significant for its development come into being without a common will directed toward establishing them?" He spoke here as well of "the error of those who reduce all institutions to acts of positive common will" and reaffirmed that "institutions are unintended creations of the human mind."

Almost everything that makes the Austrian school of economics distinctive was found in Menger—marginal utility, subjective value, emphasis on knowledge and foreknowledge, the importance of prices, spontaneous generation of societal institutions, and economic activity as a process occurring over time. From a more practical perspective, during the 1890s and early 1900s, he was the informal leader of a group of civil servants and academics who regularly met for coffee at Vienna's famous coffeehouses to discuss the issues of the day.

During this time, Menger advocated Austria's return to the gold standard. His testimony before government committees on this issue indicates an exceptionally thoughtful, intelligent, and insightful man, well aware of the problems of practical implementation of new government policies. Austrian economist Hans Sennholz describes his testimony as follows: "He urged the government to proceed most carefully and deliberately lest it disrupt the international gold market and cause the purchasing power of gold to rise. Currency redemption should commence only after years of thorough preparation when government should acquire the needed quantity of gold without disrupting or disturbing the precious metal markets."

Seager described Menger in 1893 as a teacher: "Professor Menger carries his fifty-three years lightly enough. In lecturing he rarely uses his notes except to verify a quotation or a date. His ideas seem to come to him as he speaks and are expressed in language so clear and simple, and emphasized with gestures so appropriate, that it is a pleasure to follow him. The student feels that he is being led instead of driven, and when a conclusion is reached it comes into his mind not as something from without, but as the obvious consequence of his own mental processes."

Menger retired early from the University of Vienna in 1903, after the birth of his illegitimate son, Karl Menger, by his longtime housekeeper. Carl Menger ultimately received an act of legitimacy for his son from the emperor Franz Joseph. Karl Menger became a well-known mathematician and member of the Vienna circle of logical positivists.

~

The University of Vienna was not especially distinguished during the first half of the nineteenth century. According to Mises in *The Historical Setting of the Austrian School of Economics:* "From the middle of the sixteenth to the end of the eighteenth century Austria was foreign to the intellectual effort of Europe." He also said that until after the revolution of 1848, "the Austrian universities had been sterile."

Mises traced the rise of intellectual Vienna to the semiliberal policies that were implemented in Austria during the 1860s as Emperor Franz Joseph gradually acceded to less stature and control. The Austrian Liberal Party promoted, in Mises's recitation, "civil liberties, representative government, equality of all citizens under the law, sound money, and free trade," a good platform then and now. The new constitution of 1867 was a largely liberal document. Between 1850 and 1900, Vienna quadrupled in size, from half a million to 2 million people.

Hayek considered 1867 as the year of fundamental reform for the University of Vienna, after which it greatly expanded. The general university system throughout the Austrian empire was upgraded after 1848, and scholars from all over the empire and Germany went to Vienna. It became the intellectual, as well as cultural (though no longer political), capital of the Germanic world.

Vienna's beauty and musical vitality made it a great place to live. During the latter decades of the nineteenth century censorship ended and relative freedom of expression came into existence. Jews moved to Vienna from throughout the empire to avail themselves of opportunities that did not exist in the country. The Catholic church's control over education diminished, particularly at the university level. Academic freedom was established. Intellectual greatness emerged. One of the secrets of Vienna's academic success was the *Privatdozenten* system, which kept many individuals affiliated with academic work as part-time, unpaid lecturers. The cosmopolitan atmosphere of the Austrian Empire added to the city's intellectual milieu.

Menger was not as effective as he could have been in transmitting his original economic ideas. While his *Investigations* ignited a firestorm of controversy that resulted in the long-lasting and simmering feud between the German historical and Austrian economists, his *Principles of Economics* went out of print, and copies became almost unavailable. Menger would not consent to a new printing until after he had revised the work, which he never really did. (A second, revised edition appeared after his death.) It thus fell to Menger's two chief academic followers, Friedrich von Wieser and Eugen von Böhm-Bawerk—lifelong friends and brothers-in-law as well—to popularize and to extend Menger's work.

Wieser and Böhm-Bawerk were both eleven years younger than Menger, and neither had Menger as a teacher. Both were initially exposed to their mentor's ideas through *Principles of Economics*.

Böhm-Bawerk has attracted more attention than Wieser, for a number of reasons. First, he was far more famous outside the world of academic economics, serving three times as Austrian finance minister. In fact, he was so famous that his picture remained on Austrian currency until the introduction of the Euro currency in 2002. According to Mises, Böhm-Bawerk in office followed principles of "strict maintenance of the legally fixed gold parity of the currency, and a budget balanced without any aid from the central bank." This Austrian public policy approach has been consistent for over a century.

Given the great fame that Böhm-Bawerk attained, his prominence overshadowed not just Wieser's, but even Menger's. Also, Böhm-Bawerk was a brilliant polemicist, and engaged the Austrian school in a dispute with Marxian economists. Moreover, Böhm-Bawerk taught a number of exceptional and prominent students who served in both academia and government, including Mises, Joseph Schumpeter, Otto Bauer, Rudolf Hilferding, and Otto Neurath. After Menger retired, Böhm-Bawerk's was the main seminar in economics at the University of Vienna.

Furthermore, Böhm-Bawerk's reputation benefited from the fact that Schumpeter had such a high opinion of him, for Schumpeter had great influence on the presentation of the history of economic theory. Schumpeter considered Böhm-Bawerk to be one of the five or six greatest economists of all time, and compared him to Marx. Also, Mises praised Böhm-Bawerk greatly, which has raised Böhm-Bawerk's stature among many contemporary Austrian economists.

Böhm-Bawerk, Menger, and Wieser were all exceptionally prominent in Austria. Economic historians Erich Streissler and William Weber write that "Menger, Böhm-Bawerk, and Wieser were all of them Excellencies (and even Life Members of the Upper House of Parliament)—at a time when to become an Excellency was a rare honor, hardly to be achieved by anyone not born to it." Wieser served as commerce minister in the last Austrian government during World War I.

The extent of their influence is indicated by the following description by Hans Sennholz of Menger's role during currency reform efforts in Austria in 1892: "Menger exerted a powerful influence on Austrian economic affairs.... [H]e was the most celebrated Austrian economist.... In 1892, the year of currency reform, Menger's voice was heard throughout the land, expounding and illustrating the merits of the gold standard."

Wesley Clair Mitchell, one of the leading American economists during the first half of the twentieth century, compared Wieser to John Stuart Mill in the foreword (written before Wieser's death) to the English translation of Wieser's *Social Economics* (1927). "Hours devoted to the study" of Wieser's work, Mitchell wrote, "are hours of contact with a living force in the world of thought." Hayek described Wieser in an obituary in 1926; the occasion for the article was, of course, reflected in its substance and form. Wieser was Hayek's "revered teacher": "Neither the unrivalled depth of his insight into social development ... nor even his contributions as a statesman and patriot can adequately explain how great an inspiration this man was for those who knew him personally. It was his singular human greatness and universality, which transpires from all his works, that elicited the boundless respect and admiration of all those who came into contact with this magnetic personality."

Wieser was especially effective in coining phrases and giving life to concepts. The terms "marginal utility," "indirect utility" (opportunity cost), and even "planning" are sometimes attributed to him. He also did work in (and may have coined the term) "imputation," the tracing through of value in goods. Some of Hayek's earliest work in economic theory was for Wieser in imputation, which may account for part of Hayek's emphasis on changes in the price of capital goods (influenced by changes in interest rates) as the source of economic fluctuations.

Streissler writes that "uniquely" Wieser's own idea was

> the repeated stress ... of the paramount importance of economic
> calculation and the need to have an economic measuring rod for all
> rational "planning" for the future. ... The measuring rod for Wieser
> is marginal utility in its wide sense; but it was a small step, taken by
> Mises and Hayek, to make out of this need for a measuring rod in
> all economic planning the concept of the informative nature of
> prices. Economics may even owe the (then uncommon) term "plan-
> ning" ... to Wieser via Mises. Wieser already stated repeatedly that
> even a socialist economy would have to use the same economic
> measuring rod and basically the same principles of "planning" as a
> capitalist one: out of which Mises developed the idea that, lacking
> prices, a socialist society could not plan rationally.

Natural Value (1889) is Wieser's best-known theoretical work.
Here he significantly expanded on Menger's base, introducing and developing ideas of marginal utility, indirect utility, and imputation of
value. His work in the area of opportunity cost has proven especially
lasting and valuable.

Hayek greatly esteemed *Natural Value.* He wrote in Wieser's
obituary that it was "among the most brilliantly written and organised
books on economic theory" and that it "became the definitive expression of his [Wieser's] views for the next twenty-five years and is likely
to remain one of the classic works on the subject."

In the most important chapter of *Natural Value,* which has the
same title as the book, Wieser presented an argument that should be
familiar to most readers of Hayek and Mises: "Even in a community or
state whose economic affairs were ordered on communistic principles,
goods would not cease to have value. Wants there would still be, there
as elsewhere; the available means would still be insufficient for their
full satisfaction. ... All goods which were not free would be recognised
as not only useful but valuable; they would rank in value according to
the relation in which the available stocks stood to demand; and that relation would express itself finally in the marginal utility." Wieser ad-
umbrated the socialist calculation debate.

Value, according to Wieser and other marginalists, is determined
not by such factors as labor, interest, and rent, but solely according to
the demand for and supply of goods of all sorts. Consumption of all
goods together is pursued by each individual decision maker to the
point where the marginal utility from the final unit of each good con-

sumed is the highest. This was the marginal revolution in economic theory. It consisted of a new way of considering value such that goods are not valued according to the inputs that go into them (particularly labor); neither are goods valued the same in each increment of their consumption, nor valued the same by different people (or even the same people, over time). Consumption (whether in production or final consumption) occurs as long as the opportunity cost for every forgone alternative economic action is less than the marginal utility of the final good(s) consumed. This simplification perhaps conveys essential ideas. Wieser extended Menger's concepts.

Wieser explicitly opposed the socialist theory of value, writing in *Natural Value:* "As is well known . . . the socialists have another theory of value. This we shall find again and again in contradiction with the claims that rest on natural value, and although we say nothing against socialism, but wish to remain throughout within the neutral sphere of natural value, we shall be obliged again and again to speak against the socialists."

He began "The Socialist Theory of Value" chapter in *Natural Value* in words that Mises echoed in the first paragraph of his famous "Economic Calculation in the Socialist Commonwealth" over thirty years later. According to Wieser:

> Socialist writers, however much they find to object to in value as it is in the present day, have little enough to say concerning its future. They give us very scant information as to the part it would have to play in the socialist state. Karl Marx, in explanation of this reserve, says that "the social relations of man to his labour and to the products of his labour are here transparently simple." It would appear that value, in the socialist sense, resembles those organs of the human body of whose existence, when diseased, we are painfully conscious, while in health they are scarcely noticed. Physicians, even who know their pathology thoroughly, are not able to say what vital functions they serve.

Mises wrote:

> There are many socialists who have never come to grips in any way with the problems of economics, and who have made no attempt at all to form for themselves any clear conception of the conditions which determine the character of human society. . . . They have criticized freely enough the economic structure of "free" society, but

have consistently neglected to apply to the economics of the disputed socialist state the same caustic acumen. . . . They invariably
explain how, in the cloud-cuckoo lands of their fancy, roast pigeons
will in some way fly into the mouths of the comrades, but they omit
to show how this miracle is to take place.

Wieser went on to say (though he used the terminology of
"value" rather than "price") that "knowledge of the values of goods . . .
is . . . one of the most valuable of possessions. It is almost as valuable
as the possession of the goods themselves, inasmuch as it is the key to
their use. . . . Were a nation to lose all remembrance of these, it would
be an enormous economic misfortune. An almost incalculable period
of time, an almost incalculable amount of error and loss, would have to
be gone through, before the nation could again obtain mastery over
the relations of goods formerly expressed, with numerical clearness, for
each individual good by means of value"; and: "Although no one is
able . . . to figure out the amounts of supply and demand, value shows,
with numerical exactitude and down to the finest gradations . . . the relation between supply and demand in so far as these tend to make
themselves felt in exchange. Value shows the effect of causes which in
themselves are hidden." Here he wrote much like and prefigured
Mises's and Hayek's emphases on prices.

There was a highly realistic streak in Wieser that Hayek
adopted, in the sense that Wieser was an exceptionally clear writer who
attempted to make his assumptions and simplifications manifest.
Hayek praised Wieser's methodology—his emphasis on "the scientific
relevance of terminology" and use of "reductive and idealising assumptions and decreasing levels of abstractness." Moreover, William
Smart, who had *Natural Value* translated into English in 1893, remarked in introducing the work that Wieser maintained that "the
wealth of the world is 'not a fund but a flow.' . . . To keep value in existence, wealth has to be constantly remade." Both this theoretical conception of economic activity and its emphasis on the transitoriness of
wealth influenced Hayek's thought.

Wieser was more influential in both modern microeconomics
and the classical Austrian school than is often assumed. Wesley Clair
Mitchell noted in the foreword to *Social Economics* that "when Professor William Smart was introducing the Austrian theory to English-
speaking economists, he chose Wieser's *Natural Value* for translation in
preference to Menger's." Lionel Robbins—one of the greatest eco-

nomic historians of the twentieth century, a close friend and associate of Hayek, and an economic theoretician in his own right—placed Wieser among the seven "greatest names of the marginal revolution," together with Jevons, Menger, Böhm-Bawerk, Walras, Alfred Marshall, and Wicksell.

It is, of course, difficult to say who the most influential economists have been. Certainly Wieser's star shines brighter as the entire classical Austrian school does, and as new thought—deliberately based on these individuals as predecessors—moves forward. Menger apparently thought more highly of Wieser's work in technical economic theory than of Böhm-Bawerk's.

Hayek's friend Oskar Morgenstern wrote that "Wieser as a man . . . was a great personality whose magic nobody could escape; and in a personal way he exercised an influence upon his friends and pupils the extent of which can hardly be overrated." Morgenstern considered Wieser an "ideal representative of the old Austro-Hungarian Empire." In an encyclopedia article entitled "Austrian Economics" published in 1982, another of Hayek's old Viennese friends, Fritz Machlup, wrote that in the "1890s the following four tenets were given as characteristic [of Austrian economics]: marginalism, diminishing marginal utility, costs as forgone utility, and imputation of value to complementary factors." Wieser's role in the formulation and development of all of these concepts was extensive.

Machlup also observed that while Jevons's and Walras's approach was mathematical, Menger's was verbal. "This probably explains why the Viennese had a much larger following than his colleagues in London and Lausanne" during the late nineteenth and early twentieth centuries, Machlup continued. Indeed, in his 1893 piece "Economics at Berlin and Vienna," young American economist Seager wrote that "[t]he eyes of the economists of all nations are at present directed, as to the most conspicuous representatives of our science in the country in which that science has been most assiduously and most fruitfully cultivated during the last fifty years"— in other words, Austria. Among economists influenced to greater or lesser extents by Austrian economists were Knut Wicksell and Erik Lindahl in Sweden; Philip Wicksteed, Lionel Robbins, and John Hicks in England; John Bates Clark, Irving Fisher, Frank Fetter, and David Green in the United States; and many others, including those in Italy, the Netherlands, France, and Denmark. It was an impressive group.

More recently, leaders in the contemporary Austrian school of economics such as Peter Boettke argue for a continuing Austrian school of economics from 1950 to 2000, disputing the historical view that saw an essential break in the Austrian economic tradition for forty years or so from the 1930s through 1970s. Economic historian Karen Vaughn perceptively observes of the transplantation of Austrian economics to the United States that "although Hayek emigrated to America in the late 1940s, it was his older colleague Mises who was responsible for bringing Austrian economics to America. While I believe Hayek's ideas ultimately proved more important in shaping the Austrian revival, it was because of Mises that there was a revival at all."

The history of the Austrian school remains unfinished, and what happens in the future may influence interpretations of the past as much as what has already occurred. An increasing number of economists, however, believe that a reconceptualization of the role the Austrian school has played in academic economics from the 1870s to the present would be more accurate than the prevailing view.

4

Ludwig von Mises

A PASSAGE IN *THE CONSTITUTION OF LIBERTY* SHEDS LIGHT ON Hayek's family circumstances while growing up: "As a rule, parents can do more to prepare their children for a satisfactory life than anyone else. This means not only that the benefits which particular people derive from their family environment will be different but also that these benefits may operate cumulatively through several generations. . . . There is, indeed, good reason to think that there are some socially valuable qualities which will be rarely acquired in a single generation but which will generally be formed only by the continuous efforts of two or three. . . . There is . . . neither greater merit nor any greater injustice involved in some people being born to wealthy parents than there is in others being born to kind or intelligent parents." Hayek's parents were kind and intelligent, and even somewhat wealthy.

Perhaps the most endearing passage from Hayek's autobiographical notes is when he lets the reader know that he was sexually inexperienced as a young man. Describing himself on entering the military in 1917, he remarked: "In a way of course I was even then somewhat more academic, less familiar with the everyday world (and particularly with women) and more at home with books than most of my contemporaries. But this (except for my innocence on some very worldly matters) was still much less true of me than of the one or two really intellectual and highly sophisticated among that group. Compared with these much more mature young soldiers, I was then and for some years to come still a child." He was from a good family, and he wanted his reader to know it.

He also had this exchange that sheds some light on the social milieu in which he came to early intellectual maturity at the University of Vienna:

> Q: . . . I think it's von Mises, who had this extraordinary description of Germany before the First World War, with bands of young people with the equivalent of guitars and mandolins roaming the countryside. . . . The *Wandervögel* [ramblers]. And all that they left, he said, was not a single work of art, not a single poem, nothing but wrecked lives and dope! Were you familiar with that . . . ?
>
> A: Oh, I saw it happen; it was still quite active immediately after the war. I think it reached the highest point in the early '20s. . . . In fact, I saw it happen when my youngest brother was for a time drawn into that circle; but they were still not barbarians yet. It was rather a return to nature. Their main enjoyment was going out for walks into nature and living a primitive life. . . . [I]t was not yet an outright revolt against civilization.

Hayek was from a typical academic family.

This, then, was the innocent young man who returned from the Great War in November 1918 and began studies at the University of Vienna a few weeks later. He originally thought that he might become a diplomat: "I had more or less planned . . . to combine law and economics as part of my career. I imagined it would be a diplomatic career, really. So I came to the university with only a general idea of what my career would be. My interests, even from the beginning, were—My reading was largely philosophical . . . it was method of science. You see, I had shifted from the wholly biological approach to the social field, . . . and I was searching for the scientific character of the approach to the social sciences."

At this point Hayek's comments shed light on his circumstances while growing up and his ultimate career ambitions: "And I think my career, my development, during those three years . . . was in no way governed by thoughts about my future career, except, of course, that tradition in our family made us feel that a university professor was the sum of achievement, the maximum you could hope for, but even that wasn't very likely. It reminds me that my closest friend [perhaps Walter Magg, who died during World War I] predicted that I would end as a senior official in one of the ministries." Hayek's father was a frustrated academic who never obtained a full-time position. "Behind the scenes it wasn't much talked about, but I was very much aware that in my father the great ambition of his life was to become a university professor."

Hayek remembered that when he first began in economics at the university:

> It was dreadful, but only for a year. There was nobody there. Wieser had left the university to become a minister in the last Austrian government; Böhm-Bawerk had died shortly before; [Eugen von] Philippovich, another great figure, had died shortly before; and when I arrived there was nobody but a socialist economic historian.
>
> Then Wieser came back, and he became my teacher. He was a most impressive teacher, a very distinguished man whom I came to admire very much. I think it's the only instance where, as very young men do, I just fell for a particular teacher. He was the great admired figure, sort of a grandfather figure, two generations between us. He was a very kindly man who usually, I would say, floated high above the students as a sort of God, but when he took an interest in a student, he became extremely helpful and kind. He took me into his family; I was asked to take meals with him and so on. So he was for a long time my ideal in the field, from whom I got my main general introduction to economics. . . .

Q: I know that there were three chairs at the university, and Wieser retired at what time?

A: Well, I'm afraid Wieser was responsible for rather poor appointments. The first one was Othmar Spann, a very curious mind, an original mind, himself originally still a pupil of Menger's. But he was a very emotional person who moved from an extreme socialist position to an extreme nationalist position and ended up as a devout Roman Catholic, always with rather fantastic philosophical ideas. He soon ceased to be interested in technical economics and was developing what he called a universalist social philosophy. But he, being a young and enthusiastic man, for a very short time, had a constant influence on all us young people. Well, he was resorting to taking us to a midsummer celebration up in the woods, where we jumped over fires and that sort of thing [laughter], but it didn't last long, because we soon discovered that he really didn't have anything to tell us about economics.

As long as I was there, there were really only these two professorships. . . . When Wieser retired, which happened in the year when I finished my first degree, he was succeeded by Hans Mayer, his favorite disciple. An extremely thoughtful man, but a bad neurotic. [He was] a man who could never do anything on time, who was always late for any appointment, for every lecture, who never completed things he was working on, and in a way a tragic figure, a man who had been very promising. Perhaps it's unjust to blame Wieser for appointing him because everybody thought a great deal would come from him. And probably there is still more in his very fragmentary work than is appreciated, but one of his defects was that he worked so intensely on the most fundamental, basic problems—utility and value—there was never time for anything else in economics. So he was, in a sense, a narrow figure.

The third professorship was only filled a year or two after I had left. The man, Count Degenfeld—he played a certain role when I finally got my *Privatdozenteur,* but I never had any contact with him otherwise. There were a few *Privatdozent*s, or men with the title of professor like Mises, but my contact with him was entirely outside the university. No, the faculty, except for Wieser, as a person, as an individual, was not very distinguished in economics, really. It was a great tradition, which Wieser kept up, but except for him the economics part of the university was not very distinguished.

When Hayek was at the University of Vienna, the Austrian school of economics was not what it used to be.

Mises, too, in his autobiographical *Notes and Recollections,* described an Austrian school in decline:

> After Wieser's retirement . . . , the three professorships of economics were held by Othmar Spann, Hans Mayer and Count Ferdinand Degenfeld-Schonburg. Spann barely knew modern economics; he did not teach economics, he preached a "universalism" . . . Degenfeld did not have the slightest notion of the problems of economics; the level of his instruction would have been scarcely satisfactory for a low-ranking commercial college. Mayer was the favorite pupil of Wieser. He knew the works of Wieser and also those of Böhm-Bawerk and Menger. He, himself, was totally without critical faculty, never manifested independent thought, and basically never comprehended what it was all about in economics. . . . He occupied his time with an open fight against Professor Spann and with mischievous intrigues against me. His lectures were miserable, his seminar not much better. I need not be proud of the fact that the students, young doctors and the numerous foreigners who studied in Vienna for one or two semesters, preferred my instruction.
>
> Professors Spann and Mayer were jealous of my success and sought to alienate my students from me. In major examinations, my students reported that there was discrimination against them. . . . But I always told the members of my seminar that I attached no great importance to their official registration. They frequently made use of

this permission. Of the forty to fifty who attended, only eight to ten usually had registered. The professors also made it very difficult for those doctoral candidates in the social sciences who wanted to write their theses with me; and those who sought to qualify for a university lectureship had to be careful not to be known as my students.

Students who registered for my seminar were denied access to the library of the economics department if they did not also register for a seminar of one of the three professors. . . . All such matters did not disturb me. It was much more serious that the general level of instruction at the University of Vienna was so low. The brilliance that had marked the University during my student years had long been lost.

It might be thought from these and similar passages that can be culled from *Notes and Recollections* that Mises was an unattractive personality or, even, thinker. Such an interpretation would, however, not be just. Hayek appropriately remarked of Mises and *Notes and Recollections:*

Q: Mises personally—The view here in the United States, I think, is of Mises in his old age, and he's viewed very often, particularly by his enemies . . . as very doctrinaire. Do you feel that he got doctrinaire with age? Was he a different man in Vienna back then than he became later?

A: He was always a little doctrinaire. I think he was not so susceptible to take offense as he was later. I think he had a period of—Well, he always had been rather bitter. He had been treated very badly all through his life, really, and that hard period when he arrived in New York and was unable to get an appropriate position made him very much more bitter. On the other hand, there was a counter-effect. He became more human when he married. You see, he was a bachelor as long as I knew him in Vienna, and he was in a way harder and even more intolerant of fools than he was later. If you look at his autobiography, the contempt of his for most of the . . . economists was very justified. But I think twenty years later he would have put it in a more conciliatory form. His opinion hadn't really changed, but he wouldn't have spoken up as openly as in that particular very bitter moment when he just arrived in America and didn't know what his future would be.

Hayek himself could possess a reasonably sharp tongue when discussing the successors of the original Austrian school of economics:

"There were no very good Mayer pupils. I mean, [Franz] Mayr, who became his successor, while a very well-informed person, was really a great bore. He had no original ideas of any kind." Mises's student Murray Rothbard said that it was "the lowest point of Mises's life" when Mises wrote the manuscript draft of what was published as *Notes and Recollections*. He had just arrived in the United States, a man of almost sixty with a new wife, no job, and no resources—his library seized and career wrecked in Europe, after having been chased across southern France by the Nazis during the last days of the French Republic.

Other students of some of the epigone Viennese economists remembered them in terms similar to those Mises used. Economist Earlene Craver did exceptional work on the emigration of Austrian economists before World War II. She wrote that in her interviews with fourteen individuals (including Hayek, Fritz Machlup, Oskar Morgenstern, Gottfried Haberler, Paul Rosenstein-Rodan, and Herbert Fürth) during the latter 1970s, Mayer was remembered as "bohemian," "strange," and an "absolute scoundrel." Furthermore: "All agree that Mayer was a jealous man. They say he was jealous of Spann, of Mises, and even of the young privatdozents Hayek, Haberler, and Morgenstern, whose joint seminar in 1930–31 exceeded his in popularity." The memories of Spann were more mixed. Like Hayek, a number were initially attracted to him, but then became disenchanted. Degenfeld was remembered as "not at all a brilliant man" and a "complete nonentity."

Mises was regarded, wherever he lived, as doctrinaire or extreme politically. In Austria, he was considered an extreme liberal. Later, with the same views, he was considered an extreme conservative in the United States. That Mises was considered extreme politically in two countries from two different perspectives at two times with the same views indicates both consistency in his views and the degree to which larger societal philosophies can change—and in short periods of time. Between the 1930s and 1970s the world moved sharply in a socialist direction.

∼

In his 1978 Ludwig von Mises memorial lecture at Hillsdale College, in Hillsdale, Michigan, Hayek gave one of the best summaries of his intellectual relationship with Mises. Hayek "perhaps most profited" from Mises's instruction because he initially came to him as a "trained economist, trained in a parallel branch of Austrian economics from which he gradually, but never completely, won me over"—the Wieser branch. "I am," Hayek said, "to the present moment pursuing the questions which [Mises] made me see, and that, I believe, is the greatest benefit one scientist can confer on one of the next generation." Hillsdale College Ludwig von Mises Professor of Economics Richard Ebeling remarks that "many areas in which [Hayek] later made his profoundly important mark were initially stimulated by . . . Mises. This is most certainly true of Hayek's work in monetary and business-cycle theory, his criticisms of socialism and the interventionist state, and in some of his writings on the methodology of the social sciences."

Hayek characterized his views as a young man as having been "what in England would be described as a Fabian socialist. I was especially influenced—in fact the influence very much contributed to my interest in economics—by the writings of a man called Walter Rathenau, who was an industrialist and later a statesman and finally a politician in Germany." Rathenau advocated labor legislation as a first step toward more extensive change in society. Jeremy Shearmur, a former research assistant to Karl Popper and scholar in his own right, says that Rathenau "offered a middle way between capitalism and socialism. . . . While Rathenau expressed some sympathy with socialism, he rejected the socialist movement, which he characterized as over-concerned with the material to the exclusion of the spiritual." Shearmur also writes that "Rathenau's ideas on social reform are set within a grander vision for the moral transformation of society. . . . Rathenau rejected competition as wasteful and he was critical of speculation. His positive program involved the placing of restrictions on luxury spending, on the grounds that it represented a squandering of national wealth, and the advocacy of an inheritance tax." Rathenau's program was not so dissimilar from that of a "New Deal" Democrat. Hayek apparently first read Rathenau when he was about seventeen.

Ebeling notes that the economists of the Austrian school in Austria were more politically heterogeneous than economists who identify themselves with the contemporary Austrian school in the United States: "In general the Austrian economists of the [Austrian] period shared a common belief in the relative superiority of the market as an institutional framework for economic coordination. But the school was far from any agreement as to the superiority of unadulterated laissez-faire." Hayek emphasized the political heterogeneity of classical Austrian economists, and described the perceived focus of the school through the 1920s to economist Axel Leijonhufvud:

Q: In economics . . . in the 'twenties in Vienna, was there such a thing as an Austrian school in economics? Did you and your contemporaries perceive an identification with a school?

A: Yes, yes. Although at the same time very much aware of the division between not only Mayer and Mises but already Wieser and Mises. You see, we were very much aware that there were two traditions—the Böhm-Bawerk tradition and the Wieser tradition—and Mises was representing the Böhm-Bawerk tradition, and Mayer was representing the Wieser tradition.

Q: And where did the line between the two go? Was there a political or politically ideological line involved?

A: Very little. Böhm-Bawerk had already been an outright liberal, and Mises even more, while Wieser was slightly tainted with Fabian socialist sympathies. In fact, it was his great pride to have given the scientific foundation for progressive taxation. But otherwise . . . I mean, Wieser, of course, would have claimed to be liberal, but he was using it much more in a later sense, not a classical liberal. . . .

Q: . . . [W]hat were the differences, then, between the Mayer circle and the Mises circle?

A: Oh, things like the measurability of utility and such sophisticated points. Wieser and the whole tradition really believed in a measurable utility. . . .

Q: But that doesn't explain a split between the two groups.

A: Oh, there wasn't really. You see, Mayer—and also Rosenstein, perhaps—kept away from the Mises circle for political reasons. . . .

Q: Now, in the 'twenties, were most of the economists in Vienna at that time liberals in the traditional sense?

A: No, no. Very few. . . . I think it reduces to Haberler, Machlup, and myself.

Q: So my previous question was: Was there an Austrian school? And you said yes, definitely.

A: Theoretically, yes.

Q: In theory.

A: In that sense, the term, the meaning of the term, has changed. At that time, we would use the term Austrian school quite irrespective of the political consequences which grew from it. It was the marginal utility analysis which to us was the Austrian school.

Particularly stemming as he did from a Germanic intellectual background, Hayek as a young man would have considered the Austrian school as an approach apart from other mainstream economics, primarily the German historical school and German socialist and

Marxist economic approaches. What primarily distinguished the Austrian school from other Germanic economics was its emphasis on marginal analysis, which is also what united it with English and Swedish technical economic theory.

Mises was a student in Böhm-Bawerk's seminar during the first decade of the twentieth century, a seminar that was, if anything, dominated by socialists. Mises was used to seminars in which diverse views were expressed.

According to Hayek, "contrary to his reputation, [Mises was] an extremely tolerant person. He would have anyone in his seminar who was intellectually interested." Historian Friedrich Engel-Janosi, another seminar participant, also recalled Mises's seminar as politically diverse and Mises as personally tolerant.

Seminar participants ranged from liberal to socialist. They included women at a time when this was far from universal practice. There were both Christians and Jews; Mises himself was Jewish. The group was composed not just of economists, but also of leading philosophers and others in the social sciences and humanities. According to seminar participant economist Martha Steffy Browne: "I have lived in many cities and belonged to many organizations. I am sure there does not exist a second circle where the intensity, the interest and the intellectual standard of the discussions is as high as it was in the Mises Seminar." Fritz Machlup, another participant and later president of the American Economic Association, wrote: "I wonder whether there has ever existed anywhere a group from which so large a percentage of members became internationally recognized scholars." In addition to Hayek, other participants included Engel-Janosi, Browne, and Machlup, Oskar Morgenstern, another future president of the American Economic Association, J. Herbert von Fürth, who became a member of the Federal Reserve Board in the United States, and the following, each of whom also became a distinguished philosopher, economist, or other academic or professional: Erik Vögelin, Felix Kaufmann, Gottfried Haberler, Richard Strigl, Karl Schlesinger, Helene Lieser, Konrad Zweig, Ilse Mintz, Walter Frölich, Alfred Schütz, Eric Schiff, Robert Waelder, Karl Menger, and Emanuel Winternitz. It was a truly liberal colloquium.

In his 1969 *Historical Setting of the Austrian School of Economics,* Mises wrote that "after some years all the essential ideas of the Austrian school were by and large accepted as an integral part of economic theory. About the time of Menger's demise (1921), one no longer distinguished between an Austrian school and other economics. The appellation 'Austrian School' became the name given to an important chapter of the history of economic thought; it was no longer the name of a specific sect with doctrines different from those held by other economists."

Hayek also expressed thoughts along these lines. He said in 1965 that by the 1920s, the young Viennese economists (including himself) could "hardly any longer be seen as a separate school in the sense of representing particular doctrines. A school has its greatest success when it ceases as such to exist because its leading ideals have become a part of the general dominant teaching. The Vienna school has to a great extent come to enjoy such success."

Viennese Austrian political society from the 1890s through 1920s could, with more justice than other places and times, be called an "economistocracy" (rule by economists). Through Menger, Böhm-Bawerk, Wieser, Philippovich, Schumpeter, Mises, Bauer, and others, economists in Austria from all sides of the political spectrum exerted significant practical influence on public policy.

~

In his perceptive *Philosophy of the Austrian School* (1993), Italian political philosopher Raimondo Cubeddu remarks: "Just when the hopes of socialism seemed to be about to come true, Mises voiced the thoughts uppermost in the minds of so many who lacked the courage to speak out. Socialism could not work or keep its promises, he argued, because under such a system economic calculations in terms of value were rendered impossible." Moreover, too often socialists focused "'attention solely upon painting lurid pictures of existing conditions and glowing pictures of that golden age which is the natural consequence of the New Dispensation'"—always an unfair and not necessarily apposite comparison.

Among Mises's greatest personal attributes was courage. He had the force of will and character to maintain a position that he thought true even if almost no one else did. He concluded the epilogue to *Socialism:* "Not mythical 'material productive forces,' but reason and ideas determine the course of human affairs. What is needed to stop the trend towards socialism and despotism is common sense and moral courage."

Hayek was not excessively influenced by Mises intellectually before he went to the United States in March 1923, two months shy of his twenty-fourth birthday. Although Hayek had, by this time, been working for Mises for about a year and a half, during much of this time he had also been working as a student at the University of Vienna under Wieser, for whom he was writing a thesis for which he received a second degree in political science in early 1923.

Hayek did not participate in Mises's private seminar until after he returned from the United States in May 1924. The two appear to have been more business collaborators during the time they were together before Hayek went to the United States for fourteen months than the close intellectual interlocutors they became after he returned.

Socialism was Mises's work that most influenced Hayek early in their association. It was published in late 1922; the exact month is not known. The first review of it available was published in December 1922, and there were more reviews in 1923. This would indicate that the book was perhaps published late in the fall, several months before Hayek went to the United States—though Mises's earlier famous article, "Economic Calculation in the Socialist Commonwealth" (1920), would have been available to Hayek from the time he met Mises in late 1921.

Mises gradually permeated Hayek's thought. Hayek recalled the influence of *Socialism* on him when introducing a new edition of the work in 1978:

> When *Socialism* first appeared . . . , its impact was profound. It gradually but fundamentally altered the outlook of many of the young idealists returning . . . after World War I. . . .
>
> We felt that the civilization in which we had grown up had collapsed. We were determined to build a better world, and it was this desire to reconstruct society that led many of us to the study of economics. . . . And then came this book. . . . *Socialism* told us that we had been looking for improvement in the wrong direction. . . .
>
> . . . *Socialism* shocked our generation, and only slowly and painfully did we become persuaded of its central thesis.

Hayek also said, in an interview, about Mises and *Socialism,* that it was particularly a book (*Socialism*) that

> had the decisive influence of curing us, although it was a very long struggle. At first we all felt he was frightfully exaggerating and even offensive in tone. You see, he hurt all our deepest feelings, but gradually he won us around, although for a long time. . . . I just learned

he was usually right in his conclusions, but I was not completely satisfied with his argument. That, I think, followed me right through my
life. I was always influenced by Mises' answers, but not fully satisfied
by his arguments. It became very largely an attempt to improve the
argument, which I realized led to correct conclusions. But the question of why it hadn't persuaded most other people became a problem to me; so I became anxious to put it in a more effective form.

It is not possible to ascertain with precision for how long Hayek
retained mild socialist views after he started working for Mises. His interest in socialism and economics was sparked by the course and outcome of World War I, and after flirting with psychology, he turned to
economics at the University of Vienna during 1920, when Wieser returned to teaching. This was well over a year before he began to work
for Mises and could have been influenced by him.

Mises's central issue in *Socialism* and "Economic Calculation in
the Socialist Commonwealth" was economic calculation. How, absent
prices, would production be determined in a socialist economy? This
was a good question, as many socialist economists acknowledged.

Both works did not occur in a vacuum. They were informed by
the political circumstances in which they were written. As World War I
progressed, the Austrian economy became increasingly planned as
progressively larger shares of national economic output were tied to
the war effort. Before the war, there was not much agitation for classical socialism—that is, nationalization of the means of economic production—in Austria or elsewhere. Instead, practical proposals for
economic and social reform were modest: laws to regulate working
conditions and pay, establishment of government pension and unemployment plans, health and sanitary laws, and the like.

When Hayek wrote in *The Road to Serfdom* during World War
II that it was "the product of an experience as near as possible to twice
living through the same period—or . . . twice watching a very similar
evolution of ideas," he had in mind the proposals that had been made
to nationalize Austrian and German industry during World War I. Such
proposals were then being made in Great Britain during World War II:
"There exists now in this country certainly the same determination
that the organisation of the nation we have achieved for purposes of
defence shall be retained for the purposes of creation"; "students of
the currents of ideas can hardly fail to see that there is more than a superficial similarity between the trend of thought in Germany during

and after the last war and the present current of ideas in this country."
When Mises wrote "Economic Calculation in the Socialist Commonwealth" and *Socialism,* the debate on nationalizing industry was real,
as were Hayek's experiences with *The Road to Serfdom* during World
War II in England.

Mises was influenced by Böhm-Bawerk in his argument against
socialism. According to economic historian Henry Spiegel: "In the
writings of Wieser and Böhm-Bawerk there emerged what from then
on was to become a feature characteristic of the Austrian tradition in
economics—a critical reaction to the work of Karl Marx. This reaction,
which was relatively mild in the case of Wieser, became stronger in the
writings of Böhm-Bawerk and the later Austrians. . . . Böhm-Bawerk's
main argument was that the socialist criticism of capitalism was in fact
a criticism of the human condition, that is, of the central problem of
scarcity, with which socialism would have to cope just as did capitalism." Böhm-Bawerk was the first Austrian to attack classical socialism.
Then came Mises. Then came Hayek.

Building on Böhm-Bawerk's insight, Mises emphasized the essential role of prices for rational economic calculation. For economic
calculation to occur, there must be some way to evaluate goods in relation to one another. In a market order, this relationship is established
through freely fluctuating prices. Prices reflect scarcity of goods compared to one another and the people's demand for them. Prices are the
relative value of different goods. Moreover, Mises crucially emphasized
that unless there is private property, prices cannot exist. The exclusive
ability to exchange goods is what gives them their economic value.
Therefore, rational economic activity is based on private property.

The question of the relationship between Hayek's and Mises's
technical economic thought has long interested historians of economic
theory. Hayek undoubtedly absorbed key insights from Mises with respect to the fundamental role that prices play in economic calculation.
But where this was only one aspect of Mises's system, it became
Hayek's focus.

Hayek remarked that when he first went to work for Mises,
Mises was primarily known as an anti-inflationist on the basis of *The
Theory of Money and Credit* (1912), which is typically considered a notable extension of Austrian marginal utility ideas into the realm of
monetary theory.

Recalling his time working for Mises, Hayek stated: "I came to
know him mainly as a tremendously efficient executive, the kind of

man who . . . , because he does a normal day's work in two hours, has always a clear desk and time to talk about anything. I came to know him as one of the best-educated and -informed men I had ever known, and, what was most important at the time of great inflation, as the only man who really understood what was happening."

At this time, the body of academic literature attributes Austrian business or trade cycle theory jointly to Hayek and Mises. There is, however, a significant strand of writers who argue for greater differentiation between the two men's technical economic views than is typically considered the case, of whom Foundation for Economic Education scholar Bettina Bien Greaves is among the most prominent. Misesian economist and libertarian political activist Murray Rothbard, too—while he sometimes enunciated conflicting views in the area of the relationship between Hayek's and Mises's thought—stated later in his career that "more and more, it appears necessary to advance the dehomogenization of Mises and Hayek, even of 'Hayek I' [i.e., Hayek before the mid-1930s], not just for the sake of the historiography of economic thought, but also to rediscover the essence of the Austrian paradigm and to set Austrianism on a sound basis for future development."

Of his intellectual development and trade cycle theory, Hayek himself said in 1982 that it was in "the studies of my descriptive work on American monetary policy that I was led to develop my theories of monetary fluctuations." Moreover, in a June 17, 1976, letter to Percy Greaves of the Foundation for Economic Education, Hayek claimed priority in the development of Austrian trade cycle theory over Mises.

In a revelatory conclusion to a 1980 lecture on the future of money, Hayek said: "The pursuit of a monetary policy is really a very new idea. Until some sixty years ago monetary policy simply meant securing a gold equivalent or silver equivalent. . . . My interest in monetary policy began when I found in the 1923 Annual Report of the United States Federal Reserve Bank a statement which said that the control of the quantity of money could be used to assure the stabilization of economic activity. At that time, that was a new idea. It is only over the last sixty years that money has come to be regarded as one of the prime instruments of economic policy . . . and a useful way by which political authority could contribute to prosperity."

There is always the tendency in an era to presume that its ways of doing and understanding things are universal and eternal. But this perspective, to the extent it applies to temporal things, is inevitably wrong. Meetings of the Federal Reserve Board (and its equivalent in other nations) to direct interest rates to guide economic activity are not a preordained fact of nature or ineluctable essence of the universe. They are a public policy expedient at a given point in time. They will undoubtedly go the way of other, past public policy expedients and perhaps be as difficult for future generations to understand as it is for this generation to understand many of the political-economic policies of past generations.

As Hayek stated, when he began in economic theory during the 1920s, concepts of monetary policy as they are now understood were not then generally understood by the economics profession. The concept of a national bank to direct interest rates was, in the United States, really only a concept of the twentieth century.

As a student of Wieser's for his second degree before he went to New York, Hayek's primary research focus was almost wholly abstract theory. In America, his research became more practical; he focused on down-to-earth issues and empirical research.

In 1963, he provided this informative description of his year in New York:

Probably the most instructive and solid part of current discussion was that on central bank policy, turning largely around the important 1923 Report of the Federal Reserve Board. "Stabilisation" was the general catchword under which all these problems were discussed. What intrigued me most about all these problems, and has intrigued me ever since, was how much a stabilisation of the price level, or any other observable magnitude, would really secure an elimination of those disequilibrating forces which came from money. But the only paper I wrote at the time was an attempt to demonstrate that one could not at the same time stabilise the external and the internal value of money. I never published it because, before I could get it into decent enough English to submit it to an editor, Keynes's *Tract on Monetary Reform* was published in which he made the same point. I believe it struck most economists at that time as an entirely new consideration, though you may be surprised how late such a relatively simple circumstance came to be generally understood.

Great fascination of course was exercised at the time by the attempts at economic forecasting, particularly the economic barometers of the Harvard Economic Service. . . . There can be no doubt that it was this experience on my American visit which turned me and soon many of the other visitors to this country to the problems of the relations between monetary theory and the trade cycle.

The 1920s were among the most confused times economically in the Western world in a century. Russia had moved in a revolutionary socialist direction through nationalization of land and the means of economic production. The Austro-Hungarian Empire was shattered and political boundaries changed all over middle, eastern, and southern Europe as eight new states came into being. Germany and Austria considered nationalization acts as their economies and currencies disintegrated. In western Europe and America, the United Kingdom and the United States experienced great (though not, as in the Germanic world, catastrophic) inflation immediately after World War I, then depression. As the decade progressed, issues of returning to the gold standard, debt repayment, and war reparations occupied the stage. Then came the Great Depression.

During the 1920s there was less understanding of economic theory—that is, of correlations between antecedents and subsequents in the realm of economic activity—than was later believed to have become the case. The "science" of economics was new, still in its first blush. This was among the reasons Hayek's initial lectures at the London School of Economics and Political Science in early 1931 created such a sensation. It was still thought possible that entirely new ways of considering economic activity and theory could be put forward that would become generally accepted. These were the sociological circumstances in which Hayek conducted his early work in technical economic theory.

Rothbard was right that Mises's and Hayek's economic thought should be dehomogenized. Hayek described Mises's *Theory of Money and Credit* as "for many years the most profound and satisfying work on the subject available." Certainly it was an extraordinarily prescient work, with Mises speculating in 1912 that the value of money could drop to one-hundredth of its former value within a twelve-month period. What was once thought impossible became reality within a decade.

Hayek's trade cycle theory was not in essence the same as Mises's. Mises's primary concern and emphasis were that excessive monetary stimulation leads to economic collapse through out-of-control inflation. In 1952, he wrote in a new preface of *The Theory of Money and Credit*: "Forty years have passed since the first German-language edition of this volume was published. In the course of these four decades the world has gone through many disasters and catastrophes. The policies that brought about these unfortunate events have also affected the nations' currency systems. Sound money gave way to progressively depreciating fiat money. All countries are today vexed by inflation and threatened by the gloomy prospect of a complete breakdown of their currencies." In the work itself he wrote: "Questions of currency policy are questions of the objective exchange value of money."

For Hayek, this was exactly not the case. He wrote in 1929 in *Monetary Theory and the Trade Cycle,* his *Habilitation* dissertation by which he obtained his license to lecture and which was originally published in German: "The central subject of investigation [is] not changes in general prices but the divergence of the relation of particular prices as compared with the price system of static equilibrium"—relative prices. Hayek's emphasis and focus, in contrast to Mises's, was misproduction of temporally early capital, though Mises did mention this in some passages.

It is likely that Hayek was influenced to consider the role of prices in economic activity more substantially than he otherwise would have as a result of Mises's emphasis on the necessity of prices to engage in optimal economic activity. Nevertheless, Hayek stressed that his ideas in economic theory were his own.

When he said in the preface to the published version of his 1931 London lectures, *Prices and Production,* that they "came at a time when I had arrived at a clear view of the outlines of a theory of industrial fluctuations," it is evident that Hayek thought the theory of industrial fluctuations he put forward was new and his own. He said even more explicitly in the work itself that "the effects of a divergence between the money-rate and the equilibrium-rate of interest on relative prices were originally shortly discussed by Professor Mises. On the actual working of the price mechanism which brings about the changes in the structure of production his work contains however hardly more than the sentences quoted at the beginning of this lecture ['The first effect of the increase of productive activity, initiated by the policy of the banks to lend below the natural rate of interest is . . . to raise the prices of producers' goods while the prices of consumers' goods rise only moderately. . . . But soon a reverse movement sets in: prices of consumers' goods rise and prices of producers' goods fall. . . . ']."

Perhaps even more significantly, in *Monetary Theory and the Trade Cycle* Hayek held that the "investigations of Professor Mises

represent a big step forward in this direction [of a correct understanding of the trade cycle], although he still regards the fluctuations
in the value of money as the main object of his explanation, and deals
with the phenomena of disproportionality only in so far as they can
be regarded as consequences—in the widest sense of the term—of
these fluctuations." Hayek also said—of "the effects of a rate of interest lowered by monetary influences, which must necessarily lead
to the excessive production of capital goods"—that these effects
"have been partly described already by Mises, but they can only be
clearly observed by taking as the central subject of investigation not
changes in general prices but the divergences of the relation of particular prices as compared with the price system of static equilibrium." Indeed, he went so far as to say that the "presentation of his
[Mises's] theory under the guise of a theory of fluctuation in the
value of money remains dangerous, partly because it always gives rise
to misunderstandings, but mainly because it seems to bring into the
foreground a secondary effect of cyclical fluctuations [i.e., inflation],
an effect which generally accompanies the latter but which need not
necessarily do so."

Mises's *Theory of Money and Credit* was not available in English
translation until 1934. In the British academic community, Lionel
Robbins was for a time highly influenced by Mises, but more in the
areas of methodology and the feasibility of economic calculation in socialist systems than in monetary theory. In the crucible of economic debate in England during the early 1930s, it was Hayek, not Mises, who
was the actor, and it was Hayek's work that became known as Austrian
business cycle theory.

Even later, Mises did not adopt as his own Hayek's theory that
depressions and recessions are primarily caused by real changes in the
structure of production. Mises wrote in *Human Action* (1949) of his
own "monetary or circulation credit theory of the trade cycle": "The
wavelike movement affecting the economic system, the recurrence of
periods of boom which are followed by periods of depression, is the
unavoidable outcome of the attempts, repeated again and again, to
lower the gross market rate of interest by means of credit expansion.
The alternative is only whether the crisis should come sooner as the result of a voluntary abandonment of further credit expansion, or later
as a final and total catastrophe of the currency system involved."
Mises's main point was that excessive monetary expansion leads to inflationary collapse, not Hayek's thesis that excessive monetary expan-

sion misshapes the structure of production. What were paragraphs in Mises's thought became books in Hayek's.

It could be the case that Mises's oral teaching was slightly different from his written work, and it is possible that in his lectures he may have given more emphasis, as Hayek did, to relative price relationships that are disturbed by credit manipulation as well as to changes in the general price level. If so, there would be more congruity between Mises's and Hayek's business cycle theories. Hayek indicated this possibility to some extent in his 1982 introduction to the republication of various of his early articles on technical economic theory: "One episode in the growth of my expositions may perhaps be worth recording here. In the draft of my account of American monetary policy after 1920 I had made use of what I thought was a theory of Ludwig von Mises that was familiar to us in the Vienna circle. But another member of our group with whom I was in daily contact . . . persuaded me . . . that no sufficient exposition of the theory I had used was to be found in Mises's published work. . . . Thus arose the long footnote . . . containing the first statement of my version of Mises's theory."

∾

Another area in which Ebeling identifies Hayek as having been initially influenced by Mises is methodology. Before the middle 1930s, Hayek followed Mises in adopting an a priori conception of the theory of economic activity, although Hayek said he was never an a priorist philosophically. Following Mises, however, he thought at this time that economic theory is strictly deductive from premises. Economic theory consists of laws derived from the pure logic of choice of economic actors. Economics is not an empirical science, Hayek then thought.

In the middle 1930s, particularly in his 1936 presidential address to the London Economic Club, "Economics and Knowledge," Hayek moved in a more empirical direction. Here he held that while "individual action [i]s indeed purely deductive, as soon as the explanation move[s] to the interpersonal activities of the market, the crucial processes [a]re those by which information [i]s transmitted among individuals, and as such [a]re purely empirical."

In a 1926 letter to Wesley Clair Mitchell, whose lectures he attended while in New York, Hayek wrote of his "present work which shall embody some of the slowly ripening fruits of my sojourn in the United States." As early as that year, Hayek began to emphasize the connection between economic theory and real economic activity, a connection some of his Austrian forebears did not recognize with respect to business cycle theory and activity. According to German-language Hayek biographer Hans Jörg Hennecke, whose *Friedrich August von Hayek: Die Tradition der Freiheit* (The Tradition of Freedom) in 2000 was the first full-length biographical consideration of Hayek, Hayek and Mises discussed differences in their basic positions as early as 1932. Mises did not consider his business cycle theory to have been completely enunciated in his early *Theory of Money and Credit,* and he continued to develop it through the 1920s. More so than Mises, Hayek attempted to meld logical and empirical elements in his comprehensive description of economic activity.

Mises did not consider Hayek's 1936 "Economics and Knowledge" to be a break from his own position. Hayek wrote in a 1981 letter to economic theorist and historian Terence Hutchison that Mises "insisted that it ['Economics and Knowledge'] was not incompatible with his view." As Peter Klein writes in the introduction to the fourth volume in *The Collected Works of F. A. Hayek:* "The nature of the Mises-Hayek relationship" is not yet "fully understood."

In several later interviews, Hayek said that Mises was a "rationalist utilitarian." It is worthwhile to turn to these interviews to get a better idea of what Hayek meant, where he thought the differences between himself and Mises lay, and what he considered Mises's and his own contributions to be. He said to economist Jack High in 1978:

> . . . in most instances I found he was simply right; but in some instances, particularly the philosophical background—I think I should put it that way—Mises remained to the end a utilitarian rationalist. I came to the conclusion that both utilitarianism as a philosophy and the idea of it—that we were guided mostly by rational calculations—just would not be true.
>
> That led me to my latest development, on the insight that we largely had learned certain practices which were efficient without really understanding why we did it; so that it was wrong to interpret the economic system on the basis of rational action. It was probably much truer that we had learned certain rules of conduct which were traditional in our society. As for why we did, there was a problem of selective evolution rather than rational construction.

He said to future Nobel economist James Buchanan that Mises

had great influence on me, but I always differed, first not consciously and now quite consciously. Mises was a rationalist utilitarian, and I am not. He trusted the intelligent insight of people pursuing their known goals, rather disregarding the traditional element, the element of surrounding rules. He wouldn't accept legal positivism completely, but he was much nearer it than I would be. He would believe that the legal system—no, he wouldn't believe that it was invented; he was too much a pupil of Menger for that. But he still was inclined to see [the legal system] as a sort of rational construction. I don't think the evolutionary aspect, which is very strongly in Menger, was preserved in the later members of the Austrian school. I must say 'til I came, really, in between there was very little of it.

Regardless of whether Hayek's evaluation of Mises was correct (and many Misesians do not think it was), his essential point was clear. Hayek thought that societal institutions evolve in an unplanned manner. Mises, on the other hand, Hayek believed, was more inclined to the view that societal institutions should be rationally constructed along utilitarian lines of the greatest happiness for the greatest number. Hayek nonetheless thought that Mises made a substantial contribution to the conception of the unplanned evolution of societal institutions through his emphasis on the necessity of prices to calculate. "Mises as much as anybody has helped us to understand something which we have not designed," Hayek wrote in his 1978 foreword to *Socialism.*

Hayek expressed more fully and deeply than Mises the epistemological argument for free market order. The crucial issue for Hayek became not that without prices individuals cannot calculate (though he thought this to be the case), but that the division of knowledge renders centralized control of an economy or society impossible. If Mises, "instead of saying simply that without a market, calculation is impossible, had claimed that without a market, people would not know what to produce, how much to produce, and in what manner to produce, people might have understood him. But he never put it like this," Hayek said.

Hayek concluded a tributary introduction to Mises's *Notes and Recollections* in 1977: "That they had one of the great thinkers of our time in their midst, the Viennese have never understood." Despite the place in which Hayek rendered this judgment, it was his considered view. Mises was the greater teacher. Hayek was the more effective writer.

As he aged, Hayek's appreciation for Mises increased. At one time, he considered introducing each chapter of "The Fatal Conceit" with an epigraph from Mises's work.

While it is possible to imagine Mises without Hayek, it is not possible to imagine Hayek without Mises. Hayek's great accomplishment was to enunciate the idea of the "division of knowledge" and to explore its ramifications in various areas. Many economists have been and continue to be influenced by Ludwig von Mises. A great teacher lives on in the life and work of his students and their students. Mises's contribution was lasting, which can be said of so few.

That Hayek and his colleagues as young men in Vienna would initially, for professional reasons, downplay association with Mises may have led to their tendency even in later life not to emphasize their relationship on first being asked. If so, Mises's influence was even greater than they said. Mises truly was great.

5

Money and Capital

THE QUESTION OF THE VALUE OF HAYEK'S WORK IN TECHNICAL economic theory from the middle 1920s through early 1940s is one over
which there is considerable dispute in the academic economic community. Some, such as contemporary Austrian economists Roger Garrison, Mark Skousen, and Gene Callahan, consider this work to be of
vital, continuing relevance. Others, such as Nobel Prize winners Milton
Friedman, James Buchanan, and Ronald Coase, while they have the
highest opinion of Hayek, do not consider his work in technical economic theory to be of much worth.

Hayek's first major publications in economic theory were two
articles he wrote in Vienna on his research in New York, "Stabilization
Problems in Gold Exchange Standard Countries" and "The Monetary
Policy of the United States after the Recovery from the 1920 Crisis."
Both were published, respectively in 1924 and 1925, in the *Zeitschrift
für Volkswirtschaft und Sozialpolitik* (Journal of Political Economy
and Social Policy), a number of whose editorial staff were economists
associated with the Austrian school.

Among the most interesting aspects of these early articles is that
in each Hayek put forward the inevitability of a trade or business cycle.
In the first article, he wrote of "the organization of the monetary system as such" that "[t]herein seems to lie the seed for serious economic
disruptions and business crises, as long as it is kept in its present guise."
He wrote in the second that "[d]uring the course of the last decade, at
least in the Anglo-Saxon countries, the investigation of the alternation
of periods of prosperity and stagnation that had been correctly observed by representatives of the 'currency school' almost a hundred

years ago completely displaced the analysis of the crisis viewed as an isolated phenomenon"—in other words, a business cycle, not isolated economic fluctuations.

Hayek's bedrock assumption in his early economic theorizing was that there is a business cycle and that it is caused by the organization of the monetary system. He could hardly have been more explicit than he was on these points in his later *Monetary Theory and the Trade Cycle*, his 1929 *Habilitation* dissertation and first sustained work in economic theory. Here he wrote of "the necessity of the Trade Cycle" and that "all economic phenomena present that regular wave-like appearance which we observe in cyclical fluctuations." The new general editor of Hayek's collected works, Bruce Caldwell, writes that "[f]or Hayek, the cycle was a virtually unavoidable consequence of a credit economy" and that "Hayek's fundamental point is that the business cycle is an unfortunate but unavoidable concomitant of a credit economy."

Hayek wrote many articles and works in technical economic theory from the middle 1920s through early 1940s, of which the most important include:

> "Intertemporal Price Equilibrium and Movements in the Value of Money" (1928)
> "The 'Paradox' of Saving" (1929)
> *Monetary Theory and the Trade Cycle* (1929, 1933)
> *Prices and Production* (1931, 1935)
> "Prices, Expectations, Monetary Disturbances and Malinvestments" (1933)
> *Monetary Nationalism and International Stability* (1937)
> *Profits, Interest and Investment* (1939)
> *The Pure Theory of Capital* (1941)
> "A Commodity Reserve Currency" (1943)

In addition, he had a famous exchange with John Maynard Keynes in reviewing Keynes's *Treatise on Money,* a lesser exchange with Keynes's crony Piero Sraffa that emanated from the Hayek-Keynes interchange, and controversies with Frank Knight on capital and Nicholas Kaldor on the "Ricardo Effect."

In "Intertemporal Price Equilibrium and Movements in the Value of Money," Hayek expressed an idea found in much of his later work, that "[a]ll economic activity is carried out through time." This might appear to be among the most basic of postulates, but for Hayek the idea had profound significance: "Every individual economic process occupies a certain time, and all linkages between economic processes necessarily involve longer or shorter periods of time."

The time component of economic production became vital in Hayek's work in economic theory. Essentially, his economic work could be said to rest on the idea that the price system is a method for coordinating economic activity through time. If prices, in particular interest, become distorted from their true or (in the case of interest) natural amounts or rate, then economic disequilibrium results. His primary contention was that such disequilibration was an inevitable outcome of the money and credit system as it has developed. The price system was, for Hayek, largely an "intertemporal price system."

Hayek's major works in monetary theory were *Monetary Theory and the Trade Cycle* and *Prices and Production*. Each of these companion books is quite short, no more than about 50,000 words. He described their relationship in the preface to the English version of *Monetary Theory and the Trade Cycle:* "My *Prices and Production* . . . should be considered as an essential complement to the present publication. While I have here emphasized the *monetary causes* which *start* the cyclical fluctuations, I have, in that later publication, concentrated on the *successive changes in the real structure of production,* which *constitute* those fluctuations." Significantly, Hayek considered *Monetary Theory and the Trade Cycle* to be the more important of his two primary works in monetary theory. In that preface he also wrote that "[t]his essential complement of my theory seems to me to be the more important since, in consequence of actual economic developments, the over-simplified monetary explanations have gained undeserved prominence in recent times."

Though *Monetary Theory and the Trade Cycle* was written before *Prices and Production,* and though it was the more general and, in Hayek's view, more important of the two works, it was not translated into English until after he gave his *Prices and Production* lectures at the London School of Economics in early 1931, lectures that were published later that year. Hayekian economist Gerald O'Driscoll summarizes the relationship between the two books thusly: "*Prices and Production* . . . was Hayek's first major work in English. . . . *Prices and Production* brought Hayek widespread recognition in England. . . . *Monetary Theory and the Trade Cycle* was not published until 1933. . . . Expressing, as it does, Hayek's views on monetary theory in more detail, *Monetary Theory and the Trade Cycle* should be read before *Prices and Production.* Yet English readers did not have access to the earlier work until two years after the publication of *Prices and Production.*"

In his 1962 inaugural lecture at the University of Freiburg, Hayek remarked that in "the German discussion I was regarded as a pronounced representative of monetary explanations of the trade cycle, and my efforts had indeed been directed to emphasizing the role money played in these processes. But in England I encountered a much more extreme form of a purely monetary explanation which regarded the fluctuations of the general price level as the essence of the phenomena. The consequence was that my arguments had soon to be directed against the dominant kind of monetary theory of the trade cycles and to aim at stressing the importance of the real factors, perhaps somewhat to the bewilderment of those who regarded me as a typical representative of monetary explanations." Although Hayek ascribed a primarily monetary source to economic fluctuations, he was not a monetarist as this term came to be used.

He was emphatic that the optimal policy goal was not stabilization of prices. In *Monetary Theory and the Trade Cycle* he considered it his goal to "refute certain theories which have led to the belief that, by stabilizing the general price level, all the disturbing monetary causes would be eliminated." He criticized the "superficial view which sees no other harmful effect of a credit expansion but the rise of the price level" and he argued against previous "adherents of the monetary theory of the Trade Cycle [who] have sought an explanation either exclusively or predominantly in the superficial phenomena of changes in the value of money, while failing to pursue the far more profound and fundamental effects of the process by which money is introduced into the economic system, as distinct from its effect on prices in general." He held: "*Monetary theory has by no means finished its work when it has explained the absolute level of prices . . . ; its far more important task is to explain the changes in the relative height of particular prices which are conditioned by the introduction of money.*" For Hayek, indeed: "General price changes are no essential feature of a monetary theory of the Trade Cycle; *they are not only unessential, but they would be completely irrelevant if only they were completely 'general'—that is, if they affected all prices at the same time and in the same proportion.*"

According to Hayek, the prevailing monetarist view held that the only influence of money in an economy is its effect on the general price level. Basically, according to Hayek, monetarists believe that as long as prices are stable, monetary policy is being conducted appropriately. Deflation and inflation are, from a conventional monetarist perspective, harmful, because, in the case of deflation, it is almost invariably associated with economic downturns; and in the case of inflation, because, notwithstanding the temporary fillip inflation may provide, it corrodes sustained economic growth.

His view of conventional monetary theory was contained in this paragraph from the 1932 English edition preface of *Monetary Theory and the Trade Cycle:*

> It is a curious fact that the general disinclination to explain the past boom by monetary factors has been quickly replaced by an even greater readiness to hold the present working of our monetary organization exclusively responsible for our present plight. And the same stabilizers [advocates of stable prices] who believed that nothing was wrong with the boom and that it might last indefinitely because prices did not rise, now believe that everything could be set right again if only we would use the weapons of monetary policy to prevent prices from falling. The same superficial view which sees no other harmful effect of a credit expansion but the rise of the price level, now believes that our only difficulty is a fall in the price level, caused by credit contraction.

Hayek rejected the conventional monetarist views of appropriate monetary policy during the expansion that preceded the Great Depression and during the Great Depression itself, and of what monetary policy actually was during the Great Depression. Hayek thought that the American Federal Reserve practiced an expansionary monetary policy between 1927 and at least most of 1931.

The theoretical conception underlying his view of trade or business cycle activity was that money alone injects uncertainty into a national economy:

> The problem before us [of economic fluctuations] cannot be solved by examining the effect of a certain cause within the framework, and by the methods, of equilibrium theory. Any theory which limits itself to the explanation of empirically observed interconnections by the methods of elementary theory necessarily contains a self-contradiction. For Trade Cycle theory cannot aim at the adaptation of the adjusting mechanism of static theory to a special case; this scheme of explanation must itself be extended so as to explain how such discrepancies between supply and demand can ever arise. The obvious,

and (to my mind) the only possible way out of this dilemma, is to explain the difference between the course of events described by static theory (which only permits movements towards an equilibrium, and which is deduced by directly contrasting the supply of and the demand for goods) and the actual course of events, by the fact that, with the introduction of money . . . , a new determining cause is introduced. Money . . . does away with the rigid interdependence and self-sufficiency of the "closed" system of equilibrium, and makes possible movement which would be excluded from the latter.

This passage contains the essence of Hayek's conception of trade cycle theory.

According to his understanding, in the ideal world of static equilibrium theory—a pure barter economy in which money does not exist or, at least, play a functional role—supply and demand are always in balance. There is no such thing as a trade cycle, for, according to static equilibrium theory, supply and demand are (by definition) in accord. What, then, leads to economic fluctuations in the real world, outside the world of static equilibrium theory? The answer, to Hayek, was money. Money causes the departure from equilibrium in reality that does not exist in theory. Caldwell writes: "Hayek assumed that the adjustment mechanism [of the market system], formally described in what he called 'equilibrium theory,' works faultlessly in a world in which money is absent."

Hayek always retained the view that money (at least as it has developed institutionally in advanced economies) causes the departure from equilibrium in fact that does not exist in theory. "Money by its very nature constitutes a kind of loose joint in the self-equilibrating apparatus of the price mechanism which is bound to impede its working," he wrote a decade later in *The Pure Theory of Capital.* In 1960, three decades later, he expressed this view again in *The Constitution of Liberty,* in almost exactly the same words: "Money" is "a kind of loose joint in the otherwise self-steering mechanism of the market. . . . [T]he effects of a change in the supply of money . . . do not directly lead to a new equilibrium." He said much the same in substance in one of his last major discussions of money, the 1981 "Future Unit of Value": "Our money is only a still imperfect link in the self-steering mechanism of the market. We should endeavour to learn how to make it function better." As editor Roy McCloughry wrote in introducing Hayek's 1984 collection *Money, Capital, and Fluctuations: Early Essays:* "Although

Hayek's position has changed over the years, sometimes with great subtlety, one of the most enduring qualities of his statements has been their consistency."

Vitally, for Hayek, disequilibration will occur even if the goal of monetary policy is stable prices for, as an economy expands, its money supply must increase if there is not to be deflation: "In this case, stability of the price-level presupposes changes in the volume of money: but these changes must always lead to a discrepancy between the amount of real savings and the volume of investment. *The rate of interest at which, in an expanding economy, the amount of new money entering circulation is just sufficient to keep the price-level stable, is always lower than the rate which would keep the amount of available loan-capital equal to the amount simultaneously saved by the public:* and thus, despite the stability of the price-level, it makes possible a development leading away from the equilibrium position." He also remarked that "the only point of importance is that the effects of an artificially lowered rate of interest . . . exist whether this same circumstance does or does not eventually react on the general value of money." Even stable prices lead to periodic busts. This, to Hayek, was the monetary explanation of the trade cycle.

In 1926, he wrote to Wesley Clair Mitchell at Columbia University, with whom he had studied while in New York and who so praised Wieser's *Social Economics:* "While my theoretical predilections have remained unchanged, I realize now the weak points of abstract economic theory which seem to most of you to make the pure theory more or less useless for the explanation of the more complex phenomena of the money economy. It seems to me now as if pure theory had actually neglected in a shameful way the essential differences between a barter economy and a money economy." It was essential, Hayek wrote, to "pay sufficient regard to *time.*" Hayek attempted to forge a bridge between the static barter economy of equilibrium in theory and the dynamic money economy of the trade cycle in empirical fact, writing: "I hope . . . to be on the way to supply some of the missing links between orthodox economic theory and one applicable to the explanation of the processes of modern economic life."

While *Monetary Theory and the Trade Cycle* concerned the monetary causes that start cyclical fluctuations, *Prices and Production* concerned the real changes in the structure of production that thereafter constitute cyclical fluctuations. *Prices and Production* was, Hayek said, "a continuation of an argument which I had begun in other publications that at the time of its first appearance were available only in German," referencing *Monetary Theory and the Trade Cycle* in a footnote. He noted in *Prices and Production*'s preface of "how small a section of the whole field of monetary theory is actually treated in this book." This section was "the real phenomena" that constitute economic fluctuations following their monetary source.

Hayek's point of departure in *Prices and Production,* as elsewhere throughout his economic theory across his career, was that the most significant aspect of a monetary change is where it occurs in the economic system: "Everything depends on the point where the additional money is injected into circulation (or where money is withdrawn from circulation), and the effects may be quite opposite according as the additional money comes first into the hands of traders and manufacturers or directly into the hands of salaried people employed by the State." For him, the main point was, again, not the effect of an increase in money supply on the general price level, but "the influence which an increase in the amount of money exercises upon the production of capital, either directly or through the rate of interest."

Adam Smith Institute director Eamonn Butler describes Hayek's conception of the productive consequences following a monetary stimulus through lowered interest rates: "The cheapness of capital investment causes what modern economists would call a deepening of the capital structure. It now becomes more profitable to manufacture goods of greater complexity or refinement, requiring additional stages of production. . . . The result is that the credit expansion has caused a marked change in the distribution and use of economic resources." Hayek's idea of the business cycle was strongly influenced by his Austrian school of economics background. Menger's notion of different orders of goods is very evident, as is Böhm-Bawerk's emphases on time and roundabout methods of production. In his 1925 "Monetary Policy of the United States after the Recovery from the 1920 Crisis," Hayek wrote that the result of expansionary monetary policy was, in Mengerian terms, "the excessive expansion of the producer-goods industries, in general terms the relatively greater expansion of the output of goods of higher order as compared to those of lower order." As far back as his 1923–24 sojourn in the United States, he focused on issues of the effects of stable prices. The title of his intended thesis in New York was: "Is the function of money consistent with an artificial stabilization of its purchasing power?"

Hayek was emphatic that a policy of stable prices is not economically optimal, and is, in fact, highly deleterious. He wrote in the 1928 "Intertemporal Price Equilibrium and Movements in the Value of Money": "Given what has . . . been said, it must be assumed, in sharpest contradiction to the prevailing view, that it is not any deficiency in the stability of the purchasing power of money that constitutes one of the most important sources of disturbances of the economy from the supply of money"; and: "In describing the damaging effects which can arise from money . . . , it is not changes in the value of money which should be at issue, but disturbances of the intertemporal price system."

He also held that, from the perspective of empirical fact, the United States Federal Reserve practiced an expansionary monetary policy between 1927 and 1931, when the converse is now the usually accepted view. He wrote in the June 1932 preface to *Monetary Theory and the Trade Cycle* that there could,

> of course, be little doubt that, at the present time, a deflationary process is going on and that an indefinite continuation of that deflation would do inestimable harm. But this does not, by any means, necessarily mean that the deflation is the original cause of our difficulties or that we could overcome these difficulties by compensating for the deflationary tendencies, at present operative in our economic system, by forcing more money into circulation. . . . Far from following a deflationary policy, Central Banks, particularly in the United States, have been making earlier and more far-reaching efforts than have ever been undertaken before to combat the depression by a policy of credit expansion—with the result that the depression has lasted longer and has become more severe than any preceding one.

Hayek did not believe, in June 1932, that the deflation then being experienced was necessarily a primarily monetary phenomenon: "There is no reason to assume that the crisis was started by a deliberate deflationary action on the part of the monetary authorities, or that the deflation itself is anything but a secondary phenomenon, a process induced by the maladjustments of industry left over from the boom." This deflation was "not a cause but an effect of the unprofitableness of industry." For him, it was "surely vain to hope that, by reversing the deflationary process, we can regain lasting prosperity." He also wrote in 1932 in "The Fate of the Gold Standard" that "[f]rom 1927 onward . . .

the Federal Reserve Banks were rekindling a boom . . . by further huge injections of credit"; and that these huge injections were "maintain[ed] . . . for another two years at . . . [this] previously unheard of level." He added in "The Fate of the Gold Standard" that "[a]lthough there can be no doubt that the fall in prices since 1929 has been extremely harmful, this nevertheless does not mean that the attempts made since then to combat it by a systematic expansion of credit have not done more harm than good."

Two years later, in 1934, Hayek continued to affirm that the U.S. Federal Reserve maintained a highly expansionary monetary policy at least from 1927 through 1931, as well as earlier during the 1920s. In an April article, Hayek wrote that "in that year [1927] an entirely unprecedented action was taken by the American monetary authorities. . . . The authorities succeeded, by means of an easy-money policy, inaugurated as soon as the symptoms of an impending reaction were noticed in prolonging the boom for two years [until 1929] beyond what would otherwise have been its natural end. And when the crisis finally occurred [in 1929], for almost two more years, deliberate attempts were made to prevent, by all conceivable means, the normal process of liquidation."

He wrote in his 1935 obituary of the classical liberal doyen at the London School of Economics, Edwin Cannan, that Cannan's work *Money* "is a very notable contribution to monetary theory . . . and has a close relationship to the views expounded by Mises on basic theoretical questions." In *Money,* Cannan provided the following description of—from his, more standard, perspective—the monetary source of a trade cycle:

> If prices generally are rising, recognition of the fact is very apt to induce most people to hurry up with their purchases, so that they may secure what they want, either for consumption and use or for purposes of their business, before they have to pay more for it. This causes orders to come crowding in on the producers at a rate more rapid than usual, which of course tends to increase the rise of prices due to the original cause. . . . General elation or "boom" sets in. Conversely, if prices are falling, recognition of the fact causes people to delay purchasing, whether they are buying for their own consumption and use or for business purposes. Then orders come in to the producers more slowly than usual, production is not at once correspondingly reduced, so that unsold goods accumulate, which inclines sellers to lower their prices. General depression ensues.

There was a substantial difference between Cannan's and Hayek's conceptions of the monetary source of business cycle activity. Cannan's view was of a general rise or general decline in prices affecting consumers and producers simultaneously. Hayek's view was of a particular rise in interest rate–sensitive prices affecting producers predominantly first and then shifting to affect mostly consumers.

Hayek had originally written in *Monetary Theory and the Trade Cycle* in 1929 that "there can, at the present time, be no more important task in this field [of business forecasting] than the bridging of the gulf which divides monetary from non-monetary opinions." He added in the 1933 edition, though, that "[s]ince the publication of the German edition of this book, I have become less convinced that the difference between monetary and nonmonetary explanations is *the most important* point of disagreement between the various Trade Cycle theories. On the one hand, it seems to me that within the monetary group of explanations the difference between those theorists who regard the superficial phenomena of changes in the value of money as decisive factors in determining cyclical fluctuations, and those who lay emphasis on the real changes in the structure of production brought about by monetary causes [such as Hayek himself], is much greater than the difference between the latter group and such so-called nonmonetary theorists as Prof. Spiethoff and Prof. Cassel." That is, Hayek's view was closer to certain non-monetary theorists on the continent than to many monetary theorists in England and elsewhere.

~

Regarding Hayek's "famous" Copenhagen lecture of December 7, 1933, "Price Expectations, Monetary Disturbances and Malinvestments," Israel Kirzner, the leading contemporary exponent of the Austrian tradition, remarks that, for Hayek, "[t]he concept of equilibrium assumes . . . that everybody possesses correct foresight." Hayek said in the lecture that instead of "disregarding the time element, we must make very definite assumptions about the attitude of persons towards the future. The assumptions of this kind which are implied in the concept of equilibrium are essentially that everybody foresees the future correctly."

Time is basic in Hayek's concept of economic activity and the role of capital. Production occurs over time. The price system is in part an intertemporal valuing system. If the price system for capital is disrupted through interest rates below what the amount of savings in a community will sustain, then too much capital will be built for which the investment funds do not exist to complete these capital projects. These goods of higher orders will be wasted.

In the second phase of the business cycle, consumers bid up the demand for consumer goods (goods of first order) with the sums that they have received for producing the goods of higher order. The ultimate upshot of monetary expansion "will mean a new and reversed change of the proportion between the demand for consumer goods and the demand for producer goods in favour of the former."

Hayek listed in the fourth chapter of *The Pure Theory of Capital* a series of paired propositions "intended to represent the traditional or 'Anglo-American' point of view . . . [and] the contrasting 'Austrian' view on the same problem" (see figure 5.1).

Figure 5.1

"Anglo-American" Position	*"Austrian" Position*
Stress is laid exclusively on the role of fixed capital as if capital consisted only of very durable goods.	Stress is laid on the role of circulating capital which arises out of the duration of the process of production . . .
The term capital goods is reserved to durable goods which are treated as needing replacement only discontinuously or periodically.	Non-permanence is regarded as the characteristic attribute of all capital goods, and the emphasis is accordingly laid on the need for continuous reproduction of all capital.
The supply of capital goods is assumed to be given for the comparatively short run.	It is assumed that the stock of capital goods is being constantly used up and reproduced.
The demand for capital goods is assumed to vary in the same direction as demand for consumers' goods but in an exaggerated degree.	The demand for capital goods is assumed to vary in the opposite direction from the demand for consumers' goods.
The analysis is carried out in monetary terms, and a change in demand is assumed to mean a corresponding change in the size of the total money stream.	The analysis is carried out in "real" terms, and an increased demand somewhere must therefore necessarily mean a corresponding decrease in demand somewhere else.

The gist of Hayek's position was evident. To him, capital structure is highly dynamic. It fluctuates, as an economy does—its fluctuations are, in fact, tied largely to the overall fluctuations in the economy, though in an inverse manner. The important processes are not so much monetary as "real," and the departure for analysis is theoretical equilibrium. In addition, he discounted that there are likely unused capital resources during a depression. Rather, there are misinvested capital resources.

He wrote in the concluding section of *The Pure Theory of Capital:* "Money is of course never 'neutral.' . . . [I]t always exercises some positive influence on the course of events. It would not be difficult to show how this role of money is bound to lead to constant fluctuations of economic activity. . . . And the theory of fluctuations largely consists, of course, of a study of the interaction between the monetary and the real factors." Whether in Hayek's monetary or capital theory, the argument was the same. Brian McCormick, author of the 1992 *Hayek and the Keynesian Avalanche,* writes of *The Pure Theory of Capital* that "the book failed to capture the imagination of the profession."

Hayek's last major work during the 1930s on trade cycle theory was the 1939 collection of essays and articles, *Profits, Interest and Investment: and Other Essays on the Theory of Industrial Fluctuations.* These were written over the previous decade and together comprised an attempt to "improve and develop the outline of a theory of industrial fluctuations contained in two small books on *Monetary Theory and the Trade Cycle* and *Prices and Production.*"

Hayek provided his essential view of appropriate monetary policy in the main essay that gave the book its title. Optimal monetary policy should counterbalance what he saw as the destabilizing effects of the introduction of money into the productive process. As an economy is heating up, a restrictive monetary policy should be followed, not to prevent inflation but to ensure that the productive capacities of the economy do not become mismatched with the real demand for production and real savings. Likewise, as an economy is contracting, a more expansive monetary policy should be followed for precisely the same reasons. He held:

> What amount of changes in the rate of interest would be necessary to prevent the recurrence of cumulative processes in either direction we do not know because such a policy has never been tried. And it is, of course, true that in the absence of an automatic

mechanism making rates of interest move with rates of profits it would require superhuman wisdom to adjust them perfectly by deliberate policy. But this by no means proves that we might not get much nearer to the ideal than we have done. . . .

If we have to steer a car along a narrow road between two walls, we can either keep it in the middle of the road by fairly frequent but small movements of the steering wheel; or we can wait longer when the car deviates to one side and then bring it back by more or less violent jerks, probably overshooting the mark and risking collision with the other wall; or we can try to keep the steering wheel stiff and let the car bang alternately into either wall with a good chance of leading the car and ourselves to ultimate destruction.

Hayek came to favor a policy of incremental interest rate adjustments to macromanage a nation's economy. He also remarked along these lines in *The Road to Serfdom,* though he did not discuss technical economic theory there, that

there is, finally, the supremely important problem of combating general fluctuations of economic activity and the recurrent waves of large scale unemployment which accompany them. This is, of course, one of the gravest and most pressing problems of our time. . . . Many economists [including, presumably, Hayek himself] hope indeed that the ultimate remedy may be found in the field of monetary policy, which would involve nothing incompatible even with nineteenth century liberalism. Others [including, by this time, Keynes and most economists], it is true, believe that real success can be expected only from the skilful timing of public works. . . . But this is neither the only, nor, in my opinion, the most promising way of meeting the gravest threat to economic security. In any case, the very necessary efforts to secure protection against these fluctuations do not lead to the kind of planning which constitutes such a threat to our freedom.

Hayek became considerably more integrated with the rest of economic academia, at least with respect to practical policy and personal comity—though not with respect to emerging mathematical method—after his initial grand entry at the London School of Economics. While he did not backtrack from his fundamental analyses, he countenanced and even advocated that activist monetary policies could be appropriate policy and that even public works might have a role to play in evening out the vagaries of the business cycle—though he was disinclined to take the latter direction because it "might lead to much more serious restrictions of the competitive sphere." The economic planning Hayek opposed was national government management of prices, production, land, and the means of production.

Hayek's other significant work during the 1930s was *Monetary Nationalism and International Stability*, a collection of lectures he gave in Geneva published in 1937. He was of two minds about these lectures. On one hand, he considered them hastily written and only a sketch of his views, somewhat like his later *Denationalisation of Money*. Nonetheless, as he said in this latter work decades later, *Monetary Nationalism and International Stability* "contains important arguments against flexible exchange rates between national currencies which have never been adequately answered." In addition, in the chapter of *The Constitution of Liberty* titled "The Monetary Framework," the only one of his early works in economic theory to which he referred—twice in the chapter's nineteen notes—was *Monetary Nationalism and International Stability*.

Hayek supported an international gold standard through World War II. Only such standard would, he thought, provide the discipline necessary for individual nations to maintain noninflationary policies. A system of variable exchange rates hinders international trade, he also believed.

In *Monetary Nationalism and International Stability*, he displayed his radical belief in the power of ideas and the tie between the words of economists and public policy:

> The immediate influence of the theoretical speculation is probably weak, but that it has had a profound influence in shaping these views which to-day dominate monetary policy is not open to serious question.
>
> I am profoundly convinced that it is academic discussion of this sort which in the long run forms public opinion and which in consequence decides what will be practical politics some time hence.
>
> Much must be done in the realm of ideas before we can hope to achieve the basis of a stable international system.
>
> I do believe that in the long run human affairs are guided by intellectual forces. It is this belief which for me gives abstract considerations of this sort their importance, however slight may be their bearing on what is practicable in the immediate future.

Hayek considered it his purpose, throughout his professional career, to make politically possible what was thought to be politically impossible. Ultimately he did not write for his fellow academics, but to influence public policy no matter how distantly.

Hayek's student George L. S. Shakle greatly praised Hayek for *The Pure Theory of Capital.* Shakle considered its composition heroic for the "sustained intensity of thought" it reflected which Hayek imposed on several manuscript drafts of the work written over seven years, from about 1933 to 1940.

Shakle's later *The Years of High Theory,* which was published in 1967 and which covered the development of academic economic theory during the 1930s in depth, mentioned Hayek only twice, both times as editor of Gunnar Myrdal's work. Shakle did not consider Hayek substantively in the book.

In John Hicks's 1967 retrospective "The Hayek Story," on the role of Hayek in the progression of economic theory during the 1930s, the author remarked that by the time the essay was written, "Hayek's economic writings . . . are almost unknown to the modern student." Hicks received the Nobel Prize in Economic Sciences in 1972, the fourth year the award was presented. He considered his approach in capital theory to be "neo-Austrian," as a result of his emphasis on production as a process that occurs through time.

Hayek described his conception of the history of the Austrian school of economics, including its later generations, several times during his career, in encyclopedia articles and elsewhere. He considered Menger to be the first generation and Wieser and Böhm-Bawerk leading the second generation. Mises and Schumpeter were the most prominent students of the Austrian initiators during the third generation, and Hayek and his associates were the fourth generation. Hayek's typology was not what has become standard. Typically, Wieser and Böhm-Bawerk are now considered to be founders of the Austrian school with Menger. In addition, Hayek and his young associates were often referred to as "younger" Austrians in academic economic theory during years from about the middle 1920s to 1940.

Mises's place in the history of the Austrian school is central. Mises brought Austrian economics institutionally to the United States and continued to be the school's intellectual mentor until his death in 1973. By the early 1970s Hayek had not focused on technical economic theory for over thirty years.

Hayek's view of the later development of the Austrian school of economics and of its influence after him and fourth-generation associates, including Haberler, Morgenstern, and Machlup, is interesting.

Hayek considered the fourth generation of the Austrian school as it developed in Austria to have been vitally influenced by Mises. The same can be said of the Austrian school as it has developed in the United States; many of its leaders were students of Mises. Hans Mayer, Wieser's successor and a contemporary of Mises, had formed before World War II what is now an extinct branch of the Austrian school.

Hayek considered the development of the Austrian school from a broad perspective. He believed Lionel Robbins had made an important contribution to Austrian economics during the 1930s, and he thought that Philip Wicksteed and Frank Knight made substantial contributions that were incorporated in the Austrian tradition. He considered this tradition to extend to Hicks, at least in some of his work and even though Hicks did not consider himself to be an Austrian; Hayek believed Hicks's work in marginal utility analysis to be the final statement in the field, whose initiators he considered to have included Irving Fisher and Francis Edgeworth, and Wieser. Hayek did not consider Alfred Marshall or Paul Samuelson important theoretically in the development of economic theory, though he acknowledged their prominence.

Hayek considered the fifth generation of the Austrian school to include, preeminently, Murray Rothbard and Israel Kirzner, and he wrote in 1985 that its "present most representative work [is] probably being done by Thomas Sowell." Hayek had an exceptionally high regard for Sowell, though he, too, is not typically emphasized (or even considered) as an Austrian. Hayek said of Sowell in a 1985 interview: "He's a genius." In reviewing Sowell's Hayekian *Knowledge and Decisions* in 1981, Hayek praised it as "the best book in general economics in many a year."

Hayek's emphasis on Sowell as an Austrian and his conception of the broader tradition of economic theory being Austrian-influenced merit consideration. In his autobiography, Sowell writes that he was vitally influenced by Hayek's "The Use of Knowledge in Society" (assigned to him by Milton Friedman), and that it later inspired him to write *Knowledge and Decisions,* which Sowell considered to be his leading work to that time.

Sowell perhaps explicitly states Hayek's ideas most in *A Conflict of Visions,* published in 1987 and subtitled *Ideological Origins of Political Struggles.* Here Sowell contrasts unlimited and limited visions, similar to Hayek's distinction between societies conceived as mechanical mechanisms to be directed or as organisms that naturally evolve—

sometimes in completely unexpected directions. Sowell writes of what he terms "constrained" and "unconstrained" social visions that "F. A. Hayek is exceptional among leading figures in the constrained vision in discussing social justice."

In the article "The Austrian School of Economics: 1950–2000" contemporary Austrian leader Peter Boettke and his colleague Peter Leeson discuss sixth and seventh generations of the Austrian school, including Gerald O'Driscoll, Roger Garrison, Peter Lewin, Steve Horwitz, Lawrence H. White, and Don Lavoie. Boettke and Leeson also note, in similar fashion to Hayek's attempt to place Austrian economics in a broader context, that contemporary Austrians have and can draw much sustenance from figures such as James Buchanan, especially, and Ronald Coase, Douglass North, and Gordon Tullock, who also would not consider themselves to be "Austrians."

Hayek's work is considered to be of great value to many who identify themselves as Austrian economists, who influence Austrian economists, and who are identified by economists in the Austrian tradition as having exerted great influence on thought outside of technical economic theory. Hayek's renown and the appreciation for him extend, of course, far beyond contemporary Austrian economists. Whether his thought on "the structure of production" will ultimately prove his most lasting remains to be seen; this is a view peculiar to Austrian economists.

Hayek essentially viewed capital as being multistage. This is a somewhat different conception from "heterogeneous" capital per se, which merely sees capital goods as not being able to be used for many purposes and does not necessarily emphasize the multistage aspect of capital that Hayek saw. Hayek's controversy with Frank Knight during the mid-1930s was over whether capital is best considered heterogeneous or homogeneous. Knight argued that, from an empirical perspective, capital is more homogeneous than Hayek thought; in this he criticized the Germanic and Austrian economic distinction between original and produced means of production, the difficulty of classifying capital goods, and the lack of a relationship between a period of production and the quantity of capital.

According to Hayek the multistage aspect of his conception of capital is crucial. In his response to Piero Sraffa's criticism of his early technical economic theory, Hayek wrote that the "forced saving" aspect of capital was vital in his conception—that this capital could not be used after the monetary stimulus dissipated because it was a part of longer, unfinished capital structures. If capital were homogeneous as to use in time, then Hayek's early technical economic theory would fall. Indeed, in his response to Sraffa he noted that "it is upon the truth of this point ['forced saving'] that my theory stands or falls."

Hayek's essential gist in capital theory was that capital is heterogeneous, that it cannot be put to many uses simultaneously or at different times. If these empirical assumptions as to capital's heterogeneity are false, then his theoretical system of economic activity falls. Hayek never established that changes in interest rates primarily and predominantly influence capital production of goods of higher order and their prices.

6

John Maynard Keynes

THE WORK OF JOHN MAYNARD KEYNES AND HIS FOLLOWERS dominated academic economic theory around the world from the 1930s through 1970s—and to some extent, to this day. It is valuable to consider Keynesian economics further. Delving more deeply into a rival economic understanding may provide the reader additional information on which to evaluate the presentation of Hayek's work.

Hayek described Keynes in a 1952 book review that sheds light on both subject and author:

> Whatever one may think of Keynes as an economist, nobody who knew him will deny that he was one of the outstanding Englishmen of his generation. Indeed the magnitude of his influence as an economist is probably at least as much due to the impressiveness of the man, the universality of his interests, and the power and persuasive charm of his personality, as to the originality or theoretical soundness of his contribution to economics. He owed his success largely to a rare combination of brilliance and quickness of mind with a mastery of the English language in which few contemporaries could rival him. . . . As a scholar he was incisive rather than profound and thorough, guided by a strong intuition which would make him try to prove the same point again and again by different routes.

Hayek also described Keynes as a "man who at one stage was able to divide his time between teaching economics and conducting a ballet, financial speculation and collecting pictures, running an investment trust and directing the finances of a Cambridge college, acting as the director of an insurance company and practically running the

Cambridge Arts Theatre and attending there to such details as the food and wine served in its restaurant." In a 1966 article, he said that Keynes was "endowed with supreme mental powers, [and] his thinking was as much influenced by aesthetic and intuitive as by purely rational factors." Lionel Robbins wrote in his autobiography that "I would certainly regard Maynard Keynes as the most remarkable man I have ever met."

Notwithstanding the predominant role in academic economic theory that Keynes and Keynesian economics achieved during the twentieth century, his basic outlook and policy recommendations were shaped by the particular experiences of the British Empire's waning years. Joseph Schumpeter remarked that it "cannot be emphasized too strongly that Keynes's advice was in the first instance always English advice," as, to a certain extent, was Hayek's.

Keynes's essential view was that the laissez-faire conditions that characterized the nineteenth century were dead. He wrote in the work that first brought him fame, *The Economic Consequences of the Peace* (1919): "The forces of the nineteenth century have run their course and are exhausted. The economic motives and ideals of that generation no longer satisfy us: we must find a new way and . . . a new industrial birth." This was an entirely different sentiment from that with which Hayek would conclude *The Road to Serfdom* twenty-five years later: "Though we neither can wish, nor possess the power, to go back to the reality of the nineteenth century, we have the opportunity to realise its ideals—and they were not mean. . . . The guiding principle, that a policy of freedom for the individual is the only truly progressive policy, remains as true to-day as it was in the nineteenth century."

Keynes burst onto the scene with *The Economic Consequences of the Peace*—a blistering attack on the economic aspects of the Versailles Treaty following World War I and on the makers of the treaty. He was a treasury official with the British delegation at the Versailles Conference, but resigned before the treaty was signed. He correctly predicted that excessive war reparations demanded of Germany combined with other punishments inflicted on it (such as the loss of coal mines to Poland) would lead to economic chaos in Germany, with negative repercussions for Europe and the rest of the world.

Keynes had unsurpassed influence in the world of British academic economics. From 1911 to 1945, he was editor of the *Economic Journal,* published in Cambridge, the leading periodical in British academic economics. He served as secretary of the Royal Economic Society. In addition to more strictly academic avenues of suasion, he was among the most prominent members of society. He served on committees and commissions advising the government and was chairman of the British *Nation,* a popular magazine of opinion and news. He wrote articles and opinion pieces for newspapers and other periodicals throughout the world. During the latter part of World War II, he was Britain's leading representative at talks primarily with the United States that led to the Bretton Woods agreement that established the International Monetary Fund and World Bank. He was the chief negotiator for a large U.S. loan to Great Britain following World War II.

After *The Economic Consequences of the Peace,* Keynes's next major work was *A Tract on Monetary Reform,* published in 1923. Milton Friedman calls this Keynes's "best book." *A Tract on Monetary Reform* was for the most part a collection of articles and lectures on monetary issues he had written during the three previous years. Keynes's great concern at this time was that domestic prices be stabilized from either inflation or deflation. He disagreed with the idea that the primary goal of monetary policy should be the stabilization of intercurrency exchange rates. Hayek had, in this regard, a rare and early theoretical agreement with Keynes. Hayek wrote that as a student in New York: "One of the first conclusions at which I remember I had arrived towards the end of 1923 was that stabilization of national price levels and stabilization of foreign exchange were conflicting aims. But before I could anywhere submit for publication the short article I had written on the subject, I found that Keynes had just stated the same contention in his *Tract on Monetary Reform.*" Although Hayek agreed with Keynes on the mutual incompatibility of these two policy goals, he disagreed with him with respect to which goal should be pursued. Hayek favored stable international exchange rates, while Keynes supported stable domestic prices.

Under the gold standard system of monetary policy that characterized national and international monetary thinking at this time, the key variable over which national monetary authorities were to exercise control was the exchange rate. The goal was to keep these rates fixed. National money supplies were to be adjusted so, in the case of Great Britain, as to maintain the pound at a fixed rate of international exchange—which, prior to World War I, was $4.86 to £1.

Keynes challenged the prevailing thinking, believing that national monetary authorities should focus on stable domestic prices, which were not guaranteed under a monetary policy that emphasized

fixed international exchange rates. If a nation experienced a threat to
its external exchange rate (i.e., if the value of its money were about to
decline in the international currency exchanges), then it would reduce
its internal supply of money to right the imbalance. Conversely, if a nation's exchange rate were improving, then it would expand its internal
money supply to counter the pending disequilibrium in the opposite
direction. External exchange rate stability took priority over internal
price stability in the gold standard international monetary system. This
is not to say that stable domestic prices were not a goal of the gold
standard and even a primary justification for it. Yet when there was a
conflict between these two goals, it was domestic prices and not the exchange rate that was to give way. Domestic prices fluctuated through
the expansion or contraction of money supply occasioned by deterio-
ration or improvement of intercurrency exchange rates.

Keynes thought the gold standard could be very disruptive to a
nation's economy. He believed that as a national economy becomes
more developed—as he held that Britain's was—it is characterized by
"stickiness of social and business arrangements." While wages and
prices might react harmoniously in theory to the changes in internal
money supply that stable international exchange rates require, in practice this has not been so. It is difficult to force prices and wages down
following a diminution of internal money supply, at least without economic dislocation. Keynes held that both inflation and deflation are
"evils to be shunned." With this opinion, he established himself in contemporary parlance as a "stabiliser"—one who sought stable domestic
prices as the chief end of monetary policy rather than fixed international exchange rates.

Basic to Keynes's conception of the influence of monetary policy on prices was the relative stress he placed on the speed at which
money changes hands (its velocity) compared to the amount of
money in an economy (its supply) in setting at least short-term prices.
He adhered to the fundamental monetary equation $MV = PQ$, where
M is the supply of money in an economy, V is the velocity at which it
changes hands, P is the general price level, and Q is the amount of
goods and services. Typically, more emphasis is placed in this equation on money and prices, on the assumption that velocity and the
amount of goods and services do not change as much or vary in relative balance to one another. The conventional analysis is, in other
words, more that changes in money supply lead to changes in general
price level.

Keynes believed, however, that at least in the short run, prices do not necessarily vary with alterations in money supply. He thought that, in particular, an increase in money supply does not necessarily result in inflation. Instead, the velocity of money might change, and thus a shift in the money supply might not be equilibrated with a comparable change in the general price level. Especially in times of economic downturn—when producers are not expanding and consumers are not spending money—a given increase in the money supply might have relatively little effect on aggregate prices. He granted that in the long run, it is "probably true" that prices vary with the quantity of money. He went on, however, in the most famous of all his words: "But this *long run* is a misleading guide to current affairs. *In the long run* we are all dead. Economists set themselves too easy, too useless a task if in tempestuous seasons they can only tell us that when the storm is long past the ocean is flat again."

Basic to Keynes's conception of appropriate monetary policy was his view that prices are most effectively influenced by the monetary authority through its sway over the supply of credit available through the banking system. To counteract a tendency toward lower prices, more credit should be made available. More money, consequently, would percolate through the economy. To nip in the bud a propensity toward higher prices, credit should be made less accessible, tightening the money supply. Keynes's goal was stable prices and thus stable business conditions. Government should control monetary policy so as to level economic expansion and contraction.

He believed a breakthrough in the theory of monetary management was achieved in *A Tract on Monetary Reform,* which contained, in embryonic form, key essentials of the Keynesian Revolution: the relative bifurcation of money supply from prices, the stress on immediate financial circumstances in determining policy, the prominent role for government in macromanaging the economy.

Following publication of this work, Keynes waged an unsuccessful effort to prevent Britain from returning to the gold standard at prewar parity, which it did in 1925 under Chancellor of the Exchequer Winston Churchill. Keynes considered this course madness. During the time leading up to restoration, the pound was valued somewhere in the vicinity of 10 percent less than the dollar at the prewar parity of $4.86 to £1. Closing this gap would require deflationary policies in Britain; interest rates would have to rise. This would further depress an economy that already suffered from unemployment of over 10 percent. Following the return to the gold standard Keynes wrote an attack on it, entitled "The Economic Consequences of Mr. Churchill."

The bottom really fell out of the British and all other national economies during the international depression that began in 1929. While other factors precipitated the decision to "go off gold," the gold standard appeared doomed.

On September 21, 1931, the British treasury announced that henceforth convertibility of pounds for gold was suspended. The death of nineteenth-century economics may be dated from this announcement as may, perhaps, the death of still-pretended British supremacy in the world.

Keynes, who had stood virtually alone six years before in opposing the return to gold, was proven right again—in his own as well as much of the public mind—just as he had been right about excessive German reparations demanded following World War I. Yesterday's heresy had again become tomorrow's dogma. He took to calling himself "Cassandra," after the ancient Greek mythological prophetess who spoke the truth but whom no one believed. He originally intended to publish his 1931 *Essays in Persuasion,* a collection of nontheoretical writings from the previous decade, as *Essays in Prophecy.*

$\sim$

Further understanding of the British economy between the wars is valuable to understanding why and what Keynes wrote. The essential fact is that Britain never recovered from World War I. Prior to the Great War, it had been the world leader—in land, wealth, power, ideas. It played something of the same role of world policeman that the United States does now. This was the empire on which the sun never set. Gibraltar, Malta, and Cyprus offered dominance of the Mediterranean; the Indian Ocean belonged to the British Navy; holdings throughout Africa and Asia gave London ultimate rule over one-quarter of the earth's population and landmass; dominions provided kindred nations. The United States—with which Britain became increasingly friendly during the last years of the nineteenth century—was the up-and-coming nation in the world. The British accomplishment in managing so much of the world during the nineteenth century should not be underestimated or underappreciated, though it often is both.

Keynes well expressed the pre–Great War world in *The Economic Consequences of the Peace:*

What an extraordinary episode in the economic progress of man that age was which came to an end in August, 1914! The greater part of the population, it is true, worked hard and lived at a low standard of comfort, yet were, to all appearances, reasonably contented with the lot. But escape was possible, for any man of capacity or character at all exceeding the average, into the middle and upper classes, for whom life offered, at a low cost and with the least trouble, conveniences, comforts, and amenities beyond the compass of the richest and most powerful monarchs of other ages. The inhabitant of London could order by telephone, sipping his morning tea in bed, the various products of the whole earth, in such quantity as he might see fit, and reasonably expect their delivery upon his doorstep; he could at the same moment and by the same means adventure his wealth in the natural resources and new enterprises of any quarter of the world. . . . But, most important of all, he regarded this state of affairs as normal, certain, and permanent, except in the direction of further improvement.

The era from the defeat of Napoleon at Waterloo in 1815 to the start of World War I in 1914 was as much the British century as the post–World War II era has been dominated by the United States. World War I changed everything. The European and global order, of which Britain was the mainspring part, blew apart under the stresses of the Great War. Britain did not change internally as much as many countries in Europe. Alterations in the larger world order could not, however, fail to influence it profoundly. During World War I, international financial leadership moved from London to New York, a crucial shift in the balance of world power and wealth. Following the war, Britain experienced a short economic boom, but this boom was followed by a crash and the country experienced a depression from the latter part of 1920 to 1922. Recovery from this depression was never really complete until into World War II.

Between 1900 and 1920, British unemployment averaged 3.4 percent per year. This includes World War I, when unemployment declined to 1 percent or less, but even excluding the years 1915 through 1918, unemployment averaged only 4 percent per year for the first two decades. Between 1921 and 1940, on the other hand, for a full generation, unemployment averaged 13.7 percent per year. Excluding the prime British depression years of 1921 and 1922 and 1930 through 1933, the unemployment rate during the 1920s and 1930s still averaged 12 percent during the other, "good" years. Between 1921 and 1940, unemployment nudged beneath 10 percent only twice, to 9.7 percent in both 1927 and 1940. It is quite remarkable that during 1940, the first full year of World War II for Britain, unemployment still approached one person seeking work in ten. Something had gone awry. What?

Keynes's answer was that Britain had become an old, arthritic economy. As he wrote in *The Economic Consequences of the Peace,* "the forces of the nineteenth century have run their course and are exhausted." The nation was no longer a growing and vibrant organism, it was a stultified and rigid beast. Management of the economy was now required for it to perform optimally. The days of uncoordinated development to produce maximum output—as characterized the 1800s— were over.

The primary policy tool that Keynes saw available during the 1920s to right the economy was monetary policy. As an instrument, it was relatively benign.

Keynes viscerally opposed Marxism. He declared in his essay "The End of *Laissez Faire*": "Marxian socialism [is] . . . a doctrine so illogical and so dull" that it "must always remain a portent to the historians of Opinion . . . [that it] can have exercised so powerful and enduring an influence over the minds of men, and, through them, the events of history." He asked rhetorically, as well, of Marxism: "How can I adopt a creed which, preferring the mud to the fish, exalts the boorish proletariat above the bourgeois and intelligentsia who, with whatever faults, are the quality of life and surely carry the seeds of all human advancement?" Keynes was, in his personal values, a pure elitist. He always remained a member of the Liberal Party, even after its electoral collapse in 1931. He never joined Labour.

Keynes's goal was not the redistribution of existing wealth but the creation of more wealth. In his essay "Economic Possibilities for Our Grandchildren," he put forward the idea that the people of a century hence would have a substantially higher standard of living with considerably less effort.

~

Keynes's two-volume *Treatise on Money* appeared in December 1930. He worked on it for seven years among his many other activities and as economic circumstances changed. Hayek, as is well known, criticized this work harshly in his initial review at the London School of Economics in 1931. It is unnecessary to discuss this in depth here, as it appears in many other places. Suffice it to say that, from a policy perspective, Keynes favored expansive monetary and fiscal policies, and Hayek did not.

The General Theory of Employment, Interest, and Money, published on February 4, 1936, was Keynes's magnum opus. It was a landmark event in the history of modern academic economic theory. Keynes conceived the *General Theory* as a last-chance life preserver to save capitalism from itself and the maladies that he believed were of its own making, and that could be fixed. He wrote to English author George Bernard Shaw a year before its publication, in the context of criticizing Marx and Engels (with whom Shaw, as many British intelligentsia, was infatuated):

> I've made another shot at old K[arl] M[arx] last week, reading the Marx-Engels correspondence just published, without making much progress. . . . I can see they invented a certain method of carrying on and a vile manner of writing, both of which their successors have maintained with fidelity. But if you tell me that they discovered a clue to the economic riddle, still I am beaten—I can discover nothing but out-of-date controversialising.
>
> To understand my state of mind, however, you have to know that I believe myself to be writing a book on economic theory, which will largely revolutionise—not, I suppose, at once but in the course of the next ten years—the way the world thinks about economic problems. When my new theory has been duly assimilated and mixed with politics and feelings and passions, I can't predict what the upshot will be in its effects on actions and affairs. But there will be a great change, and, in particular, the Ricardian foundations of Marxism will be knocked away.
>
> I can't expect you, or anyone else, to believe this at the present stage. But for myself I don't merely hope what I say—in my own mind I'm quite sure.

Keynes's view of himself as a prophet was not completely without merit.

Hayek agreed that Keynes saw himself as a preserver of capitalism rather than a destroyer. In one interview, Hayek commented that Keynes "believed that he was fundamentally still a classical English liberal and wasn't quite aware of how far he had moved away from it"; in another: "He wanted a controlled capitalism"; and in a third: "I think basically Keynes was . . . a free trader and an economic liberal. But with many qualifications."

The *General Theory* is at once both a book of economic theory and a font of economic prejudices—there are probably few academics in economics and political science who do not have an opinion of it, whether they have read it or not. It has reached the status—which it obtained almost immediately—where the fact of its existence is as important, if not more important, than what it actually says.

Keynes was animated by the times in which he wrote, and Hayek later criticized him for "call[ing] such a tract for the times the *General Theory.*" The phrase "general theory" had more meaning when Keynes used it than it does today. It brought to the mind of 1930s readers Einstein's general theory of relativity, which revolutionized physics, and Keynes meant to summon this association in his readers' minds. In Einstein's theory of relativity, Newtonian physics is a "special case" that applies as far as it goes but is by no means the whole of physics. Einstein's accomplishment was to erect a larger conceptual and explanatory framework within which Newtonian physics makes sense but of which it is only a part of a greater whole.

Keynes attempted to perform this same task in economics. The nineteenth century—and the classical economic theory that underlaid it—were, he argued, a special case of the larger, general theory he now put forward. Central to the classical view was that markets are always in or tending to equilibrium. As enunciated by Smith in the *Wealth of Nations,* an "invisible hand" guides production so that it meets demand. Jean-Baptiste Say developed Smith's concept into his own law of markets, Say's law.

Say's exact conception is debated, but Keynes took him to mean essentially this: Production and demand are always in balance. There can be no such thing (at least in the long run) as economic disequilibrium at less than full production, employment, and consumption because if any variable in the economic equation wobbles, another factor will move in the contrary direction to right it. If, for example, unemployment exists, the price of labor will decline and full employment will be restored. If there is a demand for more investment in an economy than savings currently exist to finance, then the return on investment as represented by the interest rate on savings will increase, more resources will be attracted to savings, and savings will increase to the point at which they equal desired investment. To cite one more example, if too much of a good is being produced, its price will decline, and less of it will be produced, once again bringing a market into balance. The key point about Say's law from a Keynesian perspective is that it propounds a universal and invariable harmony among economic actors. If left to itself, a market economy will result in supply and demand being equal over time at maximal production and employment. Keynes stated in the *General Theory:* "The classical postulates do not admit of the possibility of . . . 'involuntary' unemployment."

As Keynes surveyed the British and world economies during the 1920s and 1930s, the happy circumstance posited by Say's law did not seem to typify what he saw. Mass unemployment existed at a time when there was great amounts of work to do. From his perspective, there was not always an optimal spontaneous order among economic actors. Why? His fundamental hypothesis was that an economy does not necessarily reach a state of equilibrium at full employment and maximum output. The role of savings is, he thought, critical. If a community saves too much (more than investment), it will consume too little. Employment and output will thus become less than they would otherwise be.

Keynes attributed some of the excess savings to the older, sclerotic nature of the British economy. Speculation also played a role, as did poor monetary policies—first and foremost the gold standard. Whatever the source of excess savings, however, the result was that the economy did not find its balance at maximal production. Government had to step in to fill the breach.

The *General Theory* was different from the *Treatise on Money* largely because of the changed circumstances in which it was written. When Keynes began writing the latter work, the British economy had had a few rocky years, but his perspective was still that this was a departure from the norm rather than the rule. By the time the *General Theory* was completed, however, Britain had experienced fifteen years of poor economic conditions, including the Great Depression, when unemployment reached nearly one in four workers. The gold standard had already been abandoned. More substantial action was required.

Coincident with the Great Depression was worldwide deflation. When, in deflationary circumstances, the real value of money is increasing, the rationale of the credit and banking system in developed economies breaks down. Why put money in the bank, when it will increase in value if one merely puts it under one's mattress? Why, indeed—particularly if banks are going out of business and it appears safer to hold onto one's money than to deposit it in a bank?

The banking and credit system is an ineffective tool to correct economic problems in deflationary times. The notion of using the

capital markets to spur on and rein in investment through manipulation of interest rates becomes a meaningless policy device when individuals are avoiding savings and investment anyway as a result of
depressed economic circumstances. More to the point, in deflationary
times, even low nominal interest rates can be high real interest rates
as a result of deflation. To create low real interest rates in deflationary conditions, banks would actually have to pay borrowers to bor-
row. This would require reconceptualizations and new statements of
policy.

The answer that Keynes endorsed as economic conditions remained poor year after year during the 1930s was emphasis on fiscal
policy. Government could pick up the slack caused by excess savings
by borrowing these savings, deficit spending, creating more demand
through public works and other means. Essentially, in simplest terms,
Keynes the mild inflater became Keynes the advocate of government
deficit spending as the 1920s evolved into the 1930s, or Keynes the
monetarist became Keynes the fiscalist.

Keynes and Hayek were not as close personally as is sometimes
thought. They were friends, but not close friends. They saw each other
regularly during World War II when the London School of Economics
relocated to Cambridge. They typically did not discuss economics. They
were two great minds who enjoyed each other's company talking
about other subjects.

Hayek enjoyed telling many stories about Keynes. One was how,
if Keynes's followers became too inflationist after the war, Keynes
would cut them down; but a few weeks later, he was dead. Hayek also
liked to say how Keynes would regale Hayek and other Cambridge
colleagues during the war with stories about his extracurricular scholarly exploits on official wartime trips to the United States.

The financial institutional arrangements that developed during
the last decades of the nineteenth century and first decades of the
twentieth required new thinking about optimal economic policy and
theory. Keynes was, originally, a monetarist. For much of his career, the
force of events led him to embrace a greater role for government in
macromanaging the national economy.

Keynes ultimately placed his hopes for good government in exceptional men. The focus in Hayek's work was rules.

7

From Economic Theory
to Political Philosophy

HAYEK'S TURN FROM TECHNICAL ECONOMIC THEORY DURING THE 1920s and 1930s to political philosophy during the 1940s through, really, the rest of his career was unexpected, and he continued to write in a variety of areas during his post-1940 career, including—in addition to political philosophy—epistemology, the history of ideas, psychology, and economics. But his focus clearly changed from his career before 1940.

He gradually became less prominent as a technical economic theorist in Britain during the 1930s and the early 1940s. So much in the economic and political worlds changed. When Hayek first lectured at the London School of Economics in early 1931, Hitler's rise to power and World War II were not even on the horizon. The world as a whole was not long into the Great Depression, and its magnitude and duration had not yet been experienced. At this point, it was still often thought, not much more than a year after the New York stock market crash, that economies around the world would soon enough right themselves.

Then, during 1932 and 1933, it became apparent that world economies were experiencing their worst collective downturns in living memory as tens of millions became unemployed, banks collapsed, and deflation was experienced in more than a score of countries. Later in the decade, responses to the rise of Nazi Germany and, in time, the war effort itself greatly changed nations' economic circumstances and the topics of economic and political discussion.

During the early to middle 1930s, Hayek was one of the several most prominent academic economic theorists in Britain, though his renown was almost exclusively in academia. His theories were often presented as an alternative to Keynes's.

Hayek commenced working in capital theory because "I had been criticized . . . that in *Prices and Production* I had a very inadequate theory of capital. . . . So I . . . started writing a great book on capital and money, which ultimately dealt with the money phenomenon. It took me much longer than I thought. . . . And then war came, which finally persuaded me to put that [capital] part into a separate volume and leave for the time being the monetary part altogether, which I was intending to do another time."

To Hayek, the weakness of his former presentation was that he had not adequately described the real nature of capital that explains a business cycle, and *The Pure Theory of Capital* (1941) was intended to remedy this deficiency. In the second volume, he would have considered the influence of money on the capital structure he described in the first part. Hayek thought the real physical capital structure of production changes during a business cycle. He had a largely material conception of capital.

When Keynes's *General Theory* was published in February 1936, it obliterated all else on the scene in academic economics. Hayek was known to be working on a treatise on capital as Keynes's work was published (the work that became *The Pure Theory of Capital*). While there was some anticipation in academia for this forthcoming major work, interest even by economists in Hayek's work waned. Ludwig Lachmann, a student of Hayek's and teacher of a number of contemporary Austrian-oriented economists, recalled that when he started at the London School of Economics during the early 1930s, almost everyone was a Hayekian; at the end of the decade, there were only two Hayekians left, Hayek and himself. John Hicks, Lionel Robbins (in time), and especially younger economists such as Nicholas Kaldor and Abba Lerner moved from Hayek and in a Keynesian direction.

Economic circumstances changed significantly in Great Britain, as elsewhere, during the 1930s. The Great Depression was not as severe as it was in the United States, for Britain had already been suffering from several years of depressed and recessionary circumstances. Thus it did not experience as sharp and prolonged an economic decline after 1929 as the United States did relative to pre-1929 economic performance.

Hayek perhaps overemphasized the extent of systemic economic change in Great Britain during the 1930s. He wrote as a footnote in *The Road to Serfdom* of "the headlong plunge" Great Britain took during the "short space of the inglorious years 1931 to 1939," when it "transformed its economic system beyond recognition." On the other hand, future Conservative prime minister Harold Macmillan struck a similar note in the first chaper, of his 1938 *The Middle Way,* which sheds light on contemporary perspectives of economic circumstances and theory:

> The great depression, with the political crisis to which it gave rise, is now coming to be regarded as past history. . . . [T]he great majority of people quite clearly regard the depression . . . as a transitory and fortuitous occurrence. This is of course a profound error. The crisis was not an accident. The initial impulse may have been the result of errors of judgment on the part of the Central Banks of Britain and America. But the disastrous plunge into such a depth of depression was a result of the changes in the whole balance of production in the world which had been developing for many decades. Moreover, in order to deal with the crisis, political and economic changes of a permanent character were carried out. It was out of the crisis that the British tariff system was born. The crisis gave rise to the schemes for planning the production and marketing of a wide range of agricultural products; it gave rise to schemes for the compulsory reorganisation of industries like coal mining and cotton spinning; it made imperative voluntary schemes of reorganisation in a number of other industries; it forced Britain to abandon the gold standard, set up an exchange equalisation fund, and enter into new kinds of commercial agreements with other countries; and it led to the adoption of quite unorthodox methods of dealing with the situation in the depressed areas.
>
> These are some of the political and economic results. The psychological effects have been no less important. Great indeed were the changes which the shock of crisis brought about in the minds of men with regard to economic and political *theories.* Formerly, they had been content to accept, as the basis of their political thought, the economic theories that had been evolved in an earlier epoch of national and world history, when the basic circumstances of economic life were wholly different. Throughout the whole of the postwar [World War I] period there had been growing an uneasy consciousness of something radically wrong with the economic system; and this uneasiness had overshadowed political controversy both within and between all the political parties for many years. One of the consequences of the crisis was to confirm these suspicions and

to liberate men's minds from a continued subservience to the economic orthodoxy of the pre-war world.

And this was before World War II and the industry nationalization and
welfare state activities that followed it in Britain. Nonetheless, Macmillan's view was fundamentally in error from several perspectives. First,
the changes in governmental policy and economic activity were not as
great as he suggested. Second, the basic free market enterprise system
of private property remained in place. Third, the economic theories of
the past were not inadequate. But none of this was evident at the time.

Hayek never really departed from the essential economic theory
that he developed during the 1920s, although he expanded and deep-
ened his analysis. He remarked in a 1975 lecture that he had not altered his opinion "about the theoretical explanation of the events" of
the Great Depression that he had put forward forty years before, "but
about the practical possibility of removing the obstacles to the functioning of the system in a particular way," which led to his later policy
proposals for competition among currencies and private currencies.

Part of the reason that Hayek's economic theory received less
attention as the 1930s progressed was that his thought appeared of less
relevance to the economic circumstances at hand. The British economy
grew during most of the middle 1930s, and Hayek's explanation that
the economy suffered from real productive misequilibration and capital malinvestment was not seen as apposite. Then preparations for
World War II and its start in 1939 in Europe brought the British economy entirely out of the doldrums and into a completely different state
of organization. Government management of the economy became the
order of the day. Hayek's work in trade cycle theory was no longer of
interest.

By the time *The Pure Theory of Capital* appeared in 1941, it attracted scant attention. Britain was fighting for its life. No academic
treatise on capital theory could have attracted anything but minimal
interest at this time.

∼

Hayek's emphasis on the signaling function of interest rates to guide
economic production to longer or shorter periods of production informed and was the starting point for many of his contributions in
spontaneous order and of the crucial role of prices to guide optimal

economic activity. "Once we assume that, even at a single point, the pricing process fails to equilibrate supply and demand, so that over a more or less long period demand may be satisfied at prices at which the available supply is inadequate to meet total demand, then the march of economic events loses its determinateness and a range of indeterminateness appears, within which movements can originate leading away from equilibrium."

In a lecture given fifty years to the day after his first London School of Economics lecture, on January 27, 1981, Hayek recalled that his *Prices and Production* lectures "made use of what became the leading theme of most of my later work, an analysis of the signal function of prices in guiding production." In a 1985 interview with Gary North and Mark Skousen, one of his last, Hayek provided this description of his transition from economic to societal theory:

Q: . . . in retrospect, after *The Pure Theory of Capital,* you never went back [to technical economic theory]. . . . *The Road to Serfdom* came out [in 1944]. It was an extraordinary success, [a] political, philosophic book. And it seemed that that turned your interest to a wholly new field.

A: It's perfectly true, I became much more interested, in fact in a way as Mises had been, but not following Mises. The differences of the philosophical approach of the social sciences which led to different conclusions. I mean, it became particularly acute because Keynes, against his intentions, had stimulated the development of macroeconomics. And I was convinced that not only his particular conclusions, but the whole foundation of macroeconomics was wrong.

So I wanted to demonstrate that we had to return to microeconomics, that this whole prejudice supported by the natural scientists that could deduce anything from measurable magnitudes, the effects of aggregates and averages, came to fascinate me much more. I felt in a way, that the thing which I am now prepared to do, I don't know as there's anybody else who can do this particular task. And I rather hoped that what I had done in capital theory would be continued by others. This was a new opening which was much more fascinating. The other would have meant working for a result which I already knew, but had to prove it. Which was very dull.

The other thing was an open problem: How does economics really look like when you recognize it as the prototype of a new kind of science of complex phenomena which could not employ the simple model of mechanics or physics, but had to deal with what then I described as mere pattern predictions, certain limited prediction. That was so much more fascinating as an intellectual problem.

Hayek also remarked in his fiftieth anniversary London School of Economics lecture that he first "expounded systematically" his conception of the signaling function of prices in guiding production in his 1936 presidential lecture to the London Economic Club, "Economics and Knowledge."

As a result of several factors, Hayek moved from narrower economic to broader social thought. First, the economic and political issues of the day changed. When he went to London in 1931, the primary concern of the world was economic—the Great Depression. By the later 1930s, the greatest problem in the world was political—Hitler and Nazi Germany. Hayek initially wrote a memorandum in 1933 on themes he later developed in article form during the late 1930s, "Freedom and the Economic System." He primarily wrote *The Road to Serfdom* in 1941 and 1942, emerging from the article.

Changes in the economic and political issues of the day were not the only reason for Hayek's move from economic to broader societal thought, just as earlier in his life he moved from biology to economics because of world events. The second reason Hayek's interests shifted was more coincidental, his participation in the socialist calculation debate. There were really two phases in the socialist calculation debate, and it is important to be clear about these in order to understand Mises's and Hayek's participation in the debate, and the development of Hayek's thought. The first phase was immediately after World War I in central Europe, when both Germany and Austria considered nationalization acts that would have placed substantial amounts of industry under direct government control, and Mises argued against the technical feasibility of socialism. The second phase of the socialist calculation debate was inaugurated in England by Hayek in the middle 1930s with publication of *Collectivist Economic Planning*.

The third reason that Hayek's interests moved from technical economic to broader societal issues—in addition to the change in the times and his participation in the socialist calculation debate—was Keynes's ascendancy and the movement of technical economic theory in a mathematical direction to which Hayek was unsympathetic. Hayek opposed not merely Keynes's policy recommendations, but his technical method.

Mises's argument in the first socialist calculation debate was brilliant: How would socialism practically be organized? It was not enough merely to point to deficiencies in contemporaneous capitalism. As he stated in the introductory paragraph to his 1920 article "Economic Calculation in the Socialist Commonwealth," socialists "invariably explain how, in the cloud-cuckoo lands of their fancy, roast pigeons will in some way fly into the mouths of the comrades, but they omit to show how this miracle is to take place."

Hayek had this exchange in 1978 with James Buchanan as to the transition in his thought and work:

> Q: I'd like to shift back . . . to your basic political theory, political philosophy, position. I'd like to ask you a little bit of intellectual history here, in terms of your own position. Both of us started out, more or less, as technical economists, and then we got interested in these more political-philosophical questions. Could you trace for us a little bit the evolution of your own thinking in that respect?
>
> A: . . . It really began with my doing that volume on *Collectivist Economic Planning,* which was originally merely caused by the fact that I found that certain new insights which were known on the Continent had not reached the English-speaking world yet. It was largely Mises and his school, but also certain discussion by [Enrico] Barone and others, which were then completely unknown to the English-speaking world. Being forced to explain this development on the Continent in the introduction and the conclusion to this volume, which contained translations, I was curiously enough driven not only into political philosophy but into an analysis of the methodological misconceptions of economics. [These misconceptions] seemed to me to lead to these naïve conceptions of, "After all, what the market does we can do better intellectually." My way from there was very largely around methodological considerations, which led me back to—I think the decisive event was that essay I did . . . "Economics and Knowledge."
>
> Q: That was a brilliant essay.
>
> A: I think that was a decisive point of the change in my outlook. As I would put it now, [it elaborated] the conception that prices serve as guides to action and must be explained in determining what people ought to do—they're not determined by what people have done in the past.
>
> But, of course, psychologically the consequence of the whole model of marginal utility analysis was perhaps the decisive point which, as I now see the whole thing—[the] market as a system of the

utilization of knowledge, which nobody can possess as a whole, which only through the market situation leads people to aim at the needs of people whom they do not know, make use of facilities for which they have no direct information, all this condensed in abstract signals, and that our whole modern wealth and production could arise only thanks to this mechanism—is, I believe, the basis not only of my economic but as much of my political views. It reduces the possible task of authority very much if you realize that the market has in that sense a superiority, because the amount of information the authorities can use is always very limited, and the market uses an infinitely greater amount of information than the authorities can ever do.

In editing *Collectivist Economic Planning,* Hayek embarked on a new direction that he pursued for the rest of his career. A number of the themes that he would explore later in further depth he first considered in some detail in his contributions to *Collectivist Economic Planning.* In his introductory chapter, Hayek referred to his still-earlier, 1933 inaugural address at the London School of Economics, "The Trend of Economic Thinking." It is worthwhile to turn to that address for a moment to follow the trend of Hayek's thought.

Perhaps the most crucial line in "The Trend of Economic Thinking" was where Hayek stated that "the majority of men still remain . . . under the erroneous impression that, since all social phenomena are the product of our own actions, all that depends upon them is their deliberate object." Hayek strictly opposed the notion that individuals can create whatever societal circumstances they wish. He later noted that, even earlier, when he was a student in the United States about a decade before, "the innocent sounding formula that, since man has himself created the institutions of society and civilisation, he must also be able to alter them at will so as to satisfy his desires or wishes" is one he thought false, in large part as a result of having read Carl Menger's *Investigations into the Method of the Social Sciences with Special Reference to Economics.*

Hayek was working on an edition of Menger's collected works at about the time he wrote his inaugural lecture and chapters of *Collectivist Economic Planning,* and he wrote a number of, typically shorter, works in the history of economic theory at about this time. He was an erudite scholar as well as brilliant creative writer. He emphasized in "The Trend of Economic Thinking," in language that also could be taken almost verbatim from his final work, that from "the time of

Hume and Adam Smith, the effect of every attempt to understand economic phenomena . . . has been to show that, in large part, the coordination of individual efforts in society is not the product of deliberate planning," calling the market here an "immensely complicated mechanism" which "worked and solved problems." He also quoted Mises, in words that he would refine decades later in *Law, Legislation and Liberty:* "In the words of an eminent Austrian economist, we refuse to recognise that society is an organism and not an organization." In *Law, Legislation and Liberty* Hayek opposed society conceived as an "order" to society conceived as an "organization."

Finally, Hayek affirmed his at least still partially socialist ethic in "The Trend of Economic Thinking," when he concluded the lecture by saying that

> the economist frequently finds himself in disagreement in regard to means with those with whom he is in agreement with regard to ends; and in agreement in regard to means with those whose views regarding ends are entirely antipathetic to him—men who have never felt the urge to reconstruct the world and who frequently support the forces of stability only for reasons of selfishness. In such a situation, it is perhaps inevitable that he should become the object of dislike and suspicion. But if he recognises the circumstances from which they spring, he will be able to bear them with patience and understanding, confident that he possesses in his scientific knowledge a solvent for differences which are really intellectual, and that although, at present, his activities have little effect, yet in course of time they will come to be recognised as serving more consistently than the activities of those he opposes, the ends which they share in common.

Hayek thought that if those who supported the ends of socialism—some of the ends of which he shared—understood the actual operation and function of the market, they would depart from socialism (defined as central, government control of economic production) and embrace capitalism. Such socialism is nowhere near as productive as capitalism.

Hayek traced development of the idea that government direction of economic activity would be more effective than free market order. Historically, the great issues with respect to socialism were considered to be more ethical and psychological than practical. Are human beings good enough to live the ethic of common property that socialism requires?

When practical plans to implement socialism began to emerge during the last decades of the nineteenth century and first decades of the twentieth, it was generally contended, with great enthusiasm and surety, that socialism would be more productive economically than capitalism. Central, government direction of economic activity would, it was held, eliminate much waste and inefficiency of the competitive, anarchical market order. Socialism would be more productive than capitalism.

Mises's great accomplishment was to turn the question of socialism from a moral to an empirical one. The issue with respect to socialism is not, Mises argued, whether humanity is good enough for socialism, but how economic value and thus production would be determined in the absence of private property and freely fluctuating prices. Socialists have never really answered this question.

Indeed, as late as 1989, the American Nobel Prize–winning economist Paul Samuelson held that "the Soviet economy is proof that, contrary to what many skeptics had earlier believed, a socialist command economy can function and even thrive"—skeptics, indeed! It remained very much the view in perhaps most of international academia as recently as a decade and a half ago that command economies are more productive than free market ones and that the contrary view was held only by skeptics and cranks, such as Mises and Hayek. As Hayek so clearly summarized in *Collectivist Economic Planning:* "The distribution of available resources between different uses which is the economic problem," would be no less a problem in socialist than in capitalist economies. How would economic value be determined in the absence of private property and freely fluctuating prices?

Crucially, Mises's analysis of practical and empirical problems of socialism emphasized prices. Prices communicate information. Hayek built on the informational content of prices in his own work.

~

Hayek was a great historian of economic thought. His reading and writing in the field of economic history were among the influences that shifted his academic research focus from technical economic theory to broader societal thought.

Hayek wrote (and therefore voluminously researched) on a number of historical subjects in economic thought during the second half of the 1920s and throughout the remainder of his career. It is, indeed, to some extent accurate to perceive Hayek in large part as a historian of economic and political thought, though this would neglect his great contributions in philosophy and optimal societal order.

In the introductory essay to his later *Capitalism and the Historians,* Hayek wrote that in "the end even those who never read a book and probably have never heard the names of the historians whose views have influenced them come to see the past through their spectacles." During the early years of his career, while he was still in Vienna, he studied monetary theory and history intently. His first major foray into the history of ideas was four chapters on the development of monetary theory and policy, "Genesis of the Gold Standard in Response to English Coinage Policy in the 17th and 18th Centuries," "First Paper Money in 18th-Century France," "The Period of Restrictions, 1797–1821, and the Bullion Debate in England," and "The Dispute Between the Currency School and the Banking School, 1821–1848." These chapters, completed in 1929 but not published until 1991, were originally foreseen, as was a considerable amount of his other early work, to be part of a larger treatise on money that he never completed.

Somewhat like the later intended "The Abuse and Decline of Reason," his intended work on money was to be introduced by a historical part before moving to theory. While the four chapters on monetary history remained unpublished at the time, his research was very beneficial, leading to *Monetary Theory and the Trade Cycle,* "The 'Paradox' of Saving," *Prices and Production,* and ultimately his invitation to London.

Among the early monetary theorists whom he discussed in these chapters is David Hume, whose doctrines, he wrote, "undoubtedly constitute a first pinnacle in the development of monetary theory." Milton Friedman observes as well that Hume's work may continue to be read for "pleasure and profit."

According to Hayek:

> Hume's analysis had such a decisive influence on all subsequent developments. . . . The three (1752) essays in question, entitled "Of Money," "Of Interest," and "Of the Balance of Trade," . . . offer important contributions to all the major problems of monetary theory. Hume prefaces his inquiry with the observation that 'money is not, properly speaking, one of the subjects of commerce; but only the instrument which men have agreed upon to facilitate the exchange of

one commodity for another." The significance of this remark lies in its repudiation of the mercantilists' excessive preoccupation with money. From Hume's perspective, it is therefore a matter of indifference how great a stock of money a country has. . . . In his eyes, "it seems a maxim almost self-evident" that "the prices of every thing depend on the proportion between commodities and money, and that any considerable alteration on either has the same effect, either of heightening or lowering the price," precisely the contention of the quantity theory of the value of money. But he recognises that while the size of a country's stock of money is a matter of indifference, the process of changing the supply of money will have a significant impact. . . . [H]e develops as a complementary hypothesis the important doctrine that an increase in the supply of money affects different prices in successive phases. . . .

Hayek's early work in monetary history stimulated his theoretical views. His introduction to Hume was particularly significant, in itself and because this exposed him to a thinker who would later become more important to him generally in societal thought.

During his early career, Hayek planned two treatises in economics, neither of which he completed. The work he began for which he wrote the four chapters on the history of money was, in toto, to be a work on "monetary theory and policy." When he went to England, circumstances had changed. The Great Depression focused theory on economic fluctuations, and Hayek's academic interests accordingly moved from monetary theory in general to more particular problems of industrial fluctuation. Hayek's second intended treatise in economics was his incomplete work in capital and monetary theory, the first volume of which was published as *The Pure Theory of Capital*. (Interestingly, Hayek's intended format of his later two-part treatise on capital and money was structured like Keynes's two-volume *A Treatise on Money;* volume 1 of Keynes's work was "The Pure Theory of Money," and volume 2 was "The Applied Theory of Money." Hayek did not write a response to Keynes's *General Theory* because he was still writing a response, in what was published as *The Pure Theory of Capital,* to Keynes's earlier *Treatise on Money*.)

Among other historical writings during the later 1920s and 1930s that Hayek singled out in his autobiographical notes as of particular noteworthiness were biographical sketches of economists Hermann Heinrich Gossen, Richard Cantillon, and especially Henry Thornton, as well as of Wieser and Menger. Also, Hayek wrote an obituary article of the first classical liberal economist of the London school of economics (the "school," not the "School"), Edwin Cannan, whose succeeding members have included Lionel Robbins, Arnold Plant, Hayek himself, Ronald Coase, William Hutt, Arthur Seldon, Basil Yamey, Alan Walters, and Peter Bauer, among many others.

Gossen lived from 1810 to 1858 and was a significant predecessor to Wieser in utility analysis. From a theoretical perspective, perhaps the most relevant aspect of Hayek's essay on Gossen was his critique of the latter's conception of utility: "Gossen, contrary to classical theory, starts from the insight that has become fundamental for the modern school: namely, that the basis of the advantage which exchanging individuals expect from the exchange must be that they assess the exchanged goods differently, one valuing a good higher, the other lower." Goods do not possess value of themselves; they possess value only in the minds of their potential possessors. That individuals value goods differently is one basis of economic activity (another is that individuals can produce more in groups than individually).

Of Richard Cantillon's *Essay on the Nature of Commerce in General,* Hayek wrote that it is a "gem of economic literature . . . [and] one of the six or eight works on our science, written in the period prior to modern developments (i.e., before about 1870), with which every economist should be familiar." Cantillon had the personal misfortune to be murdered in 1734 and the professional misfortune to be overshadowed by other economists of the later eighteenth and early nineteenth centuries, most prominently Adam Smith. Hayek considered it to be "hardly overstating the case" regarding Cantillon's *Essay* when the English economist William Stanley Jevons "acclaimed it as the cradle of economics."

According to Stephen Kresge, at one time the general editor of *The Collected Works of F. A. Hayek:* "It appears that on his arrival in Britain in 1931, Hayek was still intending to complete his book on the history of monetary theory . . . , of which an examination of Thornton's work was to be an important part. In January 1932 he began to contact the surviving Thornton grandchildren, as well as the descendants of Thornton's associates. . . . After these initial contacts, Hayek prepared a draft of his article, which he then circulated among these and other relatives."

Henry Thornton, who was born in 1760 and died in 1815, was, in economic historian Henry Spiegel's words, a banker and parliamentarian, and ... a leader of the evangelical "party of Saints" ... which urged the abolition of the slave trade and other reforms. Like his father, ... Thornton was a great philanthropist. ... Thornton's book [*Paper Credit of Great Britain* (1802)] ... was not a book with one great idea but a careful and balanced analysis of the circumstances attending the expansion and contraction of money in both their domestic and international aspects. Thornton traced in detail ... the indirect link between money and prices, that is, the effect of a change in the quantity of money on the interest rate and thereby on prices. ... Like a few other writers of his time, Thornton related the quantity of money not only to the price level but also to output. ... In the field of international finance, Thornton was the first to note the inflow of short-term funds from abroad in response to an increase in the rate of interest.

According to John Hicks: "Thornton is the first great writer of the Credit School; though he wrote so long ago, he remains among the best."

In his historical chapter on monetary policy in Great Britain during the suspension of gold convertibility from 1797 to 1821, Hayek wrote that there is "one work of such disproportionate merit that it deserves to be discussed in greater detail—Henry Thornton's *An Enquiry into the Nature and Effects of the Paper Credit of Great Britain.* ... His book deserves to be ranked as one of the few outstanding achievements in the development of monetary theory." Hayek also said, in *Prices and Production,* that while the "existence of some relation between the quantity of money and the rate of interest was clearly recognised very early ... the first author known to me to enunciate a clear doctrine on this point was Henry Thornton." Given that increasing (or decreasing) the money supply through changing interest rates to influence economic activity and prices is the cardinal theorem of contemporary monetary policy, Thornton may be considered the first monetarist. Hayek wrote in his essay on Thornton that it is "not too much to say that the appearance of the *Paper Credit* in 1802 marks the beginning of a new epoch in the development of monetary theory."

Edwin Cannan significantly influenced Hayek and many other economists, although, as Hayek noted, the "part he played is little known beyond a rather narrow circle." Hayek held that Cannan—together with Mises in Vienna and Frank Knight in Chicago—was responsible for the preservation and transmission of classical liberalism during the early decades of the twentieth century. Hayek began his acknowledgments of the notes section in *The Constitution of Liberty* saying that if he had considered it his "task to acknowledge all indebtedness and to notice all agreement, these notes would have been studded with references to the work of Ludwig von Mises, Frank H. Knight, and Edwin Cannan . . ."

Hayek had read Cannan, dean of LSE economists, before moving to England. Hayek recalled of his early years at the school that it "so happened that I had become very friendly with the Cannan tradition. I had reviewed his books, and liked [them] very much, and Robbins of course was a Cannan pupil, so I fitted in much better in a group with the Edwin Cannan tradition than I would have fitted in with a Marshall tradition."

In his essay on Cantillon, Hayek called Cannan's *A Review of Economic Theory* a "fascinating book" and observed that it led him to his "own close concern with Cantillon." In a footnote to the essay, Hayek referred readers to Cannan's book for further confirmation and discussion of Cantillon's significance. There Cannan stated that Cantillon had been called "'the economists' economist,' meaning that his influence was on the leaders of thought rather than on the rank and file." Cannan additionally observed that it is in "the *Essai* that we first find the undertaker of business (translated *entrepreneur*) playing the great part which he is given in subsequent treatises." Cannan was a great historian of economic thought.

In his 1902 Presidential Address to Section F of the British Association, Cannan well enunciated Adam Smith's invisible hand. Cannan spoke of the

> wonderful way in which the people of the whole civilised world now co-operate in the production of wealth. . . . [C]onsider the daily feeding of London. There are . . . six millions of people in and about London, so closely packed together that they cannot grow anything for their own consumption, and yet every morning their food arrives with unfailing regularity . . . they use coal which has been dug from great depths hundreds of miles away . . . in consuming . . . they eat and drink products which have come from Wiltshire, Jamaica, Dakota, or China, with no more thought than an infant consuming its mother's milk. It is clear that there is in existence some machinery, some organisation for production, which, in spite of occasional failures here and there, does its work on the whole with extraordinary success.

Cannan was an exceptional scholar of Adam Smith, and through his scholarship was responsible for a considerable portion of the twentieth century's renaissance of interest in Smith's thought.

In his introductory essay of *Collectivist Economic Planning,* Hayek observed that Cannan said as early as 1893 that "the aims of socialists and Communists could only be achieved by 'abolishing both the institution of private property and the practice of exchange, without which value, in any reasonable sense of the word, cannot exist'"—private property and the ability to exchange are the fundamental constituents of economic value. Hayek also referred the reader to Cannan's 1912 essay "The Incompatibility of Socialism and Nationalism," wherein Cannan affirmed that "this identification of the nation to which a man happens to belong with the Society to which he owes a duty is a great obstacle to socialism, which must be removed before socialism can make any considerable progress. . . . Whatever may be said in favour of mankind, or Society as a whole, owning the natural and artificial means of production, there is nothing to be said for giving such means of production as happen to be situated in each of a number of small areas to the people who happen at present, and may happen in the future, to be the inhabitants of each of those areas."

So protean a figure was Cannan that one of his students was Hugh Dalton, one of the leading intellectuals in the Labour Party during the early to middle decades of the twentieth century. Many besides Hayek have praised Cannan or mentioned his influence on them; Robbins, who wrote that "[a]ll those who came in contact with him regard his teaching as perhaps the most important influence in their lives"; Coase, who calls Cannan "the teacher of my teacher," Arnold Plant; Hutt, who called Cannan "the leading influence to which I was subjected during my first three years at LSE . . . a remarkably wise and independent thinker"; and Seldon, who was first exposed to Cannan's thought by his textbook *Wealth* while still in high school. Dalton greatly praised Cannan as well.

In a 1935 obituary of Cannan, Hayek wrote that with his death, "one of the most original and most distinguished representatives of the nearly decimated great generation of economists has vanished from the scene. Cannan's rank and importance were probably never sufficiently appreciated outside his own country. . . . He was so deeply rooted in every respect in the British tradition and was at the same time so remote from all fashionable trend prevailing in his discipline. . . . Anyone for whom scholarly distinction lies in strikingly original formulations, abstract conceptual refinements, or speculations about the methodological basis of our field will never be able to understand why Edwin Cannan is honoured as one of the truly great and especially one of the most independent thinkers of his generation."

Cannan's works remain of more intrinsic, and even topical, interest than those of most of his contemporaries. In placing Cannan in influence in the same category as Mises and Knight, whom Hayek considered the two other most influential economists during the early decades of the twentieth century, Hayek wrote in 1951 that "many of his economic essays which he published in two volumes . . . deserve, even now, renewed and wider attention. . . . Their simplicity, clarity and sound common sense make them models for the treatment of economic problems, and even some that were written before 1914 are still astonishingly topical." Decades after Cannan's collection of the same title, Milton Friedman called one of his own collections *An Economist's Protest.*

As Hayek wrote, the role that Edwin Cannan has played in the transmission and development of liberalism is little known. The school of liberal thought he established at the London School of Economics has proven lasting and influential across disciplines. According to economic historian Henry Spiegel, Cannan was "the leading student of classical economics in the England of his time." Murray Rothbard, who was an excellent historian of economic theory, had a very high opinion of Cannan's work. Leading contemporary economic historian Denis O'Brien writes that "Cannan's strong critical attitude and wide scholarship are of great value to economists."

Hayek's move from economic theory to political philosophy was a natural evolution in his ideas. First, he considered the influence of prices in production. Then he considered the larger question of the role of prices in social life. The conclusion he reached was that law should guarantee to each person a protected sphere within which each could live as much as possible as he pleased. Later in his career, he progressed to the idea that whole societies through their customs, morals, and rules are engaged in macrocompetition, the survivor of which would possess the customs, morals, and rules that are the most materially productive and result in the highest standard of living for the most—the economist's goal.

8

"The Abuse and Decline of Knowledge"

HAYEK'S NOVEMBER 10, 1936, PRESIDENTIAL ADDRESS TO THE LONDON Economic Club, "Economics and Knowledge," is often considered his single greatest work. He himself considered it among his most important. He remarked in his autobiographical notes that "together with some later related papers reprinted with it in *Individualism and Economic Order,* this seems to me in retrospect the most original contribution I have made to the theory of economics."

His idea of "theory," whether he ever expressed it this way, was a verbal description of the world, of experience. His essential conceptions in "Economics and Knowledge" were that knowledge is divided among the minds of all humanity and that market order overcomes the division of knowledge—thereby rendering central government control of all of the aspects of a society's economy not maximally productive or effective.

Hayek described the importance of this address in an interview with UCLA economist and Mont Pelerin Society member Armen Alchian:

> Q: . . . Two things you wrote that had a personal influence on me, after your *Prices and Production,* were "[Economics and Knowledge]" and "The Use of Knowledge in Society." These I would regard as your two best articles, best in terms of influence on me.
>
> A: "Economics and Knowledge"—the '37 one— . . . is the one which marks the new look at things in my way.
>
> Q: It was new to you . . . ? Was it a change in your own thinking?
>
> A: Yes, it was really the beginning of my looking at things in a new light. If you asked me, I would say that up 'til that moment I was developing conventional ideas. With the '36 lecture to the Economic

Club in London, . . . "Economics and Knowledge," I started my own
way of thinking.

Sometimes in private I say I have made one discovery and
two inventions in the social sciences: the discovery is the approach
of the utilization of dispersed knowledge, which is the short formula
which I use for it; and the two inventions I have made are denationalization of money and my system of democracy.

Q: . . . How did you happen to get into that [first] topic? . . .

A: It was several ideas converging on that subject. It was . . . my essay
on socialism, the use in my trade cycle theory of the prices as guides
to production, the current discussion of anticipation, particularly in
the discussion with the Swedes on that subject, to some extent perhaps Knight's *Risk, Uncertainty and Profit,* which contains certain
suggestions in that direction—all that came together. And it was
with a feeling of a sudden illumination, sudden enlightenment, that
I—I wrote that lecture in a certain excitement. I was aware that I
was putting down things which were fairly well known in a new
form, and perhaps it was the most exciting moment in my career
when I saw it in print.

In the address Hayek noted that Frank Knight's work had "exercised"
considerable "stimulus" in the area of "foresight." For Hayek: "The
concept of equilibrium itself can be made definite and clear only in
terms of assumptions concerning foresight." Hayek considered foresight to be an important part of knowledge.

Hayek attached great importance to the issue of knowledge.
"Economics and Knowledge" led to an intended two-part great treatise to be titled "The Abuse and Decline of Knowledge." While Hayek
never completed this project, he greatly valued the immediate work
connected with it—the essays that were later published as *The
Counter-Revolution of Science, The Road to Serfdom,* and some papers
in *Individualism and Economic Order.*

In a letter written during the Battle of Britain dated June 21,
1940, Hayek wrote to his friend Fritz Machlup, who was now in the
United States, of his essays originally intended to form part of "The
Abuse and Decline of Knowledge": "It is a great subject and one could
really make a great book out of it. I believe indeed I have now found
an approach to the subject through which one could exercise some real
influence. But whether I shall ever be able to write it, depends of
course not only on whether one survives this but also on the outcome
of it all. If things go really badly I shall certainly not be able to continue

it here and since I believe that it is really important and the best I can do for the future of mankind, I should then have to try to transfer my activities elsewhere."

The stream of work that started in *The Counter-Revolution of Science, The Road to Serfdom,* and *Individualism and Economic Order* concluded later in *The Constitution of Liberty; Law, Legislation and Liberty,* and "The Fatal Conceit." It is appropriate to return to Hayek's first published work in this area, "Freedom and the Economic System."

In that work, Hayek enunciated his understanding of the tie between classical liberalism and state-run socialism: "The link between classical liberalism and present-day socialism . . . is undoubtedly the belief that the consummation of individual freedom requires relief from the most pressing economic cares." Hayek could hardly have been more explicit that he shared the goal of the highest standard of living for the most (in classical utilitarian terms, the greatest happiness of the greatest number) with classical socialism. Hayek and classical socialists—those who believe in state management and ownership of all of a society's means of economic production—were of one mind that one outcome of the optimal society is the highest standard of living shared by the most people and, perhaps, ultimately the most sentient creation.

"Freedom and the Economic System" evolved prior to most of the work later contained in *The Counter-Revolution of Science* (which, incidentally, Mises considered to be Hayek's best work), notwithstanding that in the tentative plan for the intended "The Abuse and Decline of Knowledge," the part of which "Freedom and the Economic System" was a first, initial draft would have been the second part of the work. It was from "Freedom and the Economic System" that Hayek's most famous book, *The Road to Serfdom* (1944), developed.

The essay contains one of Hayek's best statements of the importance of free thought and dissent. Here Hayek argued that free thought is not valued because all are able to make use of it, but because some are: "What is essential to make it [free thought] serve its function as the prime mover of intellectual progress is . . . that any cause or any idea may be argued by somebody. So long as dissent is not actually prevented there will always be some who will query the ideas ruling their contemporaries and put new ideas to the test of argument and propaganda." Human reason "consists of the interaction of individuals possessing different information and different views. . . . Once given the possibility of dissent there will be dissenters. . . . Only the imposition of an official doctrine which must be accepted and which nobody dare question can stop intellectual progress." The importance of free thought can hardly be stated more clearly or emphatically. All human progress and advance stem from free thought. The abuse of knowledge is the attempt to control, limit, or direct it, in part to protect official creeds or dogmas.

During the middle and late 1930s, Hayek worked on several projects. His main task was the intended two-part treatise on the statics and dynamics of capital, the first part of which was published in 1941 as *The Pure Theory of Capital.* This grew out of his earlier and continuing work in monetary theory. In 1935, Hayek's *Collectivist Economic Planning,* which he edited, appeared; and on November 10, 1936, he gave his presidential address to the London Economic Club, "Economics and Knowledge."

The classes he taught at the London School of Economics during the 1930s included economic theory (value, industrial fluctuations, and capital) and, later in the decade, socialist calculation. Hayek's joint seminar with Robbins was a great attraction for many foreign and domestic students. Hayek spent many days at the British Museum, as had Marx, writing his intended great treatise on capital and monetary theory, which, like Marx, he did not complete.

In 1937, Hayek's *Monetary Nationalism and International Stability* was published, based on lectures given at the Graduate Institute of International Studies in Geneva, Switzerland, where Mises taught from 1934 to 1940. Hayek made key contacts there that were later instrumental in founding the Mont Pelerin Society. Hayek supported the gold standard at this time and opposed flexible international exchange rates. He believed that flexible international exchange rates inevitably lead to inflation, national and international economic instability and downturns, and the diminution of international trade.

Hayek regularly traveled to the continent during the 1930s. He and his wife and children visited family in Austria, and he participated in conferences and symposia on his own. He was not much of a family man. Neither as a husband (to his first wife) nor as a father could he be considered exemplary, though he dutifully provided for his family and was concerned about his children.

~

In August 1938—five months after Hitler drove triumphantly into Vienna, and one month before the Munich Conference at which Britain and France ceded parts of Czechoslovakia to him—twenty-six academic and other intellectual liberals from around the world gathered in Paris in *La Colloque Walter Lippmann* to discuss "the crisis of liberalism" and Lippmann's *The Good Society* (1937). It cannot be said that the participants, who included Mises and Hayek, were entirely barking up the right tree. The absolutely vital issue in the geopolitical world at this time was the rise of Hitler, not the decline of liberalism. Moreover, by the later 1930s, particularly in Europe, national economies had largely revived from the Great Depression. The participants in the colloquium were academics in their respective countries who, typically, were out of touch and out of favor with the academic mainstream. Their views tended to look to the past, to the liberal, pre–Great War world. They were more likely to focus on the Soviet Union than on Nazi Germany.

Hayek was, by coincidence, in Austria during the Anschluss in March 1938, saw thousands of Austrians stream to greet and cheer Hitler at the border, and witnessed Hitler's welcome in Vienna on the Heldenplatz. Hayek's family in Austria was typical of many, perhaps most, Austrian Catholics. Hayek's mother became a strong supporter of Hitler and at least one, or possibly both, of Hayek's brothers were members of the Nazi Party during World War II. (Regarding Hayek's brothers, this appears to have been more for reasons of career advancement than political conviction.)

Most Austrians were anti-Semitic, though Hayek was not. His views perhaps placed him in the most liberal quartile or quintile of Austrian Catholics with respect to his interaction with, and opinions of appropriate civil and social rights for, Jews. He thought that there should be no legal or social distinction on the basis of religious belief and was troubled by the psychological phenomenon of Hitlerism. He remarked later in his life of an unnamed colleague who went to a Hitler rally to see what one was like and, to his disappointment later, wound up clapping and cheering.

Lippmann was an eclectic writer whose work metamorphosed over his career. One of the leading popular columnists in the United States for decades, he became a harsh critic of Franklin Roosevelt, and his influence receded as his career progressed.

Hayek's participation in the conference indicates the broadening scope of his ideas and his desire to influence practical affairs. He quoted a line from Lippmann's *The Good Society* in *The Road to Serfdom:* "'The generation to which we belong is now learning from experience what happens when men retreat from freedom to a coercive organization of their affairs. Though they promise themselves a more abundant life, they must in practice renounce it; as the organized direction increases, the variety of ends must gave way to uniformity. That is the nemesis of the planned society and the authoritarian principle in human affairs.'"

"The Abuse and Decline of Knowledge" was originally intended to consist of two parts, "Hubris of Reason" and "The Nemesis of the Planned Society," the latter a reference to Lippmann's work. The ancient Greeks believed that hubris, particularly of human presumption, was followed by Nemesis, the goddess of retribution. Reason's abuse leads to its decline. Not only is ignorance the enemy of knowledge and truth; so too are deliberate efforts to control thought. *The Road to Serfdom,* growing out of Hayek's earlier "Freedom and the Economic System" articles, was an "advance sketch" of "The Nemesis of the Planned Society."

In the preface to the 1959 German edition of *The Counter-Revolution of Science,* Hayek wrote that the essays "assembled in this volume were written as part of a greater work that, if it ever should be finished, pursues the history of the abuse and decline of reason in modern times. I wrote the first two essays in . . . relative leisure, which the early years of the last war afforded me. I wrote them on a remote subject matter in a state of intensive concentration with which I reacted to my impotence against the continuous disruptions of falling bombs."

"Hubris of Reason" would have been a largely historical presentation of the ideas of individualism, followed by the intellectual sources of hostility to individualism, and concluding with four chapters on the development of socialist ideas in France, Germany, England, and America. Though Hayek never wrote the first chapter in the form he intended, his lecture "Individualism: True and False" contained "preliminary results" of his study of eighteenth-century individualistic theories.

Hayek distinguished two types of individualism—the first, stemming mostly from British and Scottish roots, and stressing the fallibility of individual reason; and the second, having its roots in Cartesian rationalism, and emphasizing the strength of individual reason. He considered the former to be true individualism, and said of it that the

> first thing that should be said is that it is primarily a *theory* of society, an attempt to understand the forces which determine the social

life of man, and only in the second instance a set of political maxims derived from this view of society. . . . [I]ts basic contention . . . is that there is no other way of understanding social phenomena but through our understanding of individual actions. . . . The next step in the individualistic analysis of society . . . is the contention that, by tracing the combined effects of individual actions, we discover that many of the institutions on which human achievements rest have arisen and are functioning without a designing and directing mind . . . and that the spontaneous collaboration of free men often creates things which are greater than their individual minds can ever fully comprehend.

Menger's influence on Hayek was fundamental.

False individualism, by way of contrast, exalts what individuals may accomplish: I cannot better illustrate the contrast in which Cartesian or rationalistic "individualism" stands to this view than by quoting a famous passage from Part II of the *Discourse on Method*. Descartes argues that "there is seldom so much perfection in works composed of many separate parts, upon which different hands had been employed, as those completed by a single master." He then goes on to suggest . . . that "those nations which, starting from a semi-barbarous state and advancing to civilization by slow degrees, have had their laws successively determined, and, as it were, forced upon them simply by experience of the hurtfulness of particular crimes and disputes, would by this process come to be possessed of less perfect institutions than those which, from the commencement of their association as communities, have followed the appointment of some wise legislator."

True and false individualism differ, according to Hayek, not primarily about values but about facts. The question of how societies are actually ordered or organized separates them: Are communities created, or do they evolve? The answer is obviously some combination of the two, but the relative weighting is of the greatest importance. If one believes that it is possible to plan centrally an economy or society, an entirely different normative society may emerge than if one believes that such planning is not possible. Starting from different factual premises, contrasting moral systems may be built.

Hayek emphasized the importance of rules. He thought that what society should do is not to direct the individual in his or her particular actions, but to create a metaphysical structure, as it were, enforced by rules or laws, that create stable expectations and thus allow rational action: "I propose not only to undertake to defend a general principle of social organization but shall also try to show that aversion to general principles, and the preference for proceeding from particular instance to particular instance . . . leads us back from a social order resting on the general recognition of certain principles to a system in which order is created by direct commands." Rules or commands—this is the essential choice Hayek saw humanity facing with respect to its order or organization.

He gave his idea of optimal social order in "Individualism: True and False": "True individualism affirms the value of the family and all the common efforts of the small community and group, . . . it believes in local autonomy and voluntary associations, . . . indeed its case rests largely on the contention that much for which the coercive action of the state is usually invoked can be done better" through voluntary co-operation. "There can be no greater contrast to this than the false individualism which wants to dissolve all these smaller groups into atoms which have no cohesion other than the coercive rules imposed by the state, and which tries to make all social ties prescriptive, instead of using the state mainly as a protection of the individual against the arrogation of coercive powers by the smaller groups." There was a strong communitarian element in Hayek's thought, an emphasis on freely chosen communities that will emerge in the absence of government-imposed coercive authority.

Hayek thought that the state is necessary, though, because, like and following John Locke, he thought that there must be a body—government—in society that possesses the monopoly of coercive power; otherwise, the condition of men and women would be barbarous. The critical goal, in both Locke's and Hayek's minds, therefore became how to control the power of government. As James Madison wrote in *The Federalist:* "In framing a government which is to be administered by men over men, the great difficulty lies in this: you must first enable the government to control the governed; and in the next place oblige it to control itself." Both Hayek and Locke thought that this is best achieved by limiting government's potential actions and restricting these potential actions to known general rules applicable to all. Both sought a government of rules rather than commands, the latter of which, by their nature, are not known in advance and may be arbitrary—not applicable to all. Hayek's goal was the society of law.

Hayek ripped G. W. F. Hegel in *The Counter-Revolution of Science*'s third part for his "historicism"—the idea, in Hayek's terminology, that history moves in set and predictable stages. He considered this idea fatally flawed and societies that were based on it to be unsuccessful, unproductive, and unfree.

Historicism denies free will. The future is what we make of it.

9

The Road to Serfdom

IN HIS AUTOBIOGRAPHICAL NOTES, WHICH HE BEGAN TO WRITE AFTER
the success of *The Road to Serfdom,* Hayek said that the "light burden
of teaching (there were very few students) and the short distances at
Cambridge gave me more time for my own work than I ever had before." His best-known work was his response to World War II and the
rise of totalitarian, militarily aggressive dictatorships. *The Road to Serfdom* was an advance, popular sketch of the intended second part of the
larger "The Abuse and Decline of Reason" to be titled "The Nemesis
of the Planned Society." Hayek worked on *The Road to Serfdom* intensely during 1941 and 1942. In particular, he spent more time writing
its early chapters than anything else he ever wrote.

He insisted that when *The Road to Serfdom* was published in
1944, and became an international cause célebre over the next year
and a half, he was surprised at the popular response. He may have
hoped that the work would have broad impact, but it seems unlikely
that he anticipated it would make him world-famous and the leading
classical liberal.

The Road to Serfdom was not as important a work in Hayek's
thought as its popular acclaim implies. In the original preface, dated
December 1943, he noted that it was a "political book" (as distinct
from an "essay in social philosophy") and that as a "professional student of social affairs," it was his duty to say so.

He was even more explicit in the preface to the 1976 edition.
There he wrote, just after receiving the Nobel Prize in Economic Sciences in 1974, that in "spite of the wholly unexpected success of the
book—in the case of the initially not contemplated American edition

even greater than in that of the British one—I felt for a long time not altogether happy about it." Indeed, he added that he had previously felt somewhat "apologetic" with respect to the work and had not reread it for twenty years. He had "long resented being more widely known by what I regarded as a pamphlet for the time than by my strictly scientific work."

Originally, Hayek intended *The Road to Serfdom* as a polemic against the twin totalitarians of the East—Nazi Germany and the Soviet Union—contrasted to the liberal democracies of the West—the United Kingdom, United States, and France. However, then France fell, and, more significantly, the Soviet Union became an ally of Britain and America. Therefore, Hayek eliminated most negative references to the Soviet Union.

Among Hayek's possible initial titles for the intended treatise of which *The Road to Serfdom* was an advance, popular sketch of the second part was "The Abuse and Decline of Reason or Through Socialism to Fascism (From Saint Simon to Hitler)." He greatly opposed the political system of the Soviet Union, considering that country an even worse tyranny than Hitler's. Only the exigencies of the circumstances led him not to express this view.

Hayek did not intend to leave technical economic theory when he wrote *The Road to Serfdom*. It "unexpectedly" became for him the start of work in a new area, and he at first "tried hard to get back to economics proper." For about a decade after he wrote it, he did not concentrate as much on social philosophy as he did after the middle 1950s or so, when political philosophy became his focus for the rest of his career. From 1944 through the middle 1950s, he was focused on more practical endeavors, such as his divorce, moving to America from England, and starting the Mont Pelerin Society, as well as academic projects such as *The Sensory Order* and works in the history of ideas, of which his books on John Stuart Mill and his editing of *Capitalism and the Historians* were the most significant products during this period.

One of the paradoxes of Hayek is that he wrote better than he thought. That is, his writing is often more suggestive and stimulating than the thought that underlaid it. While his writing is, stylistically, difficult, it is also exceptionally profound, and its value lies in its profundity. He was one of the most significant writers on political and economic topics during the twentieth century in conveying new conceptions of optimal societal order and ways of understanding the sensory world. Hayek was, perhaps first of all, a great pure philosopher.

The idea that it is possible to write better than one thinks is truly paradoxical. What is meant by it, in this case, is that Hayek's thought was not as profound or stimulating as the writing based on it. Hayek's writings create ideas in the minds of others that were not necessarily in his own.

In the 1956 foreword to a new American paperback edition of *The Road to Serfdom,* he called "Planning and the Rule of Law," chapter 6, its "central" chapter. For this reason, it is appropriate to pay special attention to it. "Nothing distinguishes more clearly conditions in a free country," he began, "from those in a country under arbitrary government than the observance in the former of the great principles known as the Rule of Law. Stripped of all technicalities, this means that government in all its actions is bound by rules fixed and announced beforehand—rules which make it possible to foresee with fair certainty how the authority will use its coercive powers in given circumstances and to plan one's individual affairs on the basis of this knowledge."

Hayek's essential political philosophy was that liberty is the supremacy of law. To some, this may appear a paradoxical conception of liberty, for liberty is too often considered to be the absence of law. This, however, was the exact opposite of Hayek's view. He thought that liberty is not possible without law. Right law is liberty.

In "Planning and the Rule of Law," he put forward the fundamental idea that "under the Rule of Law the government is prevented from stultifying individual efforts by *ad hoc* action. Within the known rules of the game the individual is free to pursue his personal ends and desires." In addition, the "discretion left to the executive organs wielding coercive power should be reduced as much as possible." These are crucial desiderata and remain applicable today. Far too often, government in contemporary society intervenes in a discretionary manner, perhaps especially at the local level. The diminution of arbitrary government and its replacement by set and known laws remains a vital component of the libertarian program and agenda. While he was still developing his thought in this area when he wrote *The Road to Serfdom,* Hayek recognized that without the fixity that law provides—both morally and in society—positive actions are impossible. In political society, state law creates the framework of legally permissible activity.

Law creates a rational framework for individuals in society. With respect to his conception of the rule of law, the "important question is whether the individual can foresee the action of the state and make use of this knowledge as a datum in forming his own plans." The idea of prediction was important for Hayek, who wrote later in "Degrees of Explanation" that "while it is evidently possible to predict precisely without being able to control, we shall clearly not be able to control developments further than we can predict the results of our action." As Stephen Kresge, then the general editor of *The Collected Works of F. A. Hayek*, writes of this passage: "Arguments both for and against the efficacy of the central planning that socialism inevitably requires either stand or fall on the epistemological justification of the ability to predict the consequences of actions."

Hayek was a philosophical utilitarian in his ultimate moral outlook. His criterion for rules, as he wrote in *The Road to Serfdom*, was whether they are "most likely on the whole to benefit all the people affected by them." The utilitarian standard is the greatest happiness of the greatest number.

In the 1959 German edition preface of *The Counter-Revolution of Science*, he said that this "overview of the progressive abuse of reason, or socialism, was to be followed by a discussion of the decay of reason under totalitarianism, be it fascism or communism. The basic thought of this second major part was initially presented in popular form in my book *The Road to Serfdom*." Once reason attempts to control its further advance, free thought is dead. It is inevitable, Hayek thought, that government control of the economy leads to suppression of freedom of thought and speech. Economic and political liberty are coincident, just as collectivist economics and totalitarian politics are.

The Road to Serfdom was initially published in England in March 1944 with a print run of 2,000 copies, which sold out within days. Hayek became famous in Britain as a result of the work. It was reviewed in leading papers, magazines, and journals. In September 1944, the American edition of *The Road to Serfdom* was published by the University of Chicago Press. It, too, became an overnight sensation, as it was given the lead review in the *New York Times Book Review*, with a rave review by Henry Hazlitt: "Friedrich A. Hayek has written one of the most important books of our generation."

During April and May 1945, Hayek was scheduled to make an academic lecture tour of the United States. However, in April 1945, the *Reader's Digest*—then a major force on the American cultural scene—published a condensed version of *The Road to Serfdom* as its lead feature. When Hayek got off the boat in New York, he had become a celebrity.

Ludwig von Mises, who was then living in the United States, experienced and foresaw Hayek's success in this country. On July 27, 1944, he wrote Hayek that *The Road to Serfdom* was "really excellent," noting that "even before the publication of the American edition your success in this country is remarkable." Several references had been published in the *New York Times*.

On December 1, 1944, Mises wrote Hayek that *The Road to Serfdom* "has had a tremendous success in this country. . . . But don't be mistaken. The Veblen-Hansen ideology dominates public opinion in this country no less than does the Laski-Keynes ideology in Great Britain."

Mises wrote Hayek in February 1945 that "news of your impending lecture tour is very gratifying. It is almost a public sensation. You probably do not realize how great the success of your book is and how popular you are in this county. The newspaper-men will watch all your steps and publicize all your dicta."

Then the *Reader's Digest* version of *The Road to Serfdom* appeared. After Hayek returned to Britain in May, he became a celebrity there, as well. In his first speech of the 1945 general election campaign (which he lost), Winston Churchill seemed to make reference to Hayek's ideas. The next night, Labour leader Clement Attlee specifically referred to Hayek in his nationwide radio broadcast in response to Churchill's speech.

During the next several years, *The Road to Serfdom* was translated into a number of languages, sometimes in authorized editions, sometimes in underground or handwritten versions. As a result of his fame, Hayek traveled to many academic institutions in Europe and the United States during the later 1940s. This made it possible for him to start the Mont Pelerin Society in 1947, which endures to this day as an international libertarian and classical liberal organization in which a number of practical political members, mostly in Europe, have been involved, including Ludwig Erhard in West Germany, Jacques Rueff in France, and Luigi Einaudi in Italy. Erhard was chancellor of his county, Rueff, a leading economic adviser, and Einaudi, president.

The society emerged from an idea Hayek had during World War II to establish a reeducation center in Vienna for German intellectuals. In time, this idea metamorphosed into an international society of intellectuals to bring German thinkers back into the mainstream of Western thought. From this latter concept, Hayek began to write letters to individuals he met on his travels, asking if they would find it beneficial to meet. Thus was born the Mont Pelerin Society in 1947, named after the site of its first meeting. Later in his career, while he was on the Committee on Social Thought at the University of Chicago, Hayek sought to re-create the lost intellectual tradition at the University of Vienna through the establishment of an academic center there, but little came of this effort.

APPENDIX: HAYEK'S DIVORCE AND SECOND MARRIAGE

As a result of their centrality to Hayek's life, it is appropriate to pause for a moment to discuss his divorce and second marriage.

Hayek and his second wife, Helene, were unhappy in their first marriages for many years. Hayek and Helene (also known as Lena) were distant cousins and had been best friends since childhood. Hayek and Helene did not marry when they were young because of miscommunication, perhaps caused in part by Hayek's stay in the United States from March 1923 to May 1924. Whatever the reason, she married someone else, and Hayek then married someone who resembled her. Hayek and Helene remained in close contact after they were married, and both considered divorce as early as the 1930s.

Hayek did not see Helene before his divorce for over seven years, from 1939 to 1946, due to World War II. He sought a relatively high-paying position on the Committee on Social Thought at the University of Chicago, largely because this would provide the funds for his family in England, and Helene and himself. Hayek traveled to Vienna to visit Helene and other family members in 1946. In 1948, he spent the summer at the University of Vienna.

In a November 1948 letter to John Nef, chairman of the Committee on Social Thought, Hayek accepted a position there and indicated he would like to begin the following fall, in 1949. However, Hayek was unable to obtain a divorce from his first wife in England in 1949, and so had to travel to the United States to obtain one in 1950.

Hayek left his first wife and children on December 27, 1949, and flew to New York, where he attended the American Economic Association convention from December 29, 1949, to January 2, 1950. While there, he contacted Harold Dulan, chair of the economics and business department at the University of Arkansas at Fayetteville. Arkansas had permissive divorce laws. Hayek wondered whether the department would be interested in him as a visiting professor during the coming year. Dulan responded affirmatively.

Hayek spent the winter quarter in 1950 in a visiting capacity at the University of Chicago and then spent the spring quarter at the University of Arkansas at Fayetteville. He did not want a permanent position at Chicago before his divorce was granted in Arkansas, as otherwise legal challenges might have been made to his residency status in Arkansas. His divorce was granted on July 13, 1950, in Arkansas. He married Helene Bitterlich in Vienna on August 10, 1950.

Hayek's divorce was acrimonious. Hella Hayek's opposition to the divorce in response to his determined perseverance that he must have it led to highly charged personal circumstances during the last year and a half he was in England.

Hayek experienced personal fulfillment during the 1950s. While he experienced moral angst at his decision to leave his first wife and children, Helene was the love of his life. Their marriage was the realization of perhaps his longest and most deeply held vision.

Milton Friedman remembers Helene as a "very intelligent" person. She sometimes attended Hayek's seminar in Chicago. Beautiful and talented, Helene had a difficult and demanding personality. In a 1948 letter to Harold Luhnow of the Volcker Fund, which paid for Hayek's position at the University of Chicago, Hayek said that Helene had been his partner in his intellectual work prior to their separation in 1939, but this appears grossly overstated.

Hayek's children did not break with him after the divorce, though they rarely saw him. Hella Hayek lived for another decade, dying in London at age fifty-eight in 1960.

The 1961 wedding of Hayek's son, Larry, in England appears to have been a grand occasion for reconciliation. Esca Hayek, Larry's wife, remembers Larry commenting, "Now I have a father again," when Hayek and Helene moved to Freiburg in 1962.

Hayek had a great rift during the 1950s with his (former) friends in London, especially Lionel Robbins, which was caused in part by Hella Hayek's continued residence in the city while Hayek moved to Chicago. Hella remained in London, doors away from several economists, including the Robbinses. The rift was also caused, however, by Hayek's actions. He essentially abandoned Hella in London, where she was never really happy; she would have preferred never to have left Austria. Her children, Larry and Christina, were going to remain British, however, and she would not leave them to return to Vienna. Larry Hayek remembers his mother as a kind, beautiful, intelligent person. Following Hella's death and Larry's marriage, Hayek completely reconciled with Robbins.

The financial arrangements Hayek made for his first wife and children, ages fifteen and twenty at the time of the divorce, were ultimately acceptable, though not generous. Hayek was very much concerned about financial issues when he negotiated his position in Chicago. Lionel Robbins corresponded on behalf of Hella to Hayek regarding his financial settlement with her. Hayek took little with him when he left England to attend the American Economic Association convention and then go to the University of Chicago. His clothes, books, and other possessions were subsequently shipped to him, after the divorce.

In a June 1950 letter to a Mont Pelerin Society member explaining why he would no longer participate in society activities, Robbins said that Hayek "behaved in such a way which I find impossible to reconcile with the conception of his character and his standards which I have cherished through twenty years of friendship. . . . [A]s far as I am concerned, the man I knew is dead and I should find it almost intolerably painful to have to meet his successor."

Only one available interview exchange exists in which Hayek talked about his divorce, to UCLA economist Armen Alchian in 1978. While lengthy, this passage merits presentation for whatever light it may shed:

> Q: . . . I want to ask you one question which is impertinent. But it's serious, and I hope that maybe later you will be willing maybe to answer it. Forgive me for asking it, but I detect a strong respect for moral standards and their importance in society. Now, all of us . . . in our lifetime have faced problems where we have said, "Here is a moral standard, and I want to break it." I have done that, and I've thought back at times, "How did I justify that?" I said, "Well, I justified it." You must have had some; I'm assuming you've had some. Would you be willing, in that private tape of yours, to maybe indicate what some of them were? And what went through your mind at the time, if that happened, and what your response would be now to someone in the same situation?
>
> I was impressed by this when you were talking to Bob Bork about the sense in which our moral standards and restraints are part of our civilization. I liked that very much—why, I don't know—but I thought one way—I've been thinking myself of things I've done that I would not want to discuss even on a tape maybe, but still it would be interesting if in, say, fifty years we could—
>
> A: Well, if it's on that unmarked tape, I'm quite willing to talk about it. There's only one thing—

Q: I'm not trying to inquire. I just want to raise the issue.
A: There's no reason for [hesitation] when it's after your lifetime. I know I've done wrong in enforcing divorce. Well, it's a curious story. I married on the rebound when the girl I had loved, a cousin, married somebody else. She is now my present wife. But for twenty-five years I was married to the girl whom I married on the rebound, who was a very good wife to me, but I wasn't happy in that marriage. She refused to give me a divorce, and finally I enforced it. I'm sure that was wrong, and yet I have done it. It was just an inner need to do it.
Q: You'd do it again, probably.
A. I would probably do it again.

In the video portion of this tape, Hayek appears to consider making a more detailed statement about his marital situation, but he then backs off into more general, less revealing comments. Visually, Alchian's final question, "You'd do it again, probably," was met by Hayek's obvious agitation, discomfort, deliberation, and reluctance to answer.

1991 Nobel laureate Ronald Coase, a colleague in the economics department at the London School of Economics at the time, remembers the divorce as a "miserable business." Lord Desai, in economics at the school now, recalls department lore to the effect that after Hayek announced he would seek a divorce, Robbins and others would not talk to him in the senior common room.

When Hayek left the school in December 1949, there was some question about whether he would return or whether this was another of his extended leaves, as well as what was going on in his marriage. He did not officially submit his resignation from the London School of Economics until February 1950, about two months after he left England. He wrote in contemporaneous correspondence that he deferred his official letter of resignation because of the pending general election in Britain; he thought that the timing of his letter could reflect on it, which he did not wish to be the case.

In a March 6, 1950, letter to Karl Popper at the London School of Economics, Hayek said that he had first tried to persuade Hella to grant him a divorce almost fifteen years earlier. In a December 17, 1950, letter to Popper, Hayek anticipated that he might have to remain away from England for years because of his divorce.

Hayek broke down when he heard of Hella's death. According to one source, he called out her name at the point of his own death. He was a good and dutiful grandfather, well liked by his grandchildren, two girls and a boy. He always visited his son and his family at their home in southern England without Helene.

Hayek was happy in his second marriage, which lasted more than forty years. Helene survived him by four years, until 1996. When contacted for an interview in 1995 in Freiburg, she merely said, in declining, "I am now very much alone without my husband."

10

Epistemology, Psychology, and Methodology

AFTER HAYEK FINISHED *THE ROAD TO SERFDOM* AND EXPERIENCED its phenomenal success, he turned his attention to old ideas in psychology that he had explored as a student at the University of Vienna three decades before. Hayek's work in epistemology, psychology, and methodology is among the most difficult in his corpus for the noneconomist or nonpolitical scientist, and various interpretations are possible. Stemming from the Germanic philosophical heritage, Hayek was likely to place more emphasis on the act of knowing than on objects themselves. Hayek ultimately followed Kant in his ontological conception of reality—he thought that mind impresses order on existence.

He apparently still intended to return to technical economic theory in the years immediately after *The Road to Serfdom.* Another area he had reentered during the late 1930s was methodology and epistemology, philosophical areas he explored first in Mises's private seminar. All of this was background to Hayek's move into political philosophy in *The Constitution of Liberty* (1960), *Law, Legislation and Liberty* (1973–79), and "The Fatal Conceit." *The Road to Serfdom* moved Hayek from a course primarily in technical economic theory to one in broader areas of philosophical and societal inquiry.

His epistemology began from a phenomenalist base. The philosopher and physicist Ernst Mach was very important in Hayek's development and to the atmosphere at the University of Vienna when Hayek was a student there. Hayek remarked later:

> Nearly sixty years ago, when I conceived my psychological ideas, I
> never had a live teacher in psychology. For a young man returning
> from World War I to enter the University of Vienna, with his inter-
> ests having been drawn by those events from the family background
> of biology to social and philosophical issues, there was at the mo-
> ment no teaching in psychology available. To teach the subject was
> then still part of the duties of some of the professors of philoso-
> phy—not an altogether bad arrangement; but one of them . . . had
> recently died, and the other was clearly dying and the few of his lec-
> tures I heard, as painful for him to give as for the students to listen
> to. So I had to get my knowledge of psychology from . . . books. . . .
> [T]he decisive stimulus for taking up the problem on which I soon
> started to work came from Ernst Mach and particularly his *Analysis
> of Sensations.*

As noted earlier, there was a loud echo of Hume in Mach's
work, as both emphasized the tangibility of all knowledge—ultimately,
all knowledge is based in the senses. Mach also emphasized the internal nature of all knowledge, in that it is experienced in the mind. Finally, he emphasized the importance of quantitative and mathematical
methods and models to understand sensory experience.

In all of these views, Mach philosophically preceded the Vienna
circle of logical positivists. Mach wrote in the 1900 preface to the second edition of *The Analysis of Sensations* that "one and the same view
underlies both my epistemologico-physical writings and my present attempt to deal with the physiology of the senses—the view, namely, that
all metaphysical elements are to be eliminated as superfluous and as
destructive of the economy of science." The first chapter of this work is
titled "Introductory Remarks: Antimetaphysical." The Vienna circle
took up whole cloth the idea that one of the distinguishing marks of
true science is that it is antimetaphysical.

The question of the evolution of the Vienna circle, and of Ludwig Wittgenstein's influence on it, does not admit of one answer and remains of interest. The issue of the extent of the Vienna circle's
influence and accomplishment remains in dispute. The circle attempted
to achieve a scientific understanding of the world.

The intellectual (as distinct from personal) relationship between
Wittgenstein and Hayek has been of interest. While some have maintained that Wittgenstein had significant direct influence on Hayek, this
does not appear to have been the case. Though Hayek incidentally expressed conflicting thoughts about his distant cousin's intellectual in-

fluence on him, he referred very little to him in his major published works.

Nonetheless, interesting tangents that relate to Hayek's psychology and epistemology can be followed from verbal (as distinct from, necessarily, conceptual) similarities between the two men's work. Hayek rarely referred philosophically (as distinct from personally) to Wittgenstein. One place he did was the 1962 article "Rules, Perception and Intelligibility," where he quoted Wittgenstein in a footnote: "Cf. L. Wittgenstein . . . : '"Knowing" it only means: being able to describe it.'"

Regardless of what Hayek or Wittgenstein meant by this remark, it is very suggestive. The idea of knowledge encompasses more than can be expressed in words—this was Hayek's view. Wittgenstein's point, at least as could be inferred from his words in this quotation (though Hayek cited him in precisely the opposite context) was that knowledge means being able to describe something in sensile terms.

The question of the relationship between words and physical, sensory reality was taken up by the Vienna circle of logical positivists, whose leading members included Moritz Schlick, a successor of Mach at the University of Vienna and teacher of Hayek; Otto Neurath, the group's practical organizer; and Rudolf Carnap, another leading Viennese philosopher. Hayek was not a member of the Vienna circle, though he was aware of discussions there as a result of his friendship with Felix Kaufmann, a member of the circle, Hayek's *Geistkreis* (spirit circle), and Mises's "private seminar."

While it is always difficult to summarize the philosophy of a school that included diverse members over decades, prominent logical positivist themes included the essentiality of verification to knowledge; the exclusive meaningfulness of mathematics, logic, and science in knowledge; and the rejection, as knowledge, of ethics, metaphysics, and religion. Logical positivists were concerned with the philosophy of science and foundations of knowledge. They strove to answer the question: What makes something true? They drew heavily on the work of earlier British empiricists, such as Hume, and more recent philosophers of mathematics, logic, and semantics such as Wittgenstein and Bertrand Russell. They were also inspired by Einstein.

The key ideas of this group of philosophers, scientists, and mathematicians included verificationism and empiricism—that is, knowledge must be capable of being proven to the senses in order to be scientific, in order to be knowledge. Perhaps the central element of the Vienna circle and of logical positivism generally can be found in

Schlick's statement that "[t]he meaning of a proposition is its method of verification." As Carnap put it, the aim of logical positivism was "conclusive justification for every statement." Verification was basic in the logical positivist system. Propositions must be made in such a way as to be empirically testable in order to be scientific.

Hayek thought that logical positivism foundered on the shoals of verification. He wrote in *The Constitution of Liberty:* "I do not wish to underestimate the merit of the persistent and relentless fight of the eighteenth and nineteenth centuries against beliefs which are demonstrably false. But . . . extension of the concept of superstition to all beliefs which are not demonstrably true lacks the same justification and may often be harmful. That we ought not believe anything which has been shown to be false does not mean that we ought to believe only what has been demonstrated to be true."

Hayek's idea here was that it is not possible to corroborate every statement. Doing so would become philosophically absurd. At some point, statements should have meaning. Hayek's question was at what point this should be. He thought that the logical positivists did not adequately address this question, and thus they were ensnared in hopeless skepticism. On the other hand, the Vienna circle adopted the concept of "protocol statements," and Frank Knight put forward the idea of the relatively absolute absolute.

~

In a personal biographical recollection, Hayek remarked of Wittgenstein (grandson of a sister of one of Hayek's maternal great-grandfathers) and the intellectual milieu in Vienna that, on his first substantial contact with Wittgenstein in 1918, when both were officers in the Austrian army: "What struck me most in this conversation was a radical passion for truthfulness in everything (which I came to know as a characteristic vogue among the young Viennese intellectuals of the generation immediately preceding mine . . .). This truthfulness became almost a fashion in that . . . group . . . in which I came so much to move. It meant much more than truth in speech. One had to 'live' truth and not tolerate any pretence in oneself or others. . . . Every convention was dissected and every conventional form exposed as fraud. Wittgenstein merely carried this further in applying it to himself."

Truth is the great philosophical object. Philosophy ultimately concerns the search for the truth. Wittgenstein's great contribution to philosophy was his emphasis on words. In his great work, *Tractatus Logico-Philosophicus* (1921 German original edition), Wittgenstein put forward the view that "what can be said . . . can be said clearly, and what we cannot talk about we must pass over in silence." Wittgenstein's point here was empirical. He possessed a sensory conception of the world and thought that if something cannot be described through the senses, then nothing, empirically, could be said about it. It must, literally, be passed over in silence.

Schlick, in particular, was vitally influenced by Wittgenstein—whom Schlick considered to have inaugurated a new stage in philosophy. However, while there were a few contacts between members of the Vienna circle and Wittgenstein, the circle developed in largest part along separate lines than may be derived from Wittgenstein's life and words.

This, though, was the philosophical background—so well described in Malachi Haim Hacohen's exquisite 2000 *Karl Popper—The Formative Years 1902–1945*—in which Hayek developed his own philosophical, psychological, epistemological, and methodological thought. Hayek's epistemology was ultimately based on a phenomenalist perspective of sensory experience, but only as it is experienced in the mind. In this basic Kantian perspective of the nature of reality, Hayek was completely within the Germanic idealist intellectual and philosophical traditions.

Hayek's early work as a student in psychology (mostly before Wittgenstein's *Tractatus* was published) led him to ask himself the questions: "What is mind?" and "What is the place of mind in the realm of nature?" Hayek essentially adopted a Kantian view of the nature of the world. He saw mind as implanting order on the world rather than the world necessarily having any properties of, as it were, itself.

In *The Sensory Order,* Hayek wrote that if the "account of the determination of mental qualities which we have given is correct, it would mean that the apparatus by means of which we learn about the external world is itself the product of a kind of experience." Hayek did not ultimately ascribe much significance to the brain as an accurate (whatever, in this circumstance, accuracy would be) receptacle of reality. Reality, such as it is, is what brain makes of it.

This Kantian ontological (theory of being) perspective had, in Hayek's view, significant philosophical consequences or repercussions for epistemology. Since there is no ultimate reality apart from what brain makes of it, knowledge is not of ultimate essences but merely of mental states that themselves are liable to change during the lifetime of an organism or over the evolution of a species. Hayek's ontology ultimately reduces the role of absolute knowledge absolutely.

Hayek's view was that all the knowledge that is possible of a circumstance is a theory of the circumstance—that is, there is no such thing as pure sensation. There is, rather, a *theory* of sensation. As Heinrich Klüver wrote in introducing *The Sensory Order:* "In brief space, it is impossible to outline even the essentials of Dr. Hayek's theory, but from a broad point of view his theory may be said to substantiate Goethe's famous maxim 'all that is factual is already theory' for the field of sensory and other psychological phenomena."

Hayek thought that the social sciences are capable of greater knowledge than the natural. He wrote in "The Facts of the Social Sciences" in 1943—after, significantly, his "Economics and Knowledge" essay, which he considered to have constituted his decisive breakthrough and departure from Mises (though Mises, as already noted, did not think this): "While at the world of nature we look from the outside, we look at the world of society from the inside." Because we look at the world of society from, in Hayek's view, the "inside," we are capable of more knowledge of it than of the external world of nature.

Similarly, Hayek considered the fundamental divide between the social and natural worlds not to be in kind of phenomena (notwithstanding that we experience the former from the inside and the latter from the outside), but in complexity. He wrote in his "Scientism and the Study of Society" essay, which became a part of *The Counter-Revolution of Science* (again, after "Economics and Knowledge"), that the "place where the human individual stands in the order of things brings it about that in one direction [the natural world] what he perceives are the comparatively complex phenomena which he analyzes, while in the other direction [the social world] what is given to him are elements from which those more complex phenomena are composed that he cannot observe as wholes. While the method of the natural sciences is in this sense, analytic, the method of the social sciences is better described as compositive or synthetic." From Hayek's perspective, the natural sciences move from complexity to individual elements; the social sciences move from individual elements to complexity.

In "The Theory of Complex Phenomena" (completed in 1961), Hayek wrote that it "should not be difficult now to recognize the similar limitations applying to the theoretical explanations of the phenomena of mind and society. One of the chief results so far achieved by theoretical work in these fields seems to me to be the demonstration that here individual events regularly depend on so many concrete circumstances that we shall never in fact be in a position to ascertain them all." The complexity of the social world renders it impossible to plan or control.

In "Scientism and the Study of Society," first published between 1942 and 1944, Hayek gave examples of what are commonly considered societal events: "the Napoleonic Wars," "France during the Revolution," and "the Commonwealth period." While he believed that too many social scientists looked at these events inaccurately, as "definitely given objects, unique individuals which are given to us in the same manner as the natural units in which biological specimens or planets present themselves," Hayek did not fundamentally look at the world of society differently than he looked at the world of nature. Rather, he understood the complexity of social phenomena, whereas other social scientists did not.

It is, furthermore, he thought, precisely because social phenomena are so complex that only "pattern prediction" of them is possible. He had this exchange in 1978 with James Buchanan:

> Q: . . . I think pattern prediction is a very important concept that most economists still sort of miss.
> A: It's the whole question of the theory of how far can we explain complex phenomena where we do not really have the power of precise prediction. We don't know of any laws, but our whole knowledge is the knowledge of a pattern, essentially.

Earlier in his career, Hayek referred to pattern prediction as "explanation of the principle." His idea was that, as a result of the complexity of the social world, only general predictions of it are possible.

His emphasis on prediction of the principle or pattern leaves out a great deal. It is not merely that only general predictions can be made—it is that predictions often can be made only of best-guess probabilities, not even of patterns or principles. As Hayek mentioned, patterns can sometimes be expressed numerically as ranges.

Popperian Mark Notturno has written perceptively on the sociology of the Vienna circle, emphasizing its collectivist or communal outlook: "Positivism, from its very start, stressed the communal nature of scientific inquiry." Notturno quotes from the preface of Carnap's *The Logical Structure of the World* to substantiate this point: "'If we allot to the individual in philosophical work as in the special sciences only a partial task, then we can look with more confidence into the future: in slow careful construction insight after insight will be won. Each collaborator contributes only what he can endorse and justify before the whole body of his co-workers. Thus stone will be carefully added to stone and a safe building will be erected at which each following generation can continue to work.'" Notturno concludes that he himself "regard[s] this idea of science as a collective labor as part of the legacy of logical positivism. It is an idea that has led many contemporary philosophers to characterize the scientific *community* as collectively underwriting the authority of scientific knowledge—and to define scientific knowledge, if not truth itself, as the consensus of belief within the scientific community." Joseph Agassi, another Popperian philosopher, notes "the letter from Neurath to Carnap of 25 June 1935, castigating him for his support of Popper though Popper had failed to support the Vienna Circle." Logical positivism suffered from the tendency of some of its adherents to dogmatism, a common failing of intellectual movements.

~

The Sensory Order may in some respects be read almost as a tract against logical positivism. Hayek thought that his work in epistemology, psychology, and methodology and that of the logical positivists had a common foundation—the work of Ernst Mach. He said in 1985:

> A: . . . Vienna is the origin of so many schools of its own which were dominant in the 1920s. And one of the most fundamental and influential, in which we all were partially caught, was logical positivism. In fact, Mises' brother, Richard von Mises, became one of the leading figures. Now he and I all grew up in this Ernst Mach philosophy that ultimately everything must be rationally justified . . .
>
> Q: . . . You lived in this unique period of time in this remarkable city [Vienna]. . . .
>
> A: . . . [I]ntellectually, the dominating figure . . . was Ernst Mach, the physicist. That was the principle of thinking in which we all grew up, and at first all adopted it. But some of us—My psychological thinking begins directly with Ernst Mach. Mach in his famous book *The Analysis of Sensations* explains or assumes that while all our individual sensations have an original pure quality, they are constantly modified by experience. There is only an original order and then the

experiential change. Which led me to the conclusion that if you can show that experience can change the thing, why need there be an original quality? The original quality may have arisen in the same fashion. So it was only a step beyond Mach, which turns against him with the result that my own psychology developed. In this sense I began from the same thing on which the logical positivist [movement]—Schlick, Neurath, Carnap, and so on—developed from Vienna; but split at the base, led us apart very much. But these two apparently absolutely contrary trends come from a common initial viewpoint.

Q: In Mach?

A: Yes.

The difference between Hayek's view and that of the logical positivists was that he moved in an idealist direction and they emphasized verification. In the preface to *The Sensory Order,* Hayek said that the eighth and last chapter, "Philosophical Consequences," was one of four chapters in the work with which he was "tolerably satisfied" and that it contains "consequences" from his earlier speculations "for epistemology and the methodology of the sciences." The final section of chapter 8 is "The Division of the Sciences and the 'Freedom of the Will'"; in it Hayek stated that "From the fact that we shall never be able to achieve more than an 'explanation of the principle' by which the order of mental events is determined, it also follows that we shall never achieve a complete 'unification' of all sciences in the sense that all phenomena of which it treats can be described in physical terms." He then footnoted to this line: "The term 'physical' must here be understood in the strict sense in which it has been defined in the first chapter and not be confused with the sense in which it is used, e.g., by O. Neurath or R. Carnap when they speak of the 'physical language.' In our sense their 'physical language,' since it refers to the phenomenal or sensory qualities of the objects, is not 'physical' at all. Their use of this term rather implies a metaphysical belief in the ultimate 'reality' and constancy of the phenomenal world for which there is little justification."

This is an important passage for understanding Hayek's metaphysical, epistemological, philosophical, and psychological views. Hayek thought there are two orders through which individuals consider the world: the sensory order and the physical order. The sensory order is what we sense. The physical world is the real world of existence beyond our senses that every sane person who is not a solipsist accepts on faith.

According to Hayek, advances in science have rendered any correspondence between the real, physical world and the sensory world almost nonexistent. Instead, the natural, real world expresses itself in mathematical relationships.

Hayek's views tended philosophically to solipsism. While he believed in the existence of a physical world external to mind, he ascribed almost no (if any) properties to it.

He was not as opposed to positivism as to *logical* positivism, and it is important to be clear about these terms. Positivism is simply the idea that there should be some correspondence with the material world extrinsic to one's physical self that one perceives in order for statements about nature to be valid, to be true. Using this broad definition of positivism, Hayek was a positivist. Logical positivism tries to go a step beyond this position. The logical positivists sought to reduce all experience to sensory experience and to reduce every sensory experience to a conclusive or exact statement. This has proven an unattainable goal.

∾

Hayek did not completely explore the ideas of and relationships among words, prediction, control, sensory knowledge, theory, and will. In a number of essays he emphasized that civilization emerges. It is not planned in any one individual's mind before it develops, just as an economy cannot be.

The core ideas in Hayek's metaphysical and methodological thought were, in the former, that reality is complex; and in the latter, that there should be some empirical corroboration for statements about events in the realm of nature.

With respect to Hayek's methodological thought, more should be said. Hayek was a weak corroborationist philosophically ("corroboration" is not used here in a Popperian sense, but merely to indicate some use of empirical data to confirm or disconfirm theories). Hayek did not clearly identify what the empirical data were that corroborated or discorroborated his theories. In addition, he had a tendency to introduce two sorts of empirical data—data of the outside (scientific data) and data of the inside (social sciences data). He considered the latter to be more accurate than the former.

Hayek obtained much from the focus on evolution to which his studies in psychology led him. He saw the brain as a strictly physical organ that has evolved over billions of years; it is extremely limited in comprehension and attempts to impose order on (assumed) sensation from the perspective of maximizing survival. He came to see society as the peaceful and productive interaction of minds.

In 1977, twenty-five years after *The Sensory Order* appeared and three years after Hayek received the Nobel Prize for economics, a conference was held that considered his work in psychology. In response to a question he said that "Basically, I am still a Popperian. Indeed, I should tell you that in a way, I was a Popperian before he published *The Logic of Science Discovery*. We were both, in the 1920s, constantly arguing with two types of people—Marxists and Freudians—who both claimed that their theories were, in their nature, irrefutable. Now the claim that a scientific theory should be beyond the possibility of refutation is, of course, very irritating. This led Popper to the conclusion that a theory that cannot be refuted is, by definition, not scientific. When Popper stated that in detail, I just embraced his views as a statement of what I was feeling."

Hayek's point here was that what he shared in method with Popper was the view that for a theory to be considered scientific, there must be some way to refute it, some evidence that would contradict it. While this is, again, a weak corroborationist perspective without further specification of what these data would be, it is nonetheless partially in the realm of the external world from one's sensory experience of one's self.

Hayek always followed Mises that "the pure logic of choice" of the economic calculus is strictly deductive, and thus it is possible to have axiomatic laws of individual action. However, where he did not follow Mises was in Hayek's further belief that interpersonal activity is empirical from the perspective of the world outside of one's sensory experience of one's self and that the same fixity of axiomatic laws of human interaction as of individual human action is not possible. Individuals act on their understandings of the world, Hayek thought, and it is impossible to know what these are in other people with precision and complete accuracy.

In the 1937 published version of his 1936 "Economics and Knowledge," Hayek made reference to Karl Popper when he corrected a line in the main text by replacing "verification" in the published version with a footnote reference to Popper's emphasis on falsifiability. Hayek's move here was not from the sensory world external to one's self to another metaphysical sphere, but simply to the conceptual point, which he already had reached, that empirical corroboration or discorroboration is always tentative. There is no such thing as absolute verification, Hayek thought.

The utilization of knowledge is vital. Both within an organism and in society, individual units perform actions for the benefit of the whole without knowing all of the larger circumstances.

In September 1945, Hayek's "The Use of Knowledge in Society" appeared in the *American Economic Review*. Many economists, including Milton Friedman and Thomas Sowell, consider this among Hayek's greatest works. In "Economics and Knowledge," Hayek put forward the problem of the division of knowledge. Now he put forward some of the solution—the price system, which communicates information and is essential to effective economic decision-making. In turn, exclusive control over objects and the ability to exchange them are crucial to prices.

The free market system is implied, Hayek felt, by his ontology in order to attain maximum human productivity, the highest standard of living for all—the utilitarian-liberal-socialist-communist-libertarian goal. The division and paucity of individual knowledge renders a market economy necessary for optimal economic productivity. The utilization and communication of information and knowledge are critical.

Hayek is recognized for the comprehensive nature of his thought. Hayek scholar Gerald Steele writes that "Friedrich Hayek is held in the highest academic esteem for his contributions toward a genuine praxeology (a unified theory of human action) that incorporates economics, epistemology, ethics, jurisprudence, politics and psychology." Milton Friedman wrote in 1976 that Hayek's academic influence had "been tremendous. His work is incorporated in the body of technical economic theory; has had a major influence on economic history, political philosophy, and political science; has affected students of the law, of scientific methodology, and even of psychology." Steele also accurately states that "there is no doubt that Hayek's work will secure its rightful place at the apex of twentieth century philosophy."

On May 20, 1946, on one of his annual or so trips to America, Hayek gave the Stafford Little Lecture at Princeton University, entitled "The Meaning of Competition." When Hayek first sought to come to the United States on a permanent basis after the publication of *The Road to Serfdom,* he sought appointment at the Institute for Advanced Studies in Princeton, where Albert Einstein's institutional affiliation was and where he resided. However, the institute would not accept funding for Hayek, on the grounds of not allowing donors to direct appointments. Hayek was also interested in Yale when he first considered moving to the United States permanently after World War II.

11

The Constitution of Liberty

HAYEK'S YEARS IN THE UNITED STATES ON THE COMMITTEE ON SOCIAL Thought at the University of Chicago from 1950 to 1962 were productive, though his reasons for moving to the United States were almost entirely personal. He had the freedom at Chicago to do whatever he wished academically; his teaching and administrative duties were a fraction of what they would have been at the London School of Economics.

Hayek's major responsibility on the committee was to lead a seminar that was mostly composed of committee students and faculty, but which also included regular participation by leading figures from throughout the university, including in the sciences. Milton Friedman was one of the most consistent outside participants over the years. Professors sat around a large oval oak table in a mock Gothic-style room. If more attended than could fit around the table, students sat on the floor. It was an impeccably liberal colloquium.

Friedman considers Hayek's years at the University of Chicago to have been vital in Hayek's evolution. He had this exchange in 1995:

Q: How would you describe Hayek personally?

A: In terms of his personal characteristics Hayek was a very complicated personality. He was by no means a simple person. He was very outgoing in one sense but at the same time I would say very private. He did not like criticism, but he never showed that he didn't like criticism. His attitude under criticism . . . was to say "Well, that's a very interesting thing. At the moment I'm busy, but I'll write to you about it more later." And then he never would!

On the other hand, he wasn't like von Mises. He wasn't intolerant at all. You cannot conceive of Hayek doing the kind of thing that Mises did when, for example, he wouldn't talk to Machlup for three years because Machlup had come out for floating exchange rates at a Mont Pelerin meeting. Hayek did not do that. That was, I believe, because of the influence of the London School on him. He was very much tempered by the London School. . . .

Q: Would you say that he was a proud man?

A: Oh yes, no question that he was a proud man. . . . He was very sure of his own ideas. . . .

Let me emphasize, I am an enormous admirer of Hayek but not for his economics. That, again, is subject to misunderstanding. . . . I'm not talking about his understanding of economics, his application of economics to the real world, or anything like that, but his contributions to the science of economics. . . . I think *Prices and Production* was a very flawed book. I think his capital theory book is unreadable. . . .

On the other hand, *The Road to Serfdom* is one of the great books of our time. His writings in your area [political philosophy] are magnificent, and I have nothing but great admiration for them. I really believe that he found his right vocation—his right specialization—with *The Road to Serfdom.*

His earlier works were intended to be part of the literature of technical economics as a science, and, indeed, it was that characteristic of them that impressed Lionel Robbins and led Lionel to bring him from Austria to London. I never could understand why they were so impressed with the lectures that ended up as *Prices and Production,* and I still can't . . . these very confused notions of periods of production, different orders of products, and so on.

The interesting thing about that has something to do—he was part, as of that point, he had not freed himself from the methodological views of von Mises. And those methodological views have at their center that facts are not really relevant in determining, in testing, theories. They are relevant to illustrate theories but not to test them because we base economics on propositions that are self-evident. And they are self-evident because they are about human beings, and we're human beings. So we have an internal source of final knowledge, and no tests can overrule that. . . .

Now, as I said, I believe that Hayek started out as a strict Misesian, but he changed. . . . [T]he more tolerant atmosphere of Britain, then subsequently of the U.S., and his exposure to a wider range of scholars, led him to alter that position.

Friedman also observes in this interview his "big methodological difference" with Hayek, which, in his post-Misesian phase, Hayek "bridged . . . to some extent. Mises could never have written *The Constitution of Liberty*. *The Constitution of Liberty* is Hayek's descent into the Chicago school. It's the only one of his works that makes extensive references to absolute experience. . . . [I]f you look at the range of topics that he covers in *The Constitution of Liberty* and the way he goes about it, it's a different style altogether than most of his books. . . . In my opinion, Hayek could never have written *The Constitution of Liberty* if he had not come to Chicago." In a 1962 talk Hayek gave on leaving the University of Chicago, he remarked that "these twelve years, or I might say seventeen years because it will be five years preceding that I visited Chicago practically every year, have been of extraordinary importance to me."

Among the major works of Hayek's published while he was at the University of Chicago were *John Stuart Mill and Harriet Taylor* (1951), *The Counter-Revolution of Science* (1952), *The Sensory Order* (1952), *Capitalism and the Historians* (1954), and *The Constitution of Liberty* (1960), as well as many articles and reviews. As Hayek brought the first four of these major works to completion, he began to conceive a great positive statement on liberty, of which *The Road to Serfdom* had been a somewhat abbreviated and polemical presentation. Moreover, that work had been mostly a negative critique of socialism.

His ideas were beginning to take shape as early as 1953. He wrote in November 1953 to Fritz Machlup: "I'm beginning to have definite plans for that positive complement to the *Road to Serfdom* which people have so long [been] asking me to do." In 1948, he considered an extensive postscript to *The Road to Serfdom* that would have had the same epigraph that he ultimately used in *The Constitution of Liberty,* for its postscript "Why I Am Not a Conservative."

The work that eventually would become *The Constitution of Liberty* would be titled, Hayek wrote in his 1953 letter to Machlup, "Greater than Man: The Creative Powers of a Free Civilization." It would be composed of parts titled "The Role of Reason," "The Role of Morals," "The Role of Force," and "The Role of Material Resources."

In 1954, Hayek and Helene took a seven-month trip to Europe that was surely one of the high points of their lives together. As he was working on the correspondence of John Stuart Mill, the idea occurred to him to repeat a trip, a century later to the day, that Mill and his wife had taken in Italy and Greece during 1854–55.

In a March 1954 letter to the Guggenheim Foundation requesting a grant, Hayek wrote that he had for years been intending a work to be titled "The Creative Powers of a Free Civilization," and said that he wished to travel to nonindustrialized countries in order to understand the development of traditions and culture better. He thought that he could learn from the agrarian communities in southern Italy, Sicily, and Greece. To visit these still largely agricultural areas would assist his research into the nonrational, customary, and traditional framework of institutions, morals, and manners from which civilization develops. Not all knowledge is verbal. Much knowledge is embedded in customs, values, traditions, and beliefs. The important question for Hayek was, what values, morals, and customs will result in what social outcomes?

He did not think that all knowledge is precise. There is such a thing, particularly in the social sciences, as complex knowledge that is dependent on indeterminate variables and which thus is not susceptible to exact prediction. He sometimes referred to the lesser prediction to which knowledge such as the effects of societal rules is susceptible as "pattern prediction." Where prediction is limited, control is limited. Correct prediction precedes control. The greater the accuracy of prediction, the greater the control that is capable of being exercised.

On April 19, the Guggenheim Foundation approved Hayek for studies in Italy, Sicily, and Greece on John Stuart Mill's diary and the creative powers of a free civilization. He received $3,000—a considerable sum in those days—with $500 more to follow.

A year and a half after his initial Guggenheim Foundation letter, in November 1955, Hayek wrote a memorandum to himself on plans for future work. He had, by this time, traveled to southern Europe and Egypt. In this memorandum, he indicated that primary concerns in his forthcoming work in political philosophy would be equality and justice. Equal treatment is necessitated by and constitutes justice. Justice is societal equality under the rule of law. All are equal under the rule of law.

In the memorandum he noted that what he had originally intended on equality and justice would now require two separate books, the first of which could be written in the foreseeable future and the second of which which was a more indefinite project. The first book would be called *The Constitution of Liberty;* the second, "Greater than Man: The Creative Powers of a Free Civilization."

His initial outline of what *The Constitution of Liberty* would be like was quite similar to how the volume turned out. Its central chapters would be a reworking of his Cairo lectures, "The Political Ideal of the Rule of Law." Indeed, in the published book, for five of the twenty-four chapters in its three parts—chapters 11, "The Origins of the Rule of Law"; 13; 14, "The Safeguards of Individual Liberty"; 15; and 16—Hayek noted that they had been taken substantially from those lectures.

He never really finished the second part of his project. Though he included a chapter entitled "The Creative Powers of a Free Civilization" in *The Constitution of Liberty,* it was not as long or as detailed as an entire work would have been. He would have, in the second part, traced the relationship among his ideas in psychology, methodology, philosophy, and political and social order more. Some of his preliminary work in this area was published in article form and subsequently republished in the 1967 *Studies in Philosophy, Politics and Economics.*

∼

As Hayek wrote *The Constitution of Liberty,* he began to conceive it as his magnum opus on human freedom and how to achieve liberty in and through society. It was a product of his continued development away from economics and into social philosophy. He felt he was misconceived in *The Road to Serfdom* and desired to set the record straight. More than mere personal vindication, though, he sought to write a work that could guide humanity during the remainder of the twentieth century and beyond.

Hayek attached enormous influence to the power of ideas. He could not have expressed his conception more emphatically than he did in *The Constitution of Liberty:* "In the long run it is ideas and therefore the men who give currency to new ideas that govern evolution. . . . So far as direct influence on current affairs is concerned, the influence of the political philosopher may be negligible. But when his ideas have become common property, through the work of historians and publicists, teachers and writers, and intellectuals generally, they effectively guide developments."

The Constitution of Liberty was thus a very serious work. He approvingly quoted John Stuart Mill that it is "impossible to study history without becoming aware of 'the lesson given to mankind by every age, and always disregarded—that speculative philosophy, which to the superficial appears a thing so remote from the business of life and the outward interest of men, is in reality the thing on earth which most influences them.'" The book was not the ivory tower reflections of some intellectual writing primarily for his own interests or pleasure, but was a serious attempt to influence the future course of political and social life. That the work was dedicated to "the unknown civilization that is growing in America" gives some idea both of Hayek's concept of the development of civilization and his intent to influence the world at this time primarily through the United States.

He remarked in the first volume of his later *Law, Legislation and Liberty* that if he had "known when I published *The Constitution of Liberty* that I should proceed to the task attempted in the present work, I should have reserved that title for it." That is, because *Law, Legislation and Liberty* outlined the specific governmental forms he wished to see, it really contained his "constitution" for liberty. He clarified the purpose of *The Constitution of Liberty* in the latter work: "I then used the term 'constitution' in the wide sense in which we use it . . . to describe the state of fitness of a person."

He sought a wide public audience and great publicity for *The Constitution of Liberty,* though with limited success. As he wrote in the preface, his aim was to "picture an ideal, to show how it can be achieved, and to explain what its realization would mean in practice." While Hayek hoped that *The Constitution of Liberty* would be a great popular success, he said in its introduction that it was "meant to help understanding, not to fire enthusiasm." Unlike *The Road to Serfdom,* it was not a political book. In the 1976 preface to *The Road to Serfdom,* he said that he hoped "my later efforts will be more rewarding to the expert." He went on to say that in contrast to both *The Constitution of Liberty* and *Law, Legislation and Liberty, The Road to Serfdom* was a "simple and non-technical introduction." *The Constitution of Liberty* was, in contrast, a complex and sustained affirmative presentation of the philosophy he believed should guide a classical liberal society.

Hayek knew that because of who he was, his work would be considered. He therefore wished to make this major treatise as comprehensive and persuasive as he could. His statement in the preface that if "a man has, as I hope I have, pushed analysis a step forward . . ." indicates that he thought that he was an intellectual originator and creator of the first rank, capable of reviving old truths and imparting new ones. He hoped *The Constitution of Liberty* would help to fire and sustain a return to classical liberalism.

"Freedom," Hayek wrote in the book's first chapter "refers solely to a relation of men to other men." Only human relationships may involve coercion. Freedom is "the state in which a man is not subject to coercion by the arbitrary will of another or others." Essentially, by "coercion," Hayek meant the use of force. The free society is the one in which force and violence are reduced as much as possible.

"We are concerned in this book," Hayek wrote in the introduction, "with that condition of men in which coercion of some by others is reduced as much as is possible in society." He believed, however, that the complete elimination of coercion is not possible, because "the only way" to prevent coercion is by "the threat of coercion." Whether Hayek's judgment here will ultimately prove correct remains to be seen. His position was, nonetheless, clear.

"Free society" has met the problem of restricting coercion through the use of coercion, he continued,

> by conferring the monopoly of coercion on the state and by attempting to limit this power of the state to instances where it is required to prevent coercion by private persons. This is possible only by the state's protecting known private spheres . . . creating conditions under which the individual can determine his own sphere by relying on rules which tell him what the government will do in different types of situations.
>
> The coercion which a government must still use for this end is reduced to a minimum and made as innocuous as possible by restraining it through known general rules, so that in most instances the individual need never be coerced unless he has placed himself in a position where he knows he will be coerced. Even where coercion is not avoidable, it is deprived of most of its most harmful effects by being confined to limited and foreseeable duties, or at least made independent of the arbitrary will of another person. Being made impersonal and dependent upon general, abstract rules, . . . even the coercive acts of government become data on which the individual can base his own plans. Coercion according to known rules, which is generally the result of circumstances in which the person to be coerced has placed himself, then becomes an instrument assisting the individuals in the pursuit of their own ends and not a means to be used for the ends of others.

Hayek followed in the great line of British political philosophers starting with Thomas Hobbes, who, during the seventeenth century, held that the state is above all responsible to create order and peace in society so that individuals might be economically prosperous. As the twentieth-century historian of political philosophy Leo Strauss wrote:

"The modern project . . . demands that man should become the master and owner of nature," which is the same project as the original command given by God to men in his first words to Adam and Eve: "Be fruitful, and multiply, and replenish the earth, and subdue it . . ."

Hayek's conception of freedom was integrally tied to his depiction of the economic process, wherein the purpose of government should be to create a framework of laws within which economic activity takes place. He observed that the "classical argument for freedom in economic affairs rests on the tacit postulate that the rule of law should govern policy in this as in all other spheres. . . . Freedom of economic activity had meant [in classical economics] freedom under the law, not the absence of all government action."

Hayek's goal for society was a "permanent legal framework which enables the individual to plan with a degree of confidence and which reduces human uncertainty as much as possible." He criticized views that posit that a society without coercive government is possible or desirable and was emphatic throughout most of his work—until the last pages of *Law, Legislation and Liberty*—that there is an extensive role for government to play in providing social welfare services and other programs. The intervention he opposed was *arbitrary* government intervention, which would be the same as the Hobbesian or Lockean "state of nature," where anything may be done to one.

In economic production, the market is dependent on government to create the pattern of expectations within which transactions occur. If government does not provide a justice system, protect property, and enforce contracts, then the market will not be effective. Far from a properly operating government making the market infeasible, it is precisely government that makes the market possible.

He said in a 1978 interview that it is "absolutely essential—and . . . [this defines] the difference between my view and some of my friends who lean into the anarchist camp—that within the territory where I live I can assume that any person that I encounter is held to obey certain minimal rules. . . . I must know that . . . any unknown person I encounter is held to obey . . . certain common, basic rules which are known to me. . . . An open society in which I can deal with any person I encounter presupposes that certain basic rules are enforced on everybody." He said as well that "libertarianism quite easily slides into anarchism, and it's important to draw this line."

Government creates the market and law. Law is not the negation of liberty; it is its fulfillment. Right law is not a restriction on people's liberty; it makes their freedom possible. Right law is liberty; liberty is right law.

The primacy of the rule of law to liberty is the central message of *The Constitution of Liberty*. Without law, freedom has apparently not been possible. Law allows humanity to live at peace with one another and to interact effectively. Law is not the nullity of freedom—law *creates* freedom.

It is useful to cite John Locke's discussion of the relationship between law and freedom that Hayek used to preface his chapter "The Origins of the Rule of Law" in *The Constitution of Liberty:* "'The end of law is, not to abolish or restrain, but to preserve and enlarge freedom. For in all the states of created beings capable of laws, where there is no law there is no freedom. For liberty is to be free from restraint and violence from others; which cannot be where there is no law: and is not, as we are told, a liberty for every man to do as he lists [wishes]. (For who could be free when every other man's humour might domineer over him?) But a liberty to dispose, and order as he lists, his person, actions, possessions, and his whole property, within the allowance of those laws under which he is, and therein not to be the subject of the arbitrary will of another, but freely follow his own.'" Hayek completely followed Locke here.

Law is essential to liberty—it played the crucial role in Hayek's philosophy of freedom. He wrote in *The Road to Serfdom:* "Nothing distinguishes more clearly conditions in a free country from those in a country under arbitrary government than the observance in the former of the great principles known as the Rule of Law," and it was from this thought that *The Constitution of Liberty* began.

He observed that the "meaning of freedom that we have adopted seems to be the original meaning of the word. Man, or at least European man, enters history divided into free and unfree; and this distinction had a very definite meaning. The freedom of the free may have differed widely, but only in the degree of independence which the slave did not possess at all. It meant always the possibility of a person's acting according to his own decisions and plans, in contrast to the person who was irrevocably subject to the will of another. . . . [T]he original meaning . . . is a distinct meaning and . . . it describes one thing and one thing only, a state which is desirable for reasons different from those which make us desire other things also called 'freedom.'" Freedom or liberty referred originally to the state of not being a slave. Free men were not slaves. This idea of freedom had nothing to do with receiving government services or benefits, or the right to vote.

While this may be a truncated conception of liberty compared to those most common today, this was exactly Hayek's point. In the societal context, freedom means solely the greatest limitation of coercion possible. This conception of freedom does not deny that there are many other things—including wealth, power, and a share in mutual governance—that are desirable, or potentially worth pursuing by government. It simply denies that they are liberty.

Hayek's discussion of manumission revealed his conception of what liberty consists of even today: "There were four rights which the attainment of freedom regularly conferred. The manumission decrees normally gave the former slave, first, 'legal status as a protected member of the community'; second, 'immunity from arbitrary arrest'; third, the 'right to work at whatever he desires to do'; and, fourth, 'the right to movement according to his own choice.'" Adding to this list the right to own property, it "contains all the elements required to protect an individual against coercion." He also cited David Hume's "'three fundamental laws of nature, that of the stability of possession, of transference by consent, and of the performance of promises.'"

There are, of course, those who believe that there is no morally legitimate coercion—and thus that there are no morally legitimate states. Philosopher Robert Paul Wolff writes in *In Defense of Anarchism* that the "defining mark of the state is authority. . . . The primary obligation of man is autonomy. . . . It would seem, then, that there can be no resolution of the conflict between the autonomy of the individual and the putative authority of the state. Insofar as a man fulfills his obligation to make himself the author of his decisions, he will resist the state's claim to have authority over him. . . . [I]f, on the other hand, he submits to the state and accepts its claim to authority . . . he loses his autonomy." While Wolff states the conflict between autonomy and authority well, his comments are of limited relevance. No one, or at least no one who believes that people are less than perfect, should question the need for some sort of government. While angels might not require government, human beings do. The question is not whether there should be states, but what kind of states there should be. The rule of law characterizes a free state and a free society.

The purpose of law is not to issue direct, individual commands to people. It is to create a stable structure of expectations for all within which each may rationally lead his life as much as possible as he wishes. Hayek's lawful society was to create a framework for people to act within rather than to dictate their particular actions. He observed that as societies progress, rules move from "specificity and concreteness to increasing generality and abstractness." Law creates—or should create—a known environment of societal activity. Law's predictability replaces the arbitrariness of the ruler. Hayek's focus was rules, not rulers. The optimal society would be the society of law.

Private property is, he thought, an essential condition for the prevention of coercion. Its recognition is necessary for two primary purposes. First, without some control over their material circumstances, human beings cannot be free. Second, as he held: "We are rarely in a position to carry out a coherent plan of action unless we are certain of our exclusive control of some material objects; and where we do not control them, it is necessary that we know who does if we are to collaborate with others."

It is not just that individuals must possess some control over their material circumstances to be free; it is that, in order to cooperate, others must also have this control. Where there is no private property, there is no liberty. Hayek thought that the "recognition of property is clearly the first step in the delimitation of the private sphere which protects us against coercion." He approvingly quoted Sir Henry Maine, a nineteenth-century English jurist and legal historian, that "'a people averse to the institution of private property is without the first element of freedom.'"

The purpose of law is in large part to spell out "the conditions under which objects or circumstances become part of the protected sphere." The private sphere includes more than property, but Hayek thought that property is a prerequisite for individuals having private domains or spheres. Moreover, establishing the rules by which property enters each individual's private domain and may be transferred from it is crucial.

Where laws rule, people are free. Conversely, where not laws, but individuals, rule, people are unfree. Law is the indispensable tool for securing personal freedom, because only under the rule of law are individuals able to plan their lives according to known expectations about the social order. Where the will of the rulers determines what is right and wrong, individuals never know where they stand and hence are unfree. The primary function of law should be to maximize freedom by limiting coercion to the greatest extent possible, from both predatory individuals and arbitrary government.

Hayek sought the greatest freedom possible. Freedom is the highest political objective. The framework of law is an indispensable precondition for freedom. Law is the embodiment of the constitution of liberty.

∾

There is a criterion for appropriate government involvement in the affairs of others to which Hayek did not give adequate attention. This criterion is to prevent physical harm to others. Government interference in the affairs of men and women is justified in one and only one circumstance: to prevent physical force from being exerted on one by another against his will.

Hayek ultimately embraced a form of democratic welfare statism, at least in *The Constitution of Liberty,* as the optimal form of government. While he attempted through his criteria of known general laws applicable to all to articulate a consistent and coherent libertarian standard for involvement by one person in the affairs of others, he did not succeed. He ultimately placed his hope in some form of democratic limited polity as being the most likely to be the freest and most productive.

The idea of extending democratic governance was the great goal of government reformers of Hayek's time. As recently as less than a century ago, democratic government—defined as the suffrage of all adults—existed almost nowhere in the world. Women received the right to vote, even in the few nations that had previously practiced some adult male suffrage, only as recently as seventy to eighty years ago.

Most of the world, through World War II, lived under colonial administration or in semifeudal conditions. During World War II itself, democracy was almost snuffed out, being restricted almost exclusively to the English-speaking world. After World War II, decolonialization proceeded apace, though it was not typically followed by long-lasting democratic governments.

Then, during the 1980s and 1990s, the great worldwide democratic revolution occurred. Dozens—literally even scores—of countries throughout Latin America and Europe especially, but also in Asia and to a small extent Africa, that previously had practiced nondemocratic forms of government moved in a democratic direction. This accompanied, though was not entirely synonymous with, the collapse of Communism in the Soviet Union and elsewhere around the world.

Although Hayek would have protested being characterized as a democratic welfare statist in *The Constitution of Liberty,* this is what he was. While he favored less government rather than more, government at the local level rather than national level, the provision of social welfare through private charitable organizations rather than government at any level, and the private competitive provision of government services, there was much in his work that any modern, twentieth-century liberal could support.

Statements from the first two parts of *The Constitution of Liberty,* before he began more detailed consideration of the welfare state in part III, calling for a significant positive government role included:

> . . . sanitation or roads. . . . The provision of such services has long been a recognized field of public effort . . .
>
> . . . the non-coercive or purely service activities that government undertakes . . . such services as the care for the disabled or the infirm . . .
>
> . . . activities which governments have universally undertaken . . . the provision of a reliable and efficient monetary system . . . the setting of standards of weights and measures; the providing of information gathered from surveying, land registration, statistics, etc.; and the support, if not also the organization, of some kind of education.
>
> . . . services which are clearly desirable but which will not be provided by competitive enterprise because it would be either impossible or difficult to charge the individual beneficiary for them. Such are most . . . health services . . . and many of the amenities provided by municipalities for the inhabitants of cities.
>
> The effect which the use of any one piece of land often has on neighboring land clearly makes it undesirable to give the owner unlimited power to use or abuse his property as he likes.
>
> . . . the enforcement of safety regulations in buildings . . .
>
> . . . that the government may have to exercise the right of eminent domain for the compulsory purchase of land . . . can hardly be disputed.
>
> So far as the entry into different occupations is concerned, our principle does not exclude the possible advisability in some instances of permitting it only to those who possess certain ascertainable qualifications.
>
> . . . a free system does not exclude on principle all those general regulations of economic activity which can be laid down in the form of general rules specifying conditions which everybody who engages

in a certain activity must satisfy. . . . [T]he appropriateness of such
measures must be judged by comparing the over-all costs with the
gain. . . . This is true of most of the wide field of regulations known
as "factory legislation."

The range and variety of government action that is, at least in
principle, reconcilable with a free system is thus considerable.

Clearly, in *The Constitution of Liberty* as in *The Road to Serfdom* and
most of *Law, Legislation and Liberty,* he sanctioned a very significant
positive role for government.

Hayek did not really enunciate a principle for government interference. Rather he articulated the form that government interference should take, together with the preference that there be less
government rather than more. For this reason, while, from a libertarian
perspective, his heart was in the right place with respect to government
activities, his intellect was less so. The true libertarian principle is that
government involvement is justified in one circumstance and one circumstance only: to prevent harm to others.

∾

Hayek distinguished between his own position and conservatism in
the postscript to *The Constitution of Liberty,* "Why I Am Not a Conservative." He quoted Lord Acton that "at all times sincere friends of
freedom have been rare, and its triumphs have been due to minorities
that have prevailed by associating themselves with auxiliaries whose
objects have often differed from their own. . . ." Fundamental differences between classical liberalism and conservatism should be emphasized because these differences indicate that the contemporary
political alliance between classical liberals and conservatives may be
largely tactical.

Hayek considered true liberalism to differ as much from true
conservatism as from classical socialism. It is not a midpoint between
or a combination of the other two, but something distinct from either.
He considered, in fact, socialism and conservatism to share more in
common with each other than either has with classical liberalism.

He identified several primary differences between classical liberalism and conservatism. In the first place, conservatism—as its name
states—possesses "a fear of change, a timid distrust of the new as
such." "The main point about liberalism," in contrast, "is that it wants

to go elsewhere ... it has never been a backward-looking doctrine." Second, liberalism embraces spontaneous change, while conservatism insists that whatever change does occur should be foreseen and orderly. Third, liberalism exalts the individual, while conservatism has a "fondness for authority." Fourth, the conservative position demonstrates a "lack of understanding of economic forces." Like the socialist, the conservative is more likely to favor large power centers to direct an economy, though the power centers conservatives might choose for such direction differ from those of socialists. The liberal unequivocally favors competition, conversely, and is opposed to all power centers not established through competition. Finally, conservatism often exhibits "strident nationalism," while the true liberal is unabashedly internationalist.

Hayek best and succinctly stated the differences between conservatism and liberalism in the 1956 foreword to *The Road to Serfdom:*

> In the struggle against the believers in the all-powerful state the true liberal must sometimes make common cause with the conservative, and in some circumstances, as in contemporary Britain, he has hardly any other way of actively working for his ideals. But true liberalism is still distinct from conservatism, and there is danger in the two being confused. Conservatism, though a necessary element in any stable society, is not a social program; in its paternalistic, nationalist, and power-adoring tendencies it is often closer to socialism than true liberalism; and with its traditionalistic, anti-intellectual, and often mystical propensities it will never, except in short periods of disillusionment, appeal to the young and all those others who believe that some changes are desirable if this world is to become a better place. A conservative movement, by its very nature, is bound to be a defender of established privilege and to lean on the power of government for the protection of privilege. The essence of the liberal position, however, is the denial of all privilege.

It is significant that in his concluding postscript to what he considered would be his magnum opus he directed his fire not at socialists but at conservatives: "Let me now state the decisive objection to any conservatism which deserves to be called such. It is that by its very nature it cannot offer an alternative to the direction in which we are moving. It may succeed by its resistance to current tendencies in slowing down undesirable developments, but, since it does not indicate another direction, it cannot prevent their continuance.... What the liberal must ask, first of all, is not how fast or how far we should move, but where we should move."

He especially opposed conservatism because of its approach to knowledge:

> I find the most objectionable feature of the conservative attitude is its propensity to reject well-substantiated new knowledge because it dislikes some of the consequences which seem to follow from it—or, to put it bluntly, its obscurantism. I will not deny that scientists as much as others are given to fads and fashions and that we have much reason to be cautious in accepting the conclusions that they draw from their latest theories. But the reasons for our reluctance must themselves be rational and must be kept separate from our regret that the new theories upset our cherished beliefs. I can have little patience with those who oppose, for instance, the theory of evolution or what are called "mechanistic" explanations of the phenomena of life simply because of certain moral consequences which at first seem to follow from those theories, and still less with those who regard it as irreverent or impious to ask certain questions at all. By refusing to face the facts, the conservative only weakens his own position. . . . Should our moral beliefs really prove to be dependent on factual assumptions shown to be incorrect, it would be hardly moral to defend them by refusing to acknowledge facts.

Like all great philosophers, Hayek was passionately committed to the truth. Of the tendency to deny and ignore the truth, he correctly observed that this "characteristic conservative attitude . . . not only is a serious weakness of conservatism but tends to harm any cause which allies itself with it." The truth will prevail. The truth marches on. The truth will make us free.

Hayek wrote for the ages. A former student of his at Chicago, Chiaki Nishiyama, remembers that he "used to tell me then that he was writing for the next century." When he wrote it, Hayek considered *The Constitution of Liberty* to be his greatest work. It is indeed likely that he considered almost all of his later work to be more significant than his work in technical economic theory—a thought worth keeping in mind for those interested in his legacy. He considered *The Sensory Order* to be his leading work to the time that he wrote it. He believed his early essays related to "Economics and Knowledge" contained in *Individualism and Economic Order* to be his most important work in economic theory. He considered his last work, "The Fatal Conceit," to be potentially his most important work. He worked longer on *Law, Legislation and Liberty* than any other manuscript during his career, and he valued the essays that became *The Counter-Revolution of Science* highly.

As Hayek advanced in his career, he became increasingly less an economist and more a political philosopher. The view here is that Hayek's greatest contribution in the long run will likely be considered to have been in written pure philosophy. He wrote in *The Constitution of Liberty* that though he still considered himself mainly as an economist: "I have come to feel more and more that the answers to many of the pressing social questions of our time are to be found ultimately in the recognition of principles that lie outside the scope of technical economics or any other single discipline." In the 1966 preface to *Studies in Philosophy, Politics and Economics,* he commented that this volume contained "a selection from the work of the last twenty years . . . of an economist who discovered that if he was to draw from his technical knowledge conclusions relevant to the public issues of our time, he had to make up his mind on many questions to which economics did not supply an answer." In a lecture delivered on the occasion of the twenty-fifth anniversary of the opening of the Social Science Research Building at the University of Chicago in 1955, he said that "nobody can be a great economist who is only an economist—and I am even tempted to add that the economist who is only an economist is likely to become a nuisance if not a positive danger." He concluded an October 1963 lecture, "The Economics of the 1930s as Seen from London": "I do not propose . . . to continue this account into a discussion of the economics of the 1940s as seen from Cambridge . . . or a discussion of the economics of the 1950s as seen from Chicago, or the economics of the 1960s as seen from Freiburg. That I might do if you ask me . . . in twenty years' time, though I am not sure that I was still enough of an economist during that period to qualify."

12

Marx, Mill, and Freud

THE QUESTION OF HAYEK'S INTELLECTUAL RELATIONSHIP WITH THE TWO greatest political philosophers cum economists of the nineteenth century, Karl Marx and John Stuart Mill, is a subject on which misconceptions are rife. Hayek had high regard for Marx in technical economic theory and considered him a predecessor in his business cycle theory.

Hayek wrote as points in an early 1930s lecture, "The Marxian Theory of Crises," on book II of Marx's *Capital:* "magnificent wealth of material" and "almost in the position of Adam Smith in general economics." Eugen von Böhm-Bawerk, whose capital theory Hayek followed, held of the second book of Marx's *Capital* that these "parts of the system . . . by their extraordinary logical consistency permanently establish the author as an intellectual force of the first rank. This long middle part of his work is really essentially faultless."

In *The Pure Theory of Capital,* Hayek traced his business cycle theory through Marx. He wrote in *Prices and Production,* his initial 1931 lectures at the London School of Economics: "The central idea of the theory of the trade cycle which has been expounded in the preceding lecture is by no means new. That industrial fluctuations consist essentially in alternating expansions and contractions of the structure of capital equipment has often been emphasized. . . . In the German literature similar ideas were introduced mainly by the writings of Karl Marx." It was not in technical economic theory that the classical Austrians disagreed with Marx.

So towering a figure in history is Marx that discussion of his thought in summary form is always difficult, for there is so much that he said and that others have said about him. At the same time, so tendentious, ill-spirited, and just plain wrong a thinker was Marx that it is surprising that he may have had some of the influence attributed to him.

Hayek's opposition to Marx was in the realm of practical political emanations from Marx's thought. Here he considered Marx's influence to have been wholly pernicious. "Capitalism," Hayek emphasized, "gave life to the proletariat. . . . If we ask what men most owe to the moral practices of those who are called capitalists the answer is: their very lives. Socialist accounts which ascribe the existence of the proletariat to an exploitation of groups formerly able to maintain themselves are entirely fictional. . . . Karl Marx was thus right to claim that 'capitalism' created the proletariat: it gave and gives them life." "The dispute between the market order and socialism is no less than a matter of survival," Hayek held in his final work, *The Fatal Conceit:* "To follow socialist morality would destroy much of present [man]kind and impoverish much of the rest."

~

Hayek is usually considered, with John Stuart Mill, one of the greatest classical liberals in the great British classical liberal tradition, though this was not, for at least part of his career, Hayek's view. It is, however, the view here.

Placement of both Hayek and Mill in the liberal tradition is suspect to many historians of political thought for various reasons. First, Mill also expressed socialist sentiments, so to classify him as a liberal has seemed inaccurate to some more right-inclined liberals. Second, Hayek is sometimes considered more a conservative by left-inclined liberals, and not in the liberal tradition as it has evolved. Nonetheless, Mill and Hayek were the two greatest liberals of the nineteenth and twentieth centuries.

Mill's greatness stemmed from the capaciousness of his view. While this is sometimes interpreted as inconsistency, it is, rather, exemplary of Mill's perspective that truth, in the great practical matters of life especially, is the reconciling and combining of opposites.

Mill's greatest passion was freedom of thought and expression. He correctly predicted that, of all his works, *On Liberty,* published in 1859, would last the longest. In that volume Mill expressed the essential libertarian sentiment: "The object of this Essay is to assert one very simple principle, as entitled to govern absolutely the dealings of society with the individual in the way of compulsion and control, whether the means used be physical force in the form of legal penalties, or the moral coercion of public opinion. That principle is, that the sole end for which mankind are warranted in interfering with the liberty of action of any of their number, is self-protection. That the only purpose for which power can be rightfully exercised over any member of a civilized community, against his will, is to prevent harm to others."

This essential libertarian statement was confounded, however, by Mill through his simultaneous introduction merely sentences later of another standard of justification for interference with the actions of others: "The only part of the conduct of any one, for which he is amenable to society, is that which concerns others."

There is all the difference in the world between a standard for interference in the actions of others of "harm" and "concern." There is almost no action that does not "concern" others in some way. If this is the standard for interference, then almost any interference is justified. Harm is a much higher standard. If one can interfere with others' actions only if they are doing harm to others, this is a much more restrictive standard than mere concern.

Hayek's standard for coercive governmental interference in individuals' lives also has not been found satisfactory. Essentially, Hayek's view as enunciated in *The Constitution of Liberty* was that as long as a person is subject to perfectly general laws, and therefore not under the arbitrary will of another, he is free.

As many commentators on Hayek have noted, he said nothing, through his criterion of known general laws applicable to all, about the content of these general laws. Lionel Robbins criticized Hayek in reviewing *The Constitution of Liberty*: "There is a further matter in respect of which I do not feel that Professor Hayek's definitions completely catch the spirit of his general analysis. In his conception, the absence of coercion depends essentially upon the existence of known rules equally applicable to all. . . . But is this the whole of the story? Cannot law in this sense be oppressive and restrictive? Must we not distinguish between a liberal rule of law and others?"

Hayek considered this criticism of Robbins and others in *Law, Legislation and Liberty*: "This is a legitimate objection to the manner in which I have treated the subject in *The Constitution of Liberty* and I hope that the present statement will satisfy the critics who have pointed out this defect." Hayek's revision was that since for a

case to come before a judge a dispute must have arisen . . . , only
such actions of individuals as affect other persons, or, as they are
traditionally described, actions toward other persons . . . will give
rise to the formulation of legal rules. . . . [A]ctions which are clearly
not of this kind, such as what a person does alone within his four
walls, or even the voluntary collaboration of several persons, in a
manner which clearly cannot affect or harm others, can never become the subject of rules of conduct that will concern a judge. This
is important because it answers a problem that has often worried
students of these matters, namely that even rules which are perfectly
general and abstract might still be serious and unnecessary restrictions of individual liberty.

Hayek moved in *Law, Legislation and Liberty* from the criterion
of generality he presented in *The Constitution of Liberty* and substi-
tuted in its place Mill's criteria of "affect" on or "concern" to others.
Hayek enunciated this position clearly in a 1974 interview with
philosopher Tibor Machan, which, while it lacks the subtlety and precision of a written statement, makes up for this defect in spontaneity:

Q: . . . Let me turn now for a moment to another issue in your own
thinking—Professor Ronald Hamowy published an article . . . in
which he maintained that your idea that the rule of law implies only
formal commitments, only formal procedural commitments, is not
quite accurate and that these are not sufficient to retain what is necessary for a free society. . . . Could you elaborate it? Does your concept of the rule of law now admit of greater substantive implication?
A: Well I think Hamowy was right to the extent that my definition of
the rule of law which would secure freedom was too wide. It's not
sufficient that government coercion is limited to the enforcement of
general rules because that might well include such things as control
of religious beliefs and the like, but now I think the definition has to
be extended. Government coercion is to be confined to the rules
with a regard to conduct towards other persons. And in that form—
that revised form—I think it would sustain my original position.

Neither Hayek nor Mill accurately or consistently stated the libertarian standard for appropriate coercive involvement in the lives of
others. This standard is exclusively to prevent harm to others.

Hayek's conceptions of both Marx and Mill changed over time.
He was more supportive of them earlier in his career and more critical
of them later.

Hayek's work in the history of ideas was significant. He sustained interest in John Stuart Mill at a time when interest in Mill was at a low; through the 1954 *Capitalism and the Historians,* he vitally helped to reinterpret the early phase of British industrialization; his historical description of the evolution of law in *The Constitution of Liberty* and *Law, Legislation and Liberty* were enlightening; and, in addition to participating in it, he was a great historian of the Austrian school of economics. At the same time, like his early work in technical economic theory, his work in the history of ideas could be idiosyncratic, one-sided, and subject to challenge.

At a going-away party in Hayek's honor at the University of Chicago in 1962, George Stigler said to Hayek and his wife: "Mrs. Hayek, I want you each day in the future to address your husband and inquire what his progress has been in what I consider to be one of the most interesting and intriguing fields, the evolution of the work of scholars." Stigler also said on this occasion that Hayek's work in the history of economic and social thought was of truly lasting and historical importance.

~

Late in his career Hayek strongly criticized Sigmund Freud. Though Freud is unmentioned and unquoted in both *The Road to Serfdom* and *The Constitution of Liberty,* Hayek rounded on him in the epilogue of *Law, Legislation and Liberty,* originally given as a lecture in 1978 at the London School of Economics. Writing in the epilogue's penultimate section, titled "The destruction of indispensable values by scientific error: Freud," Hayek said that "the culturally most devastating effects have come from the endeavor of psychiatrists to cure people by releasing their innate instincts. After having lauded earlier my Viennese friends Popper, Lorenz, Gombrich, and Bertalanffy, I am afraid I must now concede that the logical positivism of Carnap and the legal positivism of Kelsen are far from the worst things that have come out of Vienna. Through his profound effects on education, Sigmund Freud has probably become the greatest destroyer of culture. . . . If our civilization survives, . . . I believe men will look back on our age as an age of superstition chiefly connected with the names of Karl Marx and Sigmund Freud."

Hayek similarly criticized Freud in a preliminary version of "The Fatal Conceit." He thought that through Freud's advocacy of "permissiveness and emancipation," juvenile delinquency and the rise of a "counter-culture" were born.

Hayek was too harsh on Freud. It is, indeed, one of the surprising facts of the development of intellectual thought during the twentieth century that Freud—who was so pervasive and dominating during the first half of that century—virtually dropped off the face of the map during the second half. Hayek was almost the last person still talking about Freud, in the sense of taking him as a serious living influence on civilization.

To the extent that Freud put forward specific views that were intended to be scientific, most of his thought can be relegated to the historical development of ideas. To the extent that Freud was not a scientist but a philosopher, however, his work may continue to have value.

Freud's emphasis on the unconscious is not entirely unrelated to Hayek's conception of spontaneous order and the idea of tacit, nonverbal knowledge distinct from verbal, explicit knowledge (or verbal statement). For the concepts of both the unconscious and spontaneous order, ideas of unarticulated knowledge and interpersonal knowledge and its communication are critical. There was more philosophical similarity between some of Hayek's and Freud's ideas than Hayek realized.

13

The Chicago School of Economics and Milton Friedman

As with Mill and Marx, the question of Hayek's relationship to the Chicago school of economics is one that is not always understood. When Hayek reemerged on the scene after receiving the Nobel Prize in Economics in 1974 (with socialist Gunnar Myrdal), after what seemed like almost decades of seclusion and isolation—almost as if Hayek had been punished and shunned for expressing such heterodox views in *The Road to Serfdom*—there was a tendency, in at least the popular media, to identify him with the Chicago school.

The Chicago school of economics was, at this time, popularly ascendant, particularly in the person of Milton Friedman. Friedman was against inflation, big government, and Keynesianism; Hayek was against inflation, big government, and Keynesianism. There was not the effort to distinguish between their views that their views merit.

This lack of differentiation between Hayek and Friedman continues to this day. Daniel Yergin and Joseph Stanislaw write in their popular 1998 *The Commanding Heights: The Battle Between Government and the Marketplace that Is Remaking the Modern World:* "In the postwar years, Keynes' theories of government management of the economy appeared unassailable. But a half century later, it is Keynes who has been toppled and Hayek, the fierce advocate of free markets, who is preeminent. The Keynesian 'new economics' from Harvard may have dominated the Kennedy and Johnson administrations in the 1960s, but it is the University of Chicago's free-market school that is globally influential in the 1990s."

The question of Hayek's relationship to the Chicago school of economics raises the anterior question of the Chicago school of economics itself. Here opinion is divided as to when the school first came into existence and what its nature and influence have been and are. Milton Friedman writes with respect to the Chicago school that there is "a sense in which it dates back to James Laurence Laughlin's appointment as head of the Department of Economics" in 1892, adding that "[t]hroughout the whole period from then to now, there has been a real distinction between the Department of Economics on the one hand and the Chicago school of economics on the other."

Others trace the rise of the Chicago school to the 1930s. Jacob Viner and Frank Knight, the two leading figures at Chicago who inspired what subsequently became, unambiguously, the Chicago school, respectively arrived at the school on a permanent basis in 1919 and 1927.

Still, as George Stigler wrote:

> In the 1930s economics appeared to be a little different at the University of Chicago than elsewhere, but the same statement could be made about most major universities.
>
> Frank Knight was skeptical of the moral and intellectual content of political behavior and particularly hostile to central economic planning, but he was also severely critical of the ethical basis of a competitive economy. No doctrinaire defender of private enterprise would find him a source of strength.
>
> Henry Simons [another Chicago economist, and Knight protégé] had preached a form of laissez-faire in his famous 1934 pamphlet *A Positive Program for Laissez Faire,* but what a form! He proposed nationalization of basic industries ... [and] urged an extremely egalitarian policy in the taxation of income and detailed regulation of business practices. ... Much of his program was almost as harmonious with socialism as with private-enterprise capitalism. ...
>
> Jacob Viner, the other major figure, had nineteenth-century liberal tastes, but rebelled against simplified or "extreme" positions. The rest of the faculty were highly varied in their policy preferences: Paul Douglas favored a large economic role for the state; Simeon Leland was a traditionalist in taxation; Henry Millis was an old-fashioned labor economist; Lloyd Mints wrote only on central bank policy; Henry Schultz stuck to his mathematical and statistical knitting; and Oskar Lange was a socialist.

In addition, Viner wrote in a 1969 letter that it was "not until after I left Chicago in 1946 that I began to hear rumors about a

'Chicago School' which was engaged in *organized* battle for laissez faire and 'quantity theory of money' and against 'imperfect competition' theorizing and 'Keynesianism.' I remained skeptical about this until I attended a conference sponsored by University of Chicago professors in 1951.... From then on, I was willing to consider the existence of a 'Chicago School' (but one not confined to the economics department and not embracing all of the department) and that this 'School' had been in operation, and had won many able disciples, for years before I left Chicago."

The first apparent explicit reference to a "school" associated with economics at the University of Chicago apparently occurs in Aaron Director's 1947 preface to Simons's posthumously published *Economic Policy for a Free Society*. Director, Friedman's brother-in-law, wrote that through his "writings and more especially through his teaching at the University of Chicago, Simons was slowly establishing himself as the head of a 'school.'"

Hayek wrote in 1951 of a Chicago "group" of economists, whose origins he traced to Knight. Hayek said that it is "hardly an exaggeration to state that nearly all the younger American economists who really understand and advocate a competitive economic system have at one time been Knight's students." Hayek then referred to Simons, Director, Stigler, and Friedman.

Hayek probably considered his relationship with Knight to be closer personally than Knight believed; the latter seems not to have been overly fond of Hayek. Knight scholar Ross Emmett writes that the men's personal relationship was "always more cordial than friendly. Knight, in particular, was wary of his Austrian counterpart."

Hayek greatly praised Knight on several occasions. In 1951, he grouped Knight, with Ludwig von Mises and Edwin Cannan, as one of three primary transmitters of classical liberalism during the 1920s and 1930s. Even more significantly, Hayek wrote in the beginning of the "Acknowledgments and Notes" section of *The Constitution of Liberty*: "If I had regarded it as my task to acknowledge all indebtedness and to notice all agreements, these notes would have been studded with references to the work of Ludwig von Mises, Frank H. Knight, and Edwin Cannan." Hayek referred to Knight eight times in *The Constitution of Liberty*.

Notwithstanding Hayek's praise and references to him, Knight ripped the book in a 1967 review. Viner, too, was critical of *The Constitution of Liberty* in a review. Hayek did not refer to Knight once in *Law, Legislation and Liberty*.

∽

The rise of the Chicago school of economics is tied, at least in the popular mind, to the rise of Friedman's fame during the 1960s. While Friedman writes that his teacher Homer Jones at Rutgers "introduced me to what even then" during the late 1920s and early 1930s "was known as the Chicago view," the identification of an explicit Chicago school of economics was not strong prior to the 1950s. Stigler, again, wrote in his autobiography: "There was no Chicago School of Economics . . . at the end of World War II . . . and I have found no hints of such a belief in the economics profession before about 1950, and no widespread recognition of the school for another five years."

Among the first sustained discussions of the Chicago school were a chapter in Edward Chamberlain's 1957 *Toward a More General Theory of Value,* and, in 1962, H. Laurence Miller's "On the 'Chicago School of Economics'" in the *Journal of Political Economy.* Of the latter, Stigler commented that Miller had "merely sketched, less than completely, the views of my friend Milton Friedman."

Hayek was not close to the Chicago school of economics, having left Chicago before the school reached its zenith during the later 1960s and 1970s. Frank Knight was not close to Hayek personally, and Jacob Viner left Chicago for Princeton in 1946. Henry Simons, to whom Hayek was perhaps personally closest at Chicago, died in 1946. George Stigler did not return to Chicago to teach until 1958. Aaron Director, to whom Hayek was close (Director having spent a year at the London School of Economics just before World War II and, with Simons, having handled publication negotiations for *The Road to Serfdom* in the United States), was not in the economics department at Chicago but in the law school. Milton Friedman was the person associated with the Chicago school of economics in the department of economics to whom Hayek was closest while he was at Chicago.

Thus, stories that circulate within the Hayek community of scholars (sometimes attributing Ludwig Lachmann as a source) to the effect that Friedman cast the deciding vote against Hayek at the crucial departmental meeting as Hayek was being considered for a position in the economics department at Chicago should be rejected as absurd. Not only do such stories completely misrepresent the facts (Friedman had just arrived in 1946 when Hayek was desultorily and briefly considered for a position, and played no role in this decision), but they completely misunderstand the men's relationship.

Friedman was Hayek's greatest supporter in the department of economics and the individual in the Chicago school most interested in, and perhaps most influenced by, Hayek's work, though not in technical economics.

Hayek did not participate in the money and banking workshop through which Friedman exerted much of his influence at Chicago, but the two did cooperate closely with respect to a student organization, the Intercollegiate Society of Individualists. Friedman has observed that, in contrast to the department of economics, "Hayek's influence on Chicago was much more through . . . the group that established the *New Individualist Review*—his influence there was very strong and very great."

The *New Individualist Review* was published between 1961 and 1968. Friedman writes:

> When the *New Individualist Review* was founded, belief in "free, private enterprise, and in the imposition of the strictest limits to the power of government" and in "a commitment to human liberty"— to quote from the editorial introducing volume 1, number 1 . . . — was at a low ebb even in the countries of the so-called free world. Yet, at the same time, there were many signs of an intellectual reaction against collectivist views, of a resurgence of interest in the philosophy of classical liberalism.
>
> Two organizations in particular served to channel and direct this resurgence: the Mont Pelerin Society, founded in 1947 by Friedrich Hayek, whose book *The Road to Serfdom* did so much to spark the resurgence; and the Intercollegiate Society of Individualists. . . .
>
> The Mont Pelerin Society brought together relatively mature intellectuals. . . . The Intercollegiate Society of Individualists (ISI) operated at the other end of the age scale. It promoted the establishment of chapters among undergraduate and graduate students on college campuses. . . .

The *Review* was started by members of the Intercollegiate Society of Individualists. Hayek and Friedman served on the journal's editorial advisory board. Friedman also wrote in 1981: "The *Review* quickly established itself as the outstanding publication in the libertarian cause. . . . [T]his student venture, despite its narrow base and its limited resources, sets an intellectual standard that has not yet, I believe, been matched by any of the more recent publications in the same philosophical tradition."

The reasons Friedman gives for the journal's demise are significant:

> Two . . . events played a role—one local, the other national.
>
> The local event was Friedrich Hayek's retirement from the University of Chicago and his relocation to Freiburg, Germany. His students had formed the core of the initial founders and had remained an important component of the editorial staff throughout.
>
> The national event was the Vietnam War.

Friedman has written on Hayek's thought and about Hayek on many occasions. Most prominently, in his 1976 Nobel address, Friedman said: "A second related effect of increased volatility of inflation is to render market prices a less efficient system for coordinating economic activity. A fundamental function of a price system, as Hayek emphasized so brilliantly, is to transmit compactly, efficiently, and at low cost the information that economic agents need in order to decide what to produce and how to produce it." "The crucial importance of this function," he added in a 1981 lecture, "tended to be neglected until Friedrich Hayek published his great article on 'The Use of Knowledge in Society.'"

In introducing a 1971 German edition of *The Road to Serfdom,* Friedman wrote that he had "made it a practice to inquire of believers in individualism how they came to depart from the collectivist orthodoxy of our times. For years, the most frequent answer was a reference to the book for which I have the honor of writing this introduction. . . . On rereading the book . . . , I was again impressed with what a magnificent book it is—subtle and closely reasoned yet lucid and clear, philosophical and abstract yet also concrete and realistic, analytical and rational yet animated by high ideals and a vivid sense of mission. Little wonder that it had so great an influence."

Among Friedman's most superlative and interesting comments on Hayek are his impromptu remarks at the 1962 testimonial dinner as Hayek prepared to move from Chicago to Freiburg:

> The thing that is interesting about Fritz Hayek . . . is the extent to which he has succeeded in straddling two kinds of worlds. The membership of this room consists of people who are here because of their interest in Fritz Hayek's work in science and also those who are here because of their interest in the enormous role he has

played in spreading ideas among the public at large. . . . This attempt to influence opinion is something that is very seldom combined with thorough, deep, and profound scholarly work that can influence the course of science. . . . And I think it is probably true that the people of each of the two groups here do not recognize how costly and difficult it is to bridge these two worlds. . . .

And I think it is easy to underestimate the cost involved in that . . . . And there are few men who have exercised the kind of influence which Fritz Hayek has on ideas in the whole western world and not only in the United States. I think it is a tribute to Hayek's dedication to his twin goals that his scholarly output has been so extensive despite the extent of his contribution in this other area.

I think also that there is a very big cost that is not easy to recognize in terms of the effect on the attitude of the rest of the scholarly world that derives from . . . influencing opinion. Of course, we have to recognize that the effect depends on what kind of an opinion you are trying to influence. There is no cost in terms of the attitudes of the rest of the scholarly world if one is simply expressing the majority opinion. . . . [There are] few who have been willing to take the straight and narrow path of the minority view, and a view that has not been popular among the intellectuals. . . .

I've always thought, incidentally, that many of us should welcome the fact that . . . a particular policy idea we hold does have this adverse effect on the opinions of other people. I think this is a very good thing, because it means that those of us who hold our views have to be better to get recognized than people who hold the other views. And in the long run, what matters is the quality of people who propose the ideas and not their number and not their position. It is because it is the quality of these ideas that matters so much that Hayek's ideas have been so wide-spread and have had such an influence, and that you are now seeing the rise in the scientific as well as in the other parts of the world of more people of this particular kind of persuasion. . . .

. . . I am one of those who has learned a great deal from Hayek. I hope he is as effective as I think he will be in his teaching in Germany, but I also hope that we will see him back here very often indeed.

Friedman was right—he saw Hayek often in the decades that followed.

In 1988, Friedman and his wife, Rose, wrote of three "tides" that have characterized political, societal, and economic development since the eighteenth century: the "Adam Smith tide," "the Fabian tide," and the "Hayek tide." *The Road to Serfdom,* the Friedmans then wrote, was "probably the first real inroad in the dominant intellectual view." Milton Friedman concluded a 1992 obituary of Hayek: "We are the poorer for his death, but his ideas will live on and influence the course of events long after the rest of us are gone."

14

Studies in Philosophy, Politics and Economics

IN 1962, HAYEK RETURNED TO EUROPE FROM CHICAGO, to the University of Freiburg in what was then West Germany. Hayek had been happy in Chicago. He considered it one of the leading universities in the world. In an impromptu talk on leaving the university, he called it a "very great place." He enjoyed its intellectual diversity beyond the social sciences, which he did not experience at the London School of Economics (though in 1962 he did consider that the LSE "was and probably still is preeminent in the world" in the social sciences).

Hayek's work in philosophy during the 1950s and 1960s grew out of his work in psychology. He wrote in a 1955 memorandum to himself on future work projects that his philosophical studies were a continuation of his work in *The Sensory Order*. Moreover, he noted that philosophical study preceded discussion of optimal social order. Like John Stuart Mill, he thought that speculative philosophy, though it appears on the surface so far removed from the practical affairs of life, is in fact their ruler. In the 1959 preface to the German translation of *The Counter-Revolution of Science*, he wrote that a "satisfactory execution of the original plan" of which the essays there were part (i.e., "The Abuse and Decline of Knowledge") "presupposes extensive philosophical studies."

Hayek's philosophical methodology was in accord with Karl Popper's. He made these comments in 1978 regarding Popper's *The Logic of Scientific Discovery* (originally published in German in 1934):

> It was so satisfactory because it confirmed this certain view I had already formed due to an experience very similar to Karl Popper's.

Karl Popper is four or five years [actually, three years] my junior; so we did not belong to the same academic generation. But our environment in which we formed our ideas was very much the same. It was very largely dominated by discussion, on the one hand, with Marxists and, on the other hand, with Freudians.

Both these groups had one very irritating attribute: they insisted that their theories were, in principle, irrefutable. Their system was so built up that there was no possibility—I remember particularly one occasion when I suddenly began to see how ridiculous it all was when I was arguing with Freudians, and they explained, "Oh, well, this is due to the death instinct." And I said, "But this can't be due to the [death instinct]." "Oh, then this is due to the life instinct." [laughter] Well, if you have these two alternatives, of course there's no way of checking whether the theory is true or not. And that led me, already, to the understanding of what became Popper's main systematic point: that the test of empirical sciences was that it could be refuted, and that any system which claimed that it was irrefutable was by definition not scientific . . .

Bruce Caldwell's position, thus, that "*despite* Hayek's claim, his methodological views differ quite dramatically on a number of key issues from those of Popper," expressed in Caldwell's exchange with economic theorist and historian Terence Hutchison, should be rejected. While it is correct, as Caldwell points out, that Hayek expressed inconsistent views in his methodology over his career, these inconsistent views are largely as both Hutchison and Milton Friedman describe them. Hayek started out much closer to Mises philosophically and methodologically; subsequently he moved in a more empirical and Popperian direction (regardless of the extent of Popper's influence on Hayek). Hayek also said in 1978 interviews, of Popper's *The Logic of Scientific Discovery,* that "when his book came out, I could at once embrace what he said as an articulation of things I had already been thinking and feeling. Ever since, I have followed his work very closely"; and, "Popper has had his own interesting developments, but on the whole I agree with him more than with anybody else on philosophical matters."

Hayek dedicated *Studies in Philosophy, Politics and Economics* to Popper, noting of him in its preface:

Readers of some of my earlier writings may notice a slight change in the tone of my discussion of the attitude which I then called "scientism." The reason for this is that Sir Karl Popper has taught me that natural scientists did not really do what most of them not only told us that they did but also urged the representatives of other disciplines to imitate. The difference between the two groups of disciplines has thereby been greatly narrowed and I keep up the argument only because so many social scientists are still trying to imitate what they wrongly believe to be the methods of the natural sciences. The intellectual debt which I owe to this old friend for having taught me this is but one of many . . .

By "scientism," Hayek meant misconceived efforts to apply the exactitude that is possible in the natural sciences to the social sciences.

The first article republished in *Studies in Philosophy, Politics and Economics,* "Degrees of Explanation," originally published in 1955, was largely consistent with Popper's methodology. Hayek embraced Popper's "hypothetico-deductive" approach to science: "The conception of science as a hypothetico-deductive system has been expounded by Karl Popper in a manner which brings out clearly some very important points." Here, as elsewhere in his work, Hayek distinguished between the facts of the natural and social sciences primarily on the basis of their complexity.

In "Degrees of Explanation," he wrote of "the field of physics" that its "connected variables . . . is sufficiently small to enable us to study them as if they formed a closed system for which we can observe and control all the determining factors." This was not the case, he thought, in the social sciences because of the number and complexity of factors involved there. At the same time, Hayek also distinguished between the natural and social sciences on the basis of the kinds of facts that exist in each—those in the natural sciences, we perceive from the outside; those in the social, from the inside.

Hayek embraced prediction as the criterion for scientific theories in "Degrees of Explanation." This was, indeed, his definition of the hypothetico-deductive approach: "Its basic conception lends itself to a somewhat narrow interpretation according to which the essence of *all* scientific procedure consists in the discovery of *new* statements ('natural laws' or 'hypotheses') from which testable predictions can be derived." Testable prediction was the core of Hayek's conception of scientific methodology in the natural realm. He noted that "prediction and explanation are merely two aspects of the same process" and that for "the purposes of this article it would indeed make no important difference if instead of 'degrees of explanation' we spoke throughout of 'degrees of prediction.'"

At the same time, as Hayek maintained elsewhere, the facts of the social sciences do not lend themselves to the same degree of prediction, or explanation, as the facts of the natural sciences—it is for this reason that there are degrees of prediction or explanation. Prediction may be expressed numerically, moreover, "not as a unique value or magnitude but as a range," narrow in the natural sciences and potentially very broad in the social sciences. In the social sciences, Hayek modified the conception of a numerical range to a "*range* of phenomena to expect." This was his concept of pattern prediction, or explanation of the principle, broad, general predictions.

Hayek gave an example in "Degrees of Explanation" of the type of prediction possible in the social sciences. It is instructive to turn to this example: "Economics tells us that we cannot at the same time maintain fixed rates of foreign exchange and . . . control the internal price level of a country by changing the quantity of money." This is considerably less exact prediction than is possible in the natural sciences. Nonetheless, the "practical value of such knowledge consists . . . largely in that it protects us from striving for incompatible aims." While he did not think that the social sciences are capable of the more exact prediction possible in the natural sciences, he nonetheless thought that, as in the natural sciences, predictions of a sort or degree—pattern prediction—are the mark of science in the social realm.

He emphasized prediction, whether in the social or natural realm, because "we shall clearly not be able to control developments further than we can predict the results of our actions. A limitation of prediction . . . implies a limitation of control." Prediction precedes control.

Hayek wrote in "The Theory of Complex Phenomena," also republished in *Studies in Philosophy, Politics and Economics,* that in the social field "individual events regularly depend on so many concrete circumstances that we shall never in fact be in a position to ascertain them all; and that in consequence . . . the ideal of prediction and control must largely remain beyond our reach." But to the extent that prediction is, even in the social realm, within our reach, we should grasp it.

$\sim$

Hayek's work in philosophy can be considered from another perspective than its methodology. When Hayek wrote that his philosophical studies should precede his political studies, he meant that in order to explain the sort of political system he favored, it was necessary to have greater understanding of the transmission and communication of information and knowledge. This is why he wished to travel to Italy and Greece. He thought that he might understand nonverbal knowledge better in doing so and might better understand the role of institutions in transmitting knowledge and information.

As we have seen, Hayek never really finished his "creative powers of a free civilization" project, though he included a chapter of that title in *The Constitution of Liberty*. He began this chapter by observing that the "Socratic maxim that the recognition of our ignorance is the beginning of wisdom has profound significance for our understanding of society." By this, at least two things may be inferred: first, that there is much of which individual human beings are ignorant, but second, that our verbal ignorance may be greater than our tacit, inexplicit, or unarticulated knowledge.

Though Hayek was apparently not much influenced by his cousin Ludwig Wittgenstein, much of value can be gathered from Wittgenstein's thought or expression that bears on the question of nonverbal, tacit, or unarticulated knowledge. Wittgenstein thought that whatever can be said can be said clearly, and that what cannot be said must, literally, be passed over in silence. There are many ways to interpret these words, and one of the beauties of Wittgenstein's words, as Hayek's, is that they are so evocative—they are subject to more than one meaning (which is, of course, the exact opposite of what Wittgenstein, at least literally, wished to accomplish through his communication).

It is entirely possible that Wittgenstein meant something other than the physicalist position that all that is real is ultimately reducible to sensory experience and, perhaps, capable of being expressed in sensory terms. However, this is the most coherent reading of his words and would explain the interest in him by members of the Vienna circle of logical positivists. This reading of Wittgenstein would be consistent with his second from concluding proposition in *Tractatus Logico-Philosophicus* that the "correct method in philosophy would really be the following: to say nothing except what can be said, i.e., propositions of natural science . . . and then, whenever someone else wanted to say something metaphysical, to demonstrate to him that he had failed to give a meaning to certain signs in his propositions. Although it would not be satisfying to the other person . . . this method would be the only strictly correct one."

Hayek's point with respect to nonverbal, tacit, unarticulated, and inexplicit knowledge would seem to be the exact opposite of Wittgenstein's. Hayek believed not that whatever can be known can be expressed in physical terms, but that there is much knowledge that cannot be expressed, or expressed yet, in words. This was a vital, profound, and brilliant concept.

The idea of unarticulated or nonverbal knowledge is that individuals can have knowledge of which they are not aware, in the sense that they cannot express it in words. A number of philosophers before Hayek explored this concept, and he did not complete his investigations in this area; nonetheless, his tentative research in this field is potentially of high value. The concept of nonverbal knowledge is so important in part because it undercuts the notion of central planning. Essentially, the idea of central planning was that planners would write down in words what the outcomes of economic activity would be and how these outcomes would be achieved. But what if there is knowledge that transcends or exceeds words? In this case, this conception of planning becomes otiose.

Words in some larger philosophical sense represent understandings of the world. If these understandings are faulty, then the words that represent them also will be. Hayek's argument against central planning was not that it was normatively bad; rather, it did not empirically exist as those who promoted it thought it did, and to act on this mistaken understanding was harmful.

Hayek wrote in "The Creative Powers of a Free Civilization" chapter in *The Constitution of Liberty* that the "fundamental fact of man's unavoidable ignorance of much on which the working of civilization rests has received little attention." There is knowledge that transcends words. Those who would deny this knowledge bespeak their ignorance.

15

Karl Popper

FROM ABOUT 1969 TO 1974, HAYEK SUFFERED AGAIN FROM SEVERE depression. He previously had experienced depression during 1960 and 1961. During the early 1970s, at times he could hardly get out of bed. His writing diminished greatly.

Hayek recovered from this depression and after the first half of 1974 or so, he began to feel better and write more. Then, on October 9, 1974, it was announced that he had received the Nobel Prize in Economic Sciences, with Swedish socialist Gunnar Myrdal. They received the prize on December 10, 1974.

The intellectual and personal relationships between Hayek and Karl Popper have been discussed at considerable length elsewhere. Malachi Haim Hacohen discusses both, as does, to a lesser extent, former Popper research assistant Jeremy Shearmur. Sir Ernst Gombrich has provided recollections of the publication of Popper's *The Open Society and Its Enemies* and of Hayek's other assistance to Popper during World War II. Both Popper and Hayek discussed their intellectual relationship in old age. Furthermore, Hans Jörg Hennecke discusses Hayek and Popper's relationship extensively in his German-language intellectual biography of Hayek.

Hayek and Popper met before World War II in England, when Popper introduced himself at the London School of Economics on the recommendation of Professor Hans Kelsen of the University of Vienna. Like Hayek, Popper was from Vienna, though Popper was of Jewish ancestry. Hayek had heard the year before of Popper's *The Logic of Scientific Discovery,* which was published in a collection of works that was typically an outlet for logical positivist writings.

Perhaps even moreso than Hayek, who usually kept his exceedingly high opinion of himself hidden, Popper had a huge ego and considered himself to be one of the greatest philosophers of all time. Michael Kaufman, biographer of George Soros, a Popper student, writes that Popper once told Soros that "he [i.e., Popper] himself was the only person in the world who had the knowledge necessary to critically review his own work." Hacohen notes that an epigram to one of Popper's early works, "borrowed from Kant's *Critique of Pure Reason,* intimated that, like Kant, he had solved every major problem of philosophy." Popper commenced his later *Objective Knowledge: An Evolutionary Approach:* "Of course, I may be mistaken; but I think I have solved a major philosophical problem: the problem of induction. (I may have reached the solution in 1927 or thereabouts.) This solution has been extremely fruitful, and it has enabled me to solve a good number of other philosophical problems." Popper footnoted to this opening paragraph that "I had earlier (in the winter of 1919–20) formulated and solved the problem of demarcation between science and non-science." Many similar examples of Popper's statements of the importance of his work could be adduced.

Expressed egotism is, of course, no reason necessarily to disregard someone's work, but it is a warning signal. If someone can evaluate his work so poorly, is the work itself likely to be better? In many of his areas of intellectual interest, Popper's work is wanting.

Hayek did more to advance Popper professionally early in his career than anyone else, and Popper remembered his personal debt to Hayek. Over the years, he wrote him a number of appreciative letters. In 1964, he wrote:

> You will never know how much you have done for me. When I was in New Zealand, out of the world and buried by all my philosophical colleagues, you remembered me. It was through you that I came back into the world. It was through you (and Ernst Gombrich) that *The Open Society* was published, after a period (before you interfered) which led . . . me almost to despair. And when I came to the LSE [London School of Economics], through you, you gave me so much encouragement and help. . . . There cannot be, ever, equality or reciprocity between you and me. I never could do anything for you, and it is extremely unlikely that I ever shall.

On the occasion of Hayek's seventy-fifth birthday on May 9, 1974, still during the period of Hayek's great depression, Popper wrote him:

Our intellectual productivity is declining. Still, yours is admirable. You can still lecture (I cannot). . . . I know that you feel that you cannot do the work you used to do, and although you have told me and others about it, you kept it hidden from your observant friends—even though you complain to them of it, and draw their attention to it. . . .

But apart from the field of intellectual production, you have done so much for others. There are many former students you have encouraged and helped on their way. And there are many who, like myself, have been helped by you in the most critical stages of their development.

The signature beneath the typewritten letter was: "Love, yours ever, Karl."

In 1984, Popper wrote Hayek:

I have created myself a kind of generational gulf between you and myself. Although you were only 3 years old when I was born, you became, as I now realize, a kind of father figure. . . . [E]ven now, when I am 82, and we have been friends for so many years, you still are! And, strangely enough, you yourself . . . described your feelings towards me as those towards a young man who has made good.

Popper's biographer Hacohen wrote of this last letter that to "become a surrogate father, Hayek measured up to Popper's unreasonable expectations of protection and support and overcame his chronic suspicions about friends' loyalty. Popper did not always reciprocate. He was an unreliable correspondent, and rarely went out of his way, or interrupted his schedule, to meet Hayek. Fathers and gods, it seems, also needed to abide by the demands of Popper's philosophy."

In his excellent review of Hacohen's work in the *New York Times Book Review,* philosophy professor David Papineau summarizes Hacohen's evaluation of Popper and indicates his own perspective: "By Hacohen's own account, Popper was a monster, a moral prig. He continually accused others of plagiarism, but rarely acknowledged his own intellectual debts. He expected others to make every sacrifice for him, but did little in return. In Hacohen's words, 'He remained to the end a spoiled child who threw temper tantrums when he did not get his way.' Hacohen is ready to excuse all this as the prerogative of genius. Those who think Popper a relatively minor figure are likely to take a different view."

During World War II it was exciting and unexpected for Hayek to find someone else, from Vienna, who was interested in many of the same topics that he was. *The Open Society and Its Enemies* has three main parts, on Plato, Hegel, and Marx. The next main chapters in Hayek's uncompleted "The Abuse and Decline of Reason," on which he was at work then, were to be on Hegel and Marx. In addition, Popper's scholarly style was similar to Hayek's, with extremely extensive notes.

∾

Notwithstanding the prominence it achieved, each of the three main parts of *The Open Society and Its Enemies* can be seriously faulted from the perspective of the history of political philosophy scholarship.

Though there are many who disagree with Popper's generally totalitarian presentation of Plato, especially in the *Laws,* there is little question that Plato favored thought and political control along the lines of the Spartan model and opposed the Athenian democracy of his day. The difficulty with Popper's presentation of Plato is not Popper's macroperspective; instead, Popper's incidental and gratuitous asides and comments reflect significant misunderstandings. Popper read far too much of his own time into his analysis of Plato. The circumstances of the ancient Greek city-state were very different from those of modern nation-states. To consider Plato a forerunner of Nazi Germany and the Soviet Union, from a practical perspective, struck many readers as absurd. Hacohen observes that "Popper translated 'metal' as 'blood,' and 'earth' as 'soil,' and called the 'noble lie' the 'Myth of Blood and Soil'—Plato's lie as if out of Goebbels's propaganda."

Historian of political philosophy Leo Strauss had a very low opinion of Popper. After hearing a talk by Popper in 1950, Strauss wrote in personal correspondence to fellow political philosophy scholar Eric Voegelin that the talk was "very bad," "the most washed-out, lifeless positivism"—that is, not only was Popper a positivist (which Strauss was not), but a washed-out and lifeless one to boot.

Voegelin's view of Popper is also interesting to know, as Voegelin, besides having been a prominent conservative scholar, was an old Viennese associate of Hayek's; he had been in both Mises's "private seminar" and in Hayek and J. Herbert von Fürth's *Geistkreis* group of younger men. According to Voegelin, in a letter to Strauss, *The Open Society and Its Enemies* was "impudent, dilettantish crap.

Every single sentence is a scandal," a judgment that, while perhaps too harsh, does summarize some of Popper's work in the history of political theory. By showing Voegelin's letter to others, Strauss may have prevented Popper's appointment in the United States, perhaps at the University of Chicago, had Popper wished to leave LSE.

Logical positivist Rudolf Carnap and Popper engaged in a certain amount of incidental correspondence with respect to Hayek and *The Road to Serfdom*. Because Hayek repeatedly referred to this letter of Carnap's, it is worthwhile to turn to it. Carnap wrote Popper on February 9, 1946:

> I thank you most cordially for sending me the two volumes of your great work *The Open Society and Its Enemies*. I find it extremely interesting and many parts quite fascinating. I cannot of course judge the details of your historical and philosophical analysis of Plato, but your fight for reducing his all too high authority is very welcome at the present time. The same holds also for Hegel. . . . Your analysis of Marx's method is very illuminating, and I am sure that many people, whether followers or opponents or neutral scholars, will learn much from it. . . . In many of the points which you discuss, I am not in a position to make a definitive judgment. But . . . I was somewhat surprised to see your acknowledgement to von Hayek. I have not read his book [*The Road to Serfdom*] myself; it is much read and discussed in this country, but praised mostly by the protagonists of free enterprise and unrestricted capitalism, while all leftists regard him as a reactionary. I wonder what you think about his book.

In the 1976 preface to *The Road to Serfdom,* Hayek wrote, apparently of this letter: "Just to indicate the character of a widespread reaction [to *The Road to Serfdom*] I will mention merely that one well-known philosopher who shall be nameless wrote to another to reproach him for having lauded this scandalous book which 'of course [he] had not read'!"

Popper's response to Carnap is interesting for the light it sheds on Hayek's influence on Popper and what Popper considered Hayek's purpose to be in writing the work:

> I should like to mention that I did not know Hayek's book (*The Road to Serfdom*) when I wrote mine; in fact, my book was finished about six months before his. All I knew was a little pamphlet "Freedom and the Economic System," in which he advocates "Planning

for Freedom." . . . The acknowledgement in my book refers to his practical help rather than to his influence; but since I wrote my book, I have read Hayek's book (and several excellent articles), and I can only say that I have learned a *very* great deal from it. A few leftists here in England are in the same position . . . . Hayek, who I had seen only four or five times before, has been really wonderful to me in his many repeated approaches to various publishers, and I understand from the people here in the School [the London School of Economics] that he is always so. His interest in my book was mainly due to the fact that he too is hoping for a common basis of discussion for socialists and liberals.

Much moreso than Hayek, Popper was egalitarian in his perspective of humanity (notwithstanding his exceedingly high opinion of himself). He apparently did not typically see great differences in the natural capacities of people. This was in contrast to the views of Hayek and John Stuart Mill, among others in the great liberal tradition. One does not find in Popper, as one finds in Mill and Hayek, emphasis on the great diversity of humanity.

Popper agreed with Hayek that in a totalitarian government, the worst get on top. Hacohen writes that "Hayek had little influence on his [Popper's] methodology, but he stymied the growth of his political philosophy. . . . Hayek managed to corrupt his socialism."

Popper started out, and remained, considerably to the left of Hayek politically, which may explain his greater popularity, for much of his career, than Hayek. Popper's incidental comments in economics were largely uninformed. Popper was originally a socialist, and he retained affinity for socialist ideas throughout his life. As late as the middle 1970s, he advocated substantial worker control of industry. For most of his career he supported the welfare state less reservedly than Hayek did.

Popper had a very high opinion of Hayek, who was one of the few specific individuals whom Popper ever identified as potentially having a superior intellect to, or being able to make more important intellectual contributions than, himself. Given Popper's high conception of himself, this was the highest praise he could bestow.

In 1964, Popper wrote Hayek that "I do not consider myself intellectually your equal. . . . I know that you have broken new ways quite beyond my reach." Twenty years earlier, he wrote: "I think that I have learnt more from you than from any other living thinker, except perhaps Alfred Tarski," the Polish philosopher.

Also in 1944, Popper wrote Hayek—giving some idea, perhaps, of the new ways of thinking that Popper thought Hayek had broken—that "your remark that in the engineering case 'all knowledge is concentrated in a single head' (or, at any rate, in a very few heads) 'while it is the specific character of all truly social problems that the task is to utilize knowledge which cannot be so concentrated' is one of the most illuminating and striking formulations I have ever heard on these problems." Much of Popper's later work in philosophy may be able to be traced to this idea of Hayek's, particularly with respect to his conception of "world 3."

Popper and Hayek corresponded regularly during the latter part of World War II, from the middle of 1943 through early 1945. They were in contact as much as every couple of weeks or so, or monthly, mostly about professional matters such as publishing and employment for Popper. During their wartime correspondence, their salutations were invariably "Dear Professor Hayek" and "Dear Dr. Popper." "Fritz" and "Karl" came only after the war.

In large part because they were both at the London School of Economics during the later 1940s (though Hayek was, by this time, a frequent traveler elsewhere), their correspondence substantially declined. When Hayek moved to the United States, he sent Popper copies of his work and tried to interest Popper in his psychological and philosophical work. Popper was not really interested. At one time, Hayek mentioned the possibility of Popper coming to the University of Chicago to teach, as later he would suggest that Popper come to Salzburg, but Popper was content in England at the London School of Economics. Hayek also suggested to Popper the possibility of participating in his endeavor to re-create the University of Vienna's intellectual tradition, but Popper considered this idea "a joke," in the words of his closest friend, Ernst Gombrich.

Hayek truly did get Popper his position at the London School of Economics. "I am personally anxious to get Dr. Popper to this School," Hayek wrote Gombrich as early as 1943. Given the later prominence that Popper achieved for the school, this was one of Hayek's most significant contributions to its reputation, as well as the decisive career move in Popper's life.

Hayek also genuinely influenced Popper's political philosophy. While Popper always remained to Hayek's left, he started out much further to Hayek's left than he wound up, and this movement was in no small part the result of Hayek's influence. Popper was a charter

member of the Mont Pelerin Society. He suggested, however, that socialists be brought into it. Hayek wrote Popper several deeply personal letters in connection with his divorce. It is likely that their
personal relationship was more important to and valued by Hayek
than Popper, though Popper valued highly Hayek's friendship.

Among Popper's most expansive public praise for Hayek was a
1975 letter to the *Times Literary Supplement* remonstrating it for not
reviewing the first volume of *Law, Legislation and Liberty:* "I regard
Hayek's book as a new opening of the most fundamental debate in the
field of political philosophy. It must not be allowed to pass unnoticed."
Popper wrote Hayek even more unreservedly in a personal letter
shortly after the first volume was published: "I may be too enthusiastic—probably I am—but my present feelings are that this is the greatest book on political philosophy I have ever read, Plato's unbelievable
Republic not excluded. . . . [I]ts liberal utopia has kindled a new hope.
If anything can help us, [it is] your book."

Hayek expressed the greatest praise for Popper. Whether this
was Hayek's ultimate view or a reflection of a deep, though subordinate, strain of personal modesty and humility that ran through him is
an open question. Hayek's support was vital in Popper's career. During the late 1970s and early 1980s, Hayek was involved with an unsuccessful effort to obtain the Nobel Prize in Literature for Popper.

The question of the ultimate value and worth of Popper's work
remains to be established. Dozens or even scores, perhaps even hundreds, of individuals consider it to be of the greatest value and importance. Whether this will be the view of time cannot now be said.

One of Popper's last major addresses was when he received the
Kyoto Prize (Japan's equivalent of the Nobel Prize) on November 11,
1992. He modestly said of *The Open Society and Its Enemies:* "Although this book has been in print continuously since it was published in 1945, it played only a small part in undermining Marxism
and the Soviet Empire; a far smaller part than the famous books of
my late friend Friedrich von Hayek, for example his book *The Road
to Serfdom.*"

Two months before, Popper had said at a memorial meeting in
Hayek's honor at the London School of Economics: "Hayek's open
mindedness was one of his most striking virtues. He was . . . an anti-so-
cialist. But he took great trouble to convince communist and socialist
students that they were welcome in his lectures and seminars; and they
found, indeed, that he was ready to listen to them with sympathy. . . .

Hayek's tolerance was indeed exemplary; and as far as students were concerned, he behaved with convincing tolerance, even to those who preached intolerance." Popper noted on this occasion that "[i]n this respect I had to learn a lot from Hayek, for I was far less ready to listen to ideological clichés than he was."

Popper, like Hayek, was interested in truth, but one questions whether his conception of and attachment to the truth were the same or as great as Hayek's. Hayek was the greater pure philosopher in written expression. In the same way that Hayek's written words were better than his thought, Popper's generalized verbal concepts were better than his detailed expression of them. In addition, unlike Hayek, Popper was likely a more effective personal teacher and communicator than writer.

16

Law, Legislation and Liberty

LAW, LEGISLATION AND LIBERTY WAS ONE OF THE GREATEST WORKS in political philosophy of the twentieth century. Its greatness stemmed, however, not from its proposed reorganization of representative democracy—which was highly flawed—but from its conception of the tie between liberty and law, emphasis on and description of spontaneous order, and inspiring ideal of a "universal order of peace." All of these themes were found in Hayek's earlier work, but in *Law, Legislation and Liberty,* they found their greatest expression.

Law, Legislation and Liberty was Hayek's second major attempt, following *The Constitution of Liberty,* to enunciate the principles of a free society. There was thus much in the second treatise that was similar to its predecessor. While his aim in the first book was mostly restatement of classical liberal principles, however, this was not the case with *Law, Legislation and Liberty.* It was explicitly intended, as its subtitle states, as "a new statement of the liberal principles of justice and political economy."

Hayek considered his second discussion of liberty "more original" than the first. Here he attempted to move beyond the classical liberal writers of the past and to enunciate new theories and ideals that could guide liberal polities in the future. Past writers did not have, as he had, two centuries' experience of democratic voting procedures to consider. He believed that appropriately channeling democracy was the most pressing challenge facing modern societies.

Law, Legislation and Liberty was written and published during a different period from *The Constitution of Liberty.* The earlier work was a product of the late 1950s—a generally optimistic and socially cohesive time when Hayek himself was in his late fifties, at the University of Chicago. *Law, Legislation and Liberty,* on the other hand, was a product of the 1960s and 1970s, a far more turbulent time, as he became an old man, was somewhat intellectually isolated in Freiburg and Salzburg, and experienced depression. That the later work has a different feel from the former is hardly to be unexpected. The relationship between the two works might be considered to be something like that between Plato's *Republic,* a product of his prime, and Plato's *Laws,* a product of his old age.

The bulk of *Law, Legislation and Liberty* was written between 1962 and 1969 while Hayek was in Freiburg, before he discontinued work for several years because of depression. Thus, the temporal contiguity of this volume, which was published between 1973 and 1979, and of *The Constitution of Liberty,* which was published in 1960, was substantially closer than their publication dates would indicate.

Hayek considered *Law, Legislation and Liberty* to be the subordinate of his two major treatises. In its preface he wrote: "It is definitely supplementary to and not a substitute" for *The Constitution of Liberty.* Its purpose was to "fill the gaps" left by the first volume in the area of the actual functioning of a liberal system in the twentieth and future centuries. *Law, Legislation and Liberty* depicted the constitutional arrangements that he thought would make a free society possible. In introducing this work, he said that if he had known when he wrote *The Constitution of Liberty* that he would subsequently turn to the subjects in *Law, Legislation and Liberty,* he would have reserved the former title for the latter work.

He thought that the "preservation of a society of free men depends on three fundamental insights which have never been adequately expounded," and which were the major purpose of *Law, Legislation and Liberty* to present:

> The first of these is that a self-generating or spontaneous order and an organization are distinct, and that their distinctiveness is related to the two different kinds of rules or laws which prevail in them. The second is that what today is generally regarded as "social" or distributive justice has meaning only within the second of these kinds of order, the organization; but that it is meaningless in, and wholly incompatible with, that spontaneous order [of the first kind of order]. . . . The third is that the predominant model of liberal democratic institutions [as currently practiced] . . . necessarily leads to a

gradual transformation of the spontaneous order of a free society into a totalitarian system conducted in the service of some coalition of organized interests.

The volumes of *Law, Legislation and Liberty* discussed each of these thoughts successively.

Law, Legislation and Liberty was issued in three volumes in 1973, 1976, and 1979, corresponding to each of its three parts, because Hayek feared he might not complete the work as a whole and wished to publish at least what he had finished. This publishing format severely detracted from the unity of the treatise; it was impossible to know what to expect in the unpublished volumes. In addition, Hayek acknowledged that the work had certain stylistic shortcomings as a result of its long gestation and intermittent birth. He remarked in a preliminary preface from 1977, which he discarded, of the work as a whole that "I know that instead of proceeding in a straight line to its goal it rather approaches it in a sort of ascending spiral and constitutes a series of systematically arranged essays touching repeatedly on the same topic."

In this same preliminary preface he observed the "strong influence" present throughout of Karl Popper and the absence of influence by Karl Marx and Sigmund Freud. "Theories which had built-in provisions against refutation by observed facts were wholly empty and provided no knowledge of the world in which we live," he added here.

Suffusing the treatise was a deeply pessimistic attitude with respect to the political future of Western nations: "The reader will probably gather that the whole work has been inspired by a growing apprehension about the direction in which the political world of what used to be regarded as the most advanced countries is tending." Hayek thought that Western nations were faced with a "threatening development towards a totalitarian state. . . . I am becoming more and more convinced that we are moving towards an impasse from which political leaders will offer to extricate us by desperate means." The consistency of his view from *The Road to Serfdom* forward was evident here.

He was not consistently pessimistic. In a 1977 interview, he responded to the question: "Are you optimistic about the future of freedom?" "Yes. A qualified optimism. . . . I am more optimistic than I was twenty years ago, when nearly all the leaders of opinion wanted to move in the socialist direction." That he could become more positive with respect to freedom's prospects indicates that the inadequacies he saw in Western nations and their political systems in *Law, Legislation and Liberty* may not be so deleterious after all.

The bulk of the first draft of *Law, Legislation and Liberty* was written while he was at the University of Freiburg from 1962 to 1969. Then depression and poor health caused him to delay finishing the work for several years. The first volume, *Rules and Order,* changed the least between the time he completed the first draft in 1969 and published the parts during the 1970s. The second volume, *The Mirage of Social Justice,* contained an entirely rewritten central chapter—"'Social' or Distributive Justice"—the longest chapter in this volume. The third volume, *The Political Order of a Free People,* changed the most. It contained a final chapter he had not completed when he discontinued writing in 1969, a new recapitulatory chapter, and an epilogue, "The Three Sources of Human Values," originally given as a lecture. Hayek's final work, "The Fatal Conceit," began from "The Three Sources of Human Values." Unlike *The Constitution of Liberty,* which was reviewed by twenty-seven individuals before it was published, sections of *Law, Legislation and Liberty* were read by only three. It was more his sole work.

~

Hayek stated in the first volume of *Law, Legislation and Liberty* that there are

> two ways of looking at the pattern of human activities which lead to very different conclusions concerning both its explanation and the possibilities of deliberately altering it. . . . The first gives us a sense of unlimited power to realize our wishes, while the second leads to the insight that there are limitations to what we can deliberately bring about. . . . The first view holds that human institutions will serve human purposes only if they have been deliberately designed for these purposes. . . . The other view, which has slowly and gradually advanced since antiquity but for a time was almost overwhelmed by the more glamorous constructivist view, was that that orderliness of society which greatly increased the effectiveness of individual action was not due solely to institutions and practices which had been invented or designed for that purpose, but was largely due to a process described at first as "growth" and later as "evolution," a process in which practices which had first been adopted for other reasons, or even purely accidentally, were pre-

served because they enabled the group in which they had arisen to prevail over others.

Hayek was a social evolutionist through group selection. He thought that the difference between an organization and a spontaneous order is fundamental. Organizations are deliberately planned, while spontaneous orders grow or evolve.

Much of his political, social, and economic philosophy rests on the distinction between constructivism and evolution in human society. He thought the constructivist view naively "holds that human institutions will serve human purposes only if they have been deliberately designed for these purposes, often also that the fact that an institution exists is evidence of its having been created for a purpose, and always that we should so re-design society and its institutions that all our actions will be wholly guided by known purposes." In contrast, Hayek emphasized the "Great" or "Open Society." By these appellations, he meant the society in which the spontaneous and nondeliberately coordinated actions of individuals bring about, through the appropriate legal and moral framework, continuous evolution to higher material progress and personal freedom.

He thought that the division of labor is one historical outcropping of the Great Society. This division occurs not just within but among societies as they practice free trade. He further stated, though— and it was here that his contribution lies—that much less stress has been placed on "the fragmentation of *knowledge,* on the fact that each member of society can have only a small fraction of the knowledge possessed by all, and that each is therefore ignorant of most of the facts on which the working of society rests."

The essentiality of the division of knowledge is that it destroys the entire constructivist approach to society and prepares the way for reconceptualization of optimal society in which maximizing liberty along the lines of Hayekian principles is paramount for optimal productivity. Human beings cannot design institutions according to their wishes. Facts matter. People being what they are, institutions may not work in the manner in which they were intended. For this reason, reform of institutions in a society that is working tolerably well should be approached in a tentative and humble manner. More harm than good may result from wholesale social reconfiguration.

He titled a section in *Law, Legislation and Liberty:* "All valid criticism or improvement of rules of conduct must proceed within a given system of such rules." In this section he stated that since "any established system of rules . . . will be based on experiences which we only partly know . . . , we cannot hope to improve it by reconstructing anew the whole of it." His point was twofold: first, conceptions of the future are based on present and past experiences, and thus individuals are literally incapable of entirely conceiving what the future might be like; and second, human ignorance of the purposes that rules serve (particularly within a larger system) is such that attempts to change rules may have unanticipated consequences. He had remarked in *The Constitution of Liberty* that "although we must always strive to improve our institutions, we can never aim to remake them as a whole," and: "What we must learn to understand is that human civilization has a life of its own, that all our efforts to improve things must operate within a working whole."

Constructivist approaches, by contrast, appeal to human vanity. Such approaches are, moreover, not confined to the past. Political philosopher Brian Barry wrote in his 1989 *Theories of Justice:* "Through contact with other societies, people came to realize that social arrangements are not a natural phenomenon but a human creation. And what was made by human beings can be changed by human beings." Too many intellectuals have believed that their specific conceptions can and should guide future societal development.

To be another Marx—to be a thinker putting forward conceptions that subsequent generations follow—has been the dream of too many intellectuals. Hayek said in this regard: "Organization thinking, largely as a result of the sway of the rationalist constructivism of Plato and his followers, has long been the besetting vice of social philosophers. . . . Academic philosophers . . . , imagining themselves to be Platonic philosopher-kings, . . . propose a re-organization of society on totalitarian lines."

The desire to be a philosopher-king is, however, a false vision. John Stuart Mill stated the objection to totalitarianism best in his concluding line of *On Liberty,* where he affirmed that the "worth of a State . . . is the worth of the individuals composing it . . . a State which dwarfs its men, in order that they may be more docile instruments in its hands even for beneficial purposes—will find that with small men no great thing can really be accomplished; and that the perfection of machinery to which it has sacrificed everything, will in the end avail it nothing, for want of the vital power which, in order that the machine might work more smoothly, it has preferred to banish."

There are at least two primary purposes of social life: the highest material standard of living and the greatest individual development. Both require, Hayek believed, political liberty. Without liberty, economic productivity is not possible. More important, without liberty, personal development is impossible. Individual moral development requires the ability to make choices. When the state or government attempts to make choices for individuals, it takes away what makes people most human. Much of the argument for democracy is, Hayek argued in accord with other liberal writers such as Mill and Alexis de Tocqueville, educational.

Moreover, it is not possible, Hayek thought, for one mind to organize all of society. Notwithstanding the radical inequality of humanity from some perspectives, human beings are nonetheless equal in largest part in others. We are all mortal; we have certain physical wants and needs; most of us live our individual lives according to certain routines and patterns.

An organization implies an organizer. If society is conceived as a rationally planned endeavor, then there will always exist the desire on the part of some to attempt to plan it. Such efforts can result only in human misery, Hayek thought.

This endeavor on the part of intellectuals and others must always end in failure, because no one mind is capable of conceiving all of the varieties of human experience (particularly within different societies and over time), nor is any one individual capable of conceiving all of the directions in which human experience may develop. Freedom is the ultimate value in human experience for the reason that Hayek put forward—individual human minds are, of themselves, incredibly puny. He commented in *Law, Legislation and Liberty* on "the unalterable ignorance of any single mind, or any organization that can direct human action, of the immeasurable multitude of particular facts which must determine the order of . . . [a society's] activities." He also said that in "none but the most simple kind of organization is it conceivable that all the details of all activities are governed by a single mind."

This should not be interpreted, though, as vitiation of the principle that human beings are unequal—and very much so—in other senses and that almost all that is of value that has emerged during human experience has been the result of exceptional human beings, for such Hayek believed to be the case. But (contrary to what Ayn Rand argued), Hayek thought that exceptional human beings are not so rare that they will not be continually produced through the natural workings of the species.

Consider, for example, Albert Einstein and his contributions. It can be argued that he was the most influential person of the twentieth century. Had he not thought as he did, it is entirely possible that atomic weapons would not have come to pass until several decades after they did, and the course of World War II and the whole postwar era would have been entirely different. One person—Albert Einstein—may have had more influence on the course of history during the twentieth century than billions of others.

But if Einstein, as brilliant and as influential as he was, had not come along, then someone else would have. It might have been another ten, twenty, or even thirty or fifty years, but sometime someone else would have discovered the theory of relativity and the relations among energy, mass, and the speed of light it postulates.

In Rand's novel *The Fountainhead,* the antagonist Ellsworth Toohey (whose real-life model was, unjustly, Harold Laski) reflected her view of the absolutely radical inequality of humanity through the following soliloquy—though Rand vehemently disagreed with the conclusion she had Toohey reach. Gazing out over the city lights, he says:

> Look at it. A sublime achievement, isn't it? A heroic achievement. Think of the thousands who worked to create this and of the millions who profit by it. And it is said that but for the spirit of a dozen men, here and there down the ages, but for a dozen men—less, perhaps—none of this would have been possible. And that might be true. If so, there are . . . two possible attitudes to take. We can say that these twelve were great benefactors, that we are all fed by the overflow of the magnificent wealth of their spirit, and that we are glad to accept it in gratitude and brotherhood. Or, we can say that by the splendor of their achievement which we can neither equal nor keep, these twelve have shown us what we are, that we do not want the free gifts of their grandeur, that a cave by an oozing swamp and a fire of sticks rubbed together are preferable to skyscrapers and neon lights—if the cave and the sticks are the limit of our own creative capacities.

It may be tempting to adopt an attitude of superiority, particularly for individuals who have some greater abilities or talents than their fellows. Notwithstanding very substantial human inequality on an individual level, all are radically equal in their inability to conceive of, much less possibly to direct, human society as it becomes larger and larger. Liberty is the only possible principle on which to organize societies as they grow. No other principle acknowledges the insignificance of individual human beings.

Hayek's view of humanity had congruities with Christianity, to the extent that the latter, too, emphasizes human insignificance or inadequacy. The gulf between God and man is absolute in the Old Testament. While Hayek's view of human insignificance was more from an intellectual perspective than from a moral one (though he certainly recognized human weakness in this area), his general emphasis on individual human inadequacy is shared by many conservative and religious thinkers and writers.

Societies are not planned. They evolve. Just as societies do not emerge from one person's mind, neither can they be guided by one person's mind. Liberty is the only human way forward.

~

Much of Hayek's work in *Law, Legislation and Liberty* was in the history of ideas, following in the tradition of *The Counter-Revolution of Science*. He drew a distinction between "rules of just conduct" and "the direction of government." By the former, he intended enforced rules of conduct. By the latter, he meant the service functions of government that were more or less provided everywhere around the developed world at the time he wrote *Law, Legislation and Liberty*.

He did not much criticize, from a philosophical as opposed to practical perspective, many aspects of the welfare state—a fact for which he was criticized by more libertarian-oriented writers and thinkers. Mises, for example, wrote that it was much to Hayek's credit through *The Road to Serfdom* to have "directed attention to the authoritarian character of socialist schemes. Now Professor Hayek has enlarged and substantiated his ideas in a comprehensive treatise, *The Constitution of Liberty.* . . . Unfortunately, the third part of Professor Hayek's book is rather disappointing. Here the author tries to distinguish between socialism and the Welfare State. . . . [H]e thinks that the Welfare State is under certain conditions compatible with liberty. Professor Hayek has misjudged the character of the Welfare State."

Hayek wrote in "Liberalism," published in 1973, that the "strict limitation of governmental powers to the enforcement of general rules of just conduct required by liberal principles refers only to the coercive powers of government. Government may render in addition, by the use of the means placed at its disposal, many services which involve no coercion except for the raising of the means by taxation." Political philosopher Anthony de Jasay remarks of this last passage that it "sounds almost like deadpan black humor to state that 'except for raising the means,' government need not rely on coercion to render services. . . . There is an infinity of services to be rendered; they all satisfy some need. How much should be provided? We are in an ideological void in which minimal state, maximal state and anything in between are equally admissible."

It is hard not to agree with de Jasay's and others' criticism here. Hayek did not provide a firm criterion or standard for government involvement in social welfare areas. While he undoubtedly preferred fewer government services to more, his underlying principles could allow far more government activity than he wished to see. Lionel Robbins noted this criticism of Hayek: "Side by side with his critique of *étatiste* [statist] policies, there are developed a series of alternatives which, set out in a more systematic form, might well be regarded as [a] liberal agenda for state action."

Hayek's distinction between enforced rules of conduct and government services was nonetheless vital. While it may be desirable that less government services are provided rather than more, and that, as a percentage of gross domestic product, the government taxes and spends 10 to 15 percent rather than 60 to 80 percent, it is nonetheless the case that what is truly to be feared from government is arbitrary and capricious rule, rather than high taxation, no matter how onerous the latter may be. Sweden, during the height of its welfare state, may have taxed and spent 60 to 80 percent of its gross domestic product on government activities, but it was in no way thereby comparable to the Soviet Union, which allowed its workers some comparable share of their individual effort. What is most to be feared from government is the midnight knock at the door, not poor taxation and spending policies, no matter how irksome and nonproductive the latter may be. There was a difference, in 1975, between living in Sweden and the Soviet Union. Libertarians and others who do not acknowledge this difference demonstrate the poverty of their positions.

All of this should not be considered endorsement of high taxation and spending policies, for Hayek neither intended nor advocated this outcome. It is to say instead that his distinction between enforced rules of conduct and government services was of great merit.

Hayek would have restricted the term "law" to enforced rules of conduct. He saw this concept of law as having evolved over centuries and even millennia. He believed that in times past: "Nobody . . . conceived of law as something which men could make at will. . . . It is no accident that we still use the same word 'law' for the invariable rules which govern nature and for the rules which govern men's conduct. They were both conceived at first as something existing independently of human will. . . . [T]hey were regarded as eternal truths that man could try to discover but which he could not alter."

This was a very different conception of the laws that govern human conduct than is now current. Hayek did not consider the best or most important law to be made. Instead, where true law has reigned, a "body of law grew up through the gradual articulation of prevailing conceptions of justice rather than by legislation." Genuine law, he thought, in the sense of enforced rules of conduct, is not manufactured; it evolves through the gradual evolution of previous legal conceptions and practices.

He stated his almost reverence for law defined as rules of enforced conduct that have gradually evolved best in *The Constitution of Liberty,* where he said that the "conception of the law which made it the basis of freedom" has largely been lost. He observed further that though "individual liberty in modern times can hardly be traced back farther than the England of the seventeenth century," this did not imply that the "heritage of the Middle Ages is irrelevant to modern liberty." He commented eloquently on the "common medieval ideal of the supremacy of law," which, because it was most preserved in England at the dawn of the modern age, allowed it to become the fountainhead of liberty throughout the world:

> This medieval view, which is profoundly important as background for modern developments, though completely accepted perhaps only during the early Middle Ages, was that "the state can not itself create or make law, and of course as little abolish or violate law, because this would mean to abolish justice itself; it would be absurd, a sin, a rebellion against God who alone creates law." For centuries it was recognized doctrine that kings or any other human authority could only declare or find the existing law, or modify abuses that had crept in, and not create law. Only gradually, during the later Middle Ages, did the conception of deliberate creation of new law—legislation as we know it—come to be accepted.

Hayek continued in *Law, Legislation and Liberty* that Roman law, which has so influenced subsequent European law, was "even less the product of deliberate law-making" than in Greece. As with other early law, Roman law was "formed at a time when 'law and the institutions of social life were considered to have always existed and nobody asked for their origin.' . . . Until the rediscovery of Aristotle's *Politics* in the thirteenth century and the reception of Justinian's code in the fifteenth . . . Western Europe passed through another epoch of nearly a thousand years when law was again regarded as something given independently of human will, something to be discovered, not made, and when the conception that law could be deliberately made or altered seemed almost sacrilegious." This was a highly different concept of law from that which prevailed during the twentieth century, when the idea that law, in the sense of enforced rules of conduct, could be changed at will was prevalent.

The medieval conception of law was very different from our own. Hayek, to be sure, was no idolater of this earlier conception, but it represented a position that was essential for him. Law, to be respected and create a stable framework for individuals—within which they are free—must in largest part be fixed.

Stability and fixity of law assist its proper function to limit the power of government, as well as to create a pattern of expectations for individuals within which rational action and cooperation are possible. Hayek remarked specifically concerning the constitution of a state in *Law, Legislation and Liberty:* "Ideally the Constitution ought to be intended for all time, though of course, as is true of any product of the human mind, defects will be discovered which will need correction by amendment." In *The Constitution of Liberty,* he approvingly quoted William Blackstone's definition of "law": "'a rule, not a transient sudden order from a superior or concerning a particular person; but something permanent, uniform and universal.'" Though Hayek decried Plato, these were sentiments not so dissimilar from those enunciated by him in the *Laws:* "Then [after the lawgiver's death] the customs are to be made unchangeable, and adhered to along with the rest of the laws the lawgiver laid down . . . . They [successors] are never voluntarily to change a single one of them."

There was a great distinction in Hayek's mind between law per se (rules of enforced conduct) and government services. He disapproved of and considered dangerous the modern tendency to conflate all acts that representative assemblies perform with law. This conflation destroys the concept of law proper on which societal freedom is based: "By calling 'law' every decision of [an] assembly, whether it lays down a rule or authorizes particular measures, the very awareness that these are different things has been lost." He emphasized: "Today legislatures are no longer so called because they make the laws, but laws are so called because they emanate from legislatures."

∿

Hayek repeatedly has been considered to have moved from a more liberal position to a more conservative position as his career advanced, and this perspective is worth considering. In his emphasis on the slow, gradual evolution of societal institutions, opposition to constructivism, and conception of society as a spontaneous order rather than organization, he is often considered to have abandoned the liberal principles of experimentation and change in favor of an almost irrationalist position that whatever societal institutions have developed through the historical process are best. Hayek, however, rejected this position.

Economist Leland Yeager has considered this criticism: "The very fact that Hayek develops *arguments* for personal and political freedom and for Western capitalist and democratic institutions shows that he does not preach smug, nonrational acceptance of whatever appears to have stood the test of time." William Bartley, Hayek's intended biographer and coauthor/editor of the published version of Hayek's *The Fatal Conceit: The Errors of Socialism,* also defended Hayek from the charge of reactionary conservatism, saying, "Hayek is emphatically not an irrationalist,"and:

> His critique of socialism in *The Fatal Conceit* is based on a sophisticated acceptance of evolutionary theory; and he reminds us in the Introduction to *The Fatal Conceit*[:] "Although I attack the *presumption* of reason on the part of socialists, my argument is in no way directed against reason properly used. By 'reason properly used' I mean reason that recognizes its own limitations and, itself taught by reason, faces the implications of the astonishing fact, revealed by economics and biology, that order generated without design can far outstrip plans men consciously contrive. How, after all, could I be attacking reason in a book arguing that socialism is factually and even logically untenable?"

Hayek stated a similar view in *The Constitution of Liberty:* "Reason undoubtedly is man's most precious possession. Our argument is intended to show merely that it is not all-powerful and the belief that it can become its own master and control its own development may yet destroy it."

Hayek's argument was not against reason. He rejoiced in reason, rightly understood. This right understanding is that there are great limitations on individual human reason. He wrote in *Law, Legislation and Liberty* that he did "not maintain that all tradition as such is sacred and exempt from criticism, but merely that the basis of criticism of any one product of tradition must always be other products of tradition which we either cannot or do not want to question. . . . [W]e can always examine a part of the whole only in terms of that whole which we cannot entirely reconstruct and the greater part of which we must accept unexamined. As it might also be expressed: we can always only tinker with the parts of a given whole but never entirely redesign it."

His point here was largely philosophical, and profound. It was connected to his argument that classification of an entity can occur only by another entity of greater complexity and of the difference between what can be said about a system and what can be said within a system. Mind's conceptions of the future are limited to what it has already experienced. Though mind can rearrange pieces of what it has experienced hypothetically as to the future, it cannot experience what the future will actually be like until it has actually experienced it. The new data in combination with the completely new experiences that mind may in the future experience can lead to a wholly different future from what one imagines possible or likely at the present.

Hayek's argument was not in favor of conservatism; it was in favor of individual humility. Moreover, it was an argument, though he did not develop it as much as he could have, in support of tacit, unarticulated, and nonverbal knowledge as opposed to verbal knowledge. It is not just that we do not and cannot know what the future has in store; it is that our words may be inadequate to describe and understand the present, much less the future. To reduce all potential knowledge of the future to words in the present is doubly unwise.

Hayek expressed his perspective of the kind of social change, as opposed to specific social changes, he favored in *Law, Legislation and Liberty* when he remarked in a footnote that his idea was "the same as what Karl Popper calls 'piecemeal social engineering,' on which I wholly agree, though I still dislike the particular expression." He referenced in this regard a section from Popper's *Open Society and Its Enemies,* which sheds further light on Hayek's conception of desirable social change: "The only course open to the social sciences is to forget all about the verbal fireworks and to tackle the practical problems of our time with the help of the theoretical methods which are fundamentally the same in *all* sciences. I mean the methods of trial and error, of inventing hypotheses which can be practically tested, and of submitting them to practical tests. *A social technology is needed whose results can be tested by piecemeal social engineering.*" In *The Poverty of Historicism,* Popper also had this to say: "The term 'social technology' (and even more the term 'social engineering' . . .) is likely to arouse suspicion, and to repel those whom it reminds of the 'social blueprints' of the collectivist planners, or perhaps even of the 'technocrats.' I realize this danger, and so I have added the word 'piecemeal,' both to offset undesirable associations and to express my conviction that 'piecemeal tinkering' (as it is sometimes called), combined with critical analysis, is the main way to practical results in the social as well as in the natural sciences."

Hayek's, and Popper's, main point here was that complete reorganization of societies in the fashion of Marx, Hegel, or Plato are as impossible as they are undesirable. Complete reorganization can be attempted, but it will never turn out entirely as it was intended. Individual human minds are simply too insignificant and too puny to execute the rational reconstruction of a whole society.

The liberal way, by contrast, is here a little, there a little, step by step approaching the ineluctable yet unattainable goal of truth. American political scientist William Ebenstein wrote of this conception of truth:

> Francis Bacon, Hume, and Locke challenged the Platonic concept of Truth with the more modern view of truth (with a small "t") as something tentative, hypothetical, and changeable, subject to constant checking, verification, modification, or rejection. It is an endless process of testing old and new hypotheses against new experience. Truth is not discovered in the sudden Platonic flash of mystical insight and intuition. It is pieced together, step by step, in the process of observing. The modern view does not regard truth as a mountain peak that will eventually be conquered. Each new discovery of knowledge opens up new areas of ignorance. The more we find out about nature and reality, the more we are aware of what we do not know. Truth is not the visible peak of the mountain (high as it may be). It is no more than a way-station in an endless journey on an endless road.

Hayek used utilitarian reasoning in *Law, Legislation and Liberty,* as elsewhere in his career, as many Hayek scholars have maintained. Since he claimed not to be a utilitarian, it is appropriate to consider his views.

He remarked in *Law, Legislation and Liberty* that "[t]he constructivist interpretation of rules of conduct is generally known as 'utilitarianism.'" This was an entirely different conception of utilitarianism from the standard one. The typical definition of utilitarianism involves maximization of the good—the greatest good for the greatest number, or the greatest happiness of the greatest number—not the rational construction of societal rules.

Using the maximizationist definition of utilitarianism, Hayek was a utilitarian. He wrote in *Law, Legislation and Liberty:*

> Which expectations ought to be protected must . . . depend on how we can maximize the fulfillment of expectations as a whole.
>
> Every change must disappoint some expectations, but . . . this very change which disappoints some expectations creates a situation in which again the chance to form correct expectations is as great as possible. . . . [T]he central problem is which expectations must be assured in order to maximize the possibility of expectations in general being fulfilled.
>
> Policy need not be guided for the striving for the achievement of particular results, but may be directed towards securing an abstract overall order of such character that it will secure for the members the best chance of achieving their different and largely unknown particular ends. . . . The aim will have to be an order which will increase everybody's chances as much as possible—not at every moment, but only "on the whole" and in the long run.
>
> *The Good Society is one in which the chances of anyone selected at random are likely to be as great as possible.*
>
> What it [the free market] tends to bring about is . . . a state of affairs in which no need is served at the cost of withdrawing a greater amount of means from the use for other needs than is necessary to satisfy it. The market is the only known method by which this can be achieved without an agreement on the relative importance of the different ultimate ends, and solely on the basis of a principle of reciprocity through which the opportunities of any person are likely to be greater than they would otherwise be.

Accordingly, when he criticized utilitarianism in his work, he did not do so because he was opposed to what is typically considered the core aspect of utilitarianism—maximization of the good—but because he opposed the rationalistic reconstruction of the body of Western civilization's societal institutions. He clarified this in a note: "It is misleading to represent as utilitarians all authors who account for the existence of certain institutions by their utility, because writers like Aristotle or Cicero, Thomas Aquinas or Mandeville, Adam Smith or Adam Ferguson, when they spoke of utility appear to have thought of this utility favouring a sort of natural selection of institutions, not determining their deliberate choice by men."

∽

Hayek had this exchange in 1978 about his career and *Law, Legislation and Liberty*. Asked why he departed from his work in capital theory, he responded:

> A: I've become much more interested in the semi-philosophical policy problems—the interaction between economics and political structure.
>
> Q: Those are much more difficult problems.
>
> A: They are in a way more difficult, and . . . much more difficult to come to clear conclusions. But I have been engaged in them so long—You know, it was *The Road to Serfdom* which led me to *The Constitution of Liberty*. Having done *The Constitution of Liberty,* I found that I had only restated in modern language what had been the classical liberal view; but I discovered there were . . . three issues which I had not answered systematically. . . .
>
> So I felt I had to fill the gaps, and I believe that in a way the thing on which I have now been working for seventeen years, which I have now at last finished, *Law, Legislation and Liberty,* is probably a much more original contribution. . . . It's not merely a restatement, but I have developed my own views on several issues—on the . . . relation between rules and order, on democracy, and the critique of the social justice concept, which were absolutely essential as complements to the original ideas, answering questions which traditional liberalism had not answered.

He concluded the text proper of *Law, Legislation and Liberty* (before its epilogue) with the thought that government had become far too extensive and intrusive during the twentieth century: "It can scarcely be doubted that quite generally politics has become much too important, much too costly and harmful, absorbing much too much mental energy and material resources, and that at the same time it is losing more and more the respect and sympathetic support of the public at large who have come to regard it increasingly as a necessary but incurable evil that must be borne."

This problem of government is different from the one he presented earlier. He sanctioned a considerable positive role for the state in *The Road to Serfdom* and *The Constitution of Liberty*, as well as earlier in *Law, Legislation and Liberty* (most of which was written by 1969). These last words did not appear until 1979, and were likely written about 1977 or so.

In a section titled "The abolition of the government monopoly of services" in *Law, Legislation and Liberty*'s final chapter, Hayek continued this theme:

> Any governmental agency allowed to use its taxing power to finance such services ought to be required to refund any taxes raised for these purposes to all those who prefer to get the services in some other way. This applies without exception to all those services of which today government possesses or aspires to a legal monopoly, with the only exception of maintaining and enforcing the law and maintaining for this purpose (including defence against external enemies) an armed force, i.e., all those from education to transport and communications, including post, telegraph, telephone and broadcasting services, all the so-called "public utilities," the various "social" insurances and, above all, the issue of money.

This was a significantly more libertarian position than he took earlier. Hayek's practical thought was flawed over his career not when he allowed a significant government social welfare role, but when he did not recognize (as he came to late in his career) that the government that governs least governs best. Hayek's practical political thought was flawed not where he postulated too small a role for government, but where he sanctioned too great a role. In his late work, Hayek the classical liberal became Hayek the libertarian.

17

Later Monetary Work

IN THE PREFACE TO THE THIRD VOLUME of *Law, Legislation and Liberty*, Hayek wrote that the volume led to a "proposal of basic alteration of the structure of democratic government . . . [which] is meant to provide a sort of intellectual stand-by equipment for the time, which may not be far away, when the breakdown of the existing institutions becomes unmistakable." His idea on the reform of democratic government has not proven persuasive. Essentially, he advocated a bipartite legislature in which one house would be elected, as at present, and the other, the more important "legislative assembly," would be comprised of individuals who were elected to single fifteen-year terms at age 45, elected only by other individuals who were themselves 45. One-fifteenth of the legislative assembly would be elected each year. An individual would thus be able to vote and run for the legislative assembly once in his life, at age 45.

Hayek continued in the third volume preface that "[t]ogether with the similar stand-by scheme I have proposed for depriving government of the monopolistic powers of control of the supply of money, equally necessary if we are to escape the nightmare of increasingly totalitarian powers, which I have recently outlined in another publication (*Denationalisation of Money* . . .), it proposes what is a possible escape from the fate which threatens us." In *Denationalisation of Money*, he wrote that inflation will "lead to the destruction of our civilisation unless we change the political framework. In this sense I will admit that my radical proposal concerning money [in the third volume of *Law, Legislation and Liberty*] will probably be practicable only as part of much more far-reaching change in our political institutions." He considered his later work in monetary institutions to be potentially of the highest value.

Indeed, Hayek's later monetary work constitutes some of his most creative practical policy suggestions, though his thought in the area was, by his own admission, undeveloped. Though Hayek's general productivity substantially diminished later in his career, he remained capable of great ideas. The increase in inflation around the world during the late 1960s and early 1970s caused him to return to practical consideration of monetary issues.

He first broached the idea that became *Denationalisation of Money* in a 1975 address, "Choice in Currency: A Way to Stop Inflation." He here blamed his old friend John Maynard Keynes for the inflation that was then being experienced around the world. His view of Keynes's essential public policy advice was monetary expansion combined with fiscal stimulation—an increasing money supply and government budget deficits.

There is little question that by the early 1970s, national economies throughout the developed world were collectively in their worst shape since the Great Depression. Inflation reached double-digit levels in many countries, yet—despite significant deficit spending—national economies foundered. Something had gone wrong. What?

Hayek's answer, stemming from his work in monetary theory four decades earlier, was that an increased money supply distorts the structure of economic production. Because an increased money supply is implemented through reduced interest rates, the structure of capital becomes misshapen. Too much investment occurs in temporally early capital. Slowing inflation would require a recession (as a result of raising interest rates). Moreover, reducing government budget deficits would require politically difficult reductions in spending or increases in taxation.

Early in his career, Hayek had begun a work on the history and theory of money that he never completed. He gave his notes to one of his graduate students, Vera Smith (later Lutz), who used them in writing her dissertation, published in 1936 as *The Rationale of Central Banking.* In her concluding chapter, Smith stated that the origin of central banking is to be "found in the establishment of monopolies, either partial or complete, in the note issue." She also observed that "monopolies in this sphere outlasted the abolition of protectionism in other branches of economic activity." Late in his career Hayek came to advocate the elimination of the government monopoly of money.

In his 1975 "Choice in Currency," he quoted himself from thirty-six years before in *Profits, Interest and Investment:* "It may perhaps be pointed out that it has, of course, never been denied that employment can be rapidly increased, and a position of 'full employment' achieved in the shortest possible time, by means of monetary expansion. . . . All that has been contended is that the kind of full employment which can be created in this way is inherently unstable." Hayek's theoretical views of economic activity did not change significantly between the 1930s and 1970s. What did change was his hope that governments could be persuaded to pursue optimal monetary policies. He therefore put forward a "somewhat startling suggestion"—competitive, and ultimately even private, currencies.

British Prime Minister Margaret Thatcher and her Chancellor of the Exchequer, Nigel Lawson, attempted to implement Hayek's idea in European monetary negotiations during the 1980s. Rather than there becoming one European currency, Lawson and Thatcher proposed the elimination of exchange charges for European currencies and that residents of any European nation should be able to use the currency of any other nation in the European Union for domestic purposes. Lawson described this proposal as an intended "happy reversal of Gresham's law," in which good money would drive out bad. This Hayekian path was, however, not taken.

Political economist Benjamin Cohen believes that for technological reasons having to do with the Internet, private currencies may become feasible in the near future: "For years, the followers of Friedrich Hayek have been calling for denationalization of money, to little avail. Governments have, quite understandably, been resistant to any voluntary surrender of authority. Yet what could not be achieved by intellectual persuasion now seems about to be produced instead by technological development and the rush of events. With the arrival of electronic money, money creation will become increasingly privatized. Hayek's vision of a world of unrestricted currency competition could, for better or worse, soon become reality."

The first edition of *Denationalisation of Money* was published by the Institute of Economic Affairs in England in 1976. Hayek played a crucial role in the institute's founding. Arthur Seldon, the institute's longtime editor, sagely reported that when Hayek's idea of competing private issuers of money was first broached: "An august personage in the British banking system . . . [said,] 'That may be for the day after tomorrow.'" Now this day may be no later than tomorrow.

Cohen also writes that among "e-money's main impact . . . will be to *expand the population* of currencies circulating within each country, further eroding an already increasingly tenuous connection between nominal demand and supply of national money. As more substitute currencies become available, variations of home-currency monetary aggregates will have even less influence on overall spending. Policy will become even more attentuated." Central banks may become, if not a thing of the past, then considerably less influential than they have been, particularly in some countries with weaker currencies. This trend has already begun.

Competing and private currencies would likely lead to deflationary international monetary circumstances and high economic growth, which characterized the world during the Pax Britannica of the half century between 1860 and 1910, when the international gold standard was in place. During a prospective Pax Americana, similar circumstances could subsist.

While Hayek considered his later work in monetary theory to be highly important, he did not continue it because he came to the view that his final work, "The Fatal Conceit," was even more important. He sent out a memo in 1980 to all contributors to two collections on his thought saying that he had found "some of the elaborations of the ideas I had sketched in the Epilogue to *Law, Legislation and Liberty* so important and exciting that for the time being I have even completely put aside that other book on money which my friends tell me it is my duty to do."

Whether private or nationally competitive currencies (within countries) come to pass remains to be seen. If either does transpire, though, Hayek will have been among the very first to have suggested them and foreseen their possibilities. He wrote in the 1976 preface to *Denationalisation of Money* that his efforts were a "foray into a wholly unexplored field." He could do no more than present "some discoveries made in the course of a first survey of the terrain." For a man of seventy-seven, he retained exceptional intellectual powers.

In the 1978 second edition of that work, he replied to a comment made by Milton Friedman at a Mont Pelerin Society meeting. Since this reply constitutes one of Hayek's most substantial considerations of Friedman's ideas, it deserves attention. Hayek agreed with Friedman in decrying Keynesians, who disputed that "'an inflationary or deflationary movement [i]s normally caused or necessarily accompanied' by 'changes in the quantity of money and velocity of its circulation.'" It is hard to remember now that as recently as a quarter of a century ago, the majority of professional economists and the mainstream of the academic profession disputed the most basic postulates of monetary theory.

Where Hayek disagreed with Friedman was not in this appraisal of Keynesianism, nor in the overarching truth of the monetarist perspective, but in the failure of the macroeconomic monetarist perspective to consider the microeconomic effects of injections of money on the economic system. The "chief defect" of Friedman's monetarism, he held, is that by "its stress on the effects of changes in the quantity of money on the general level of prices it . . . disregards the even more important and harmful effects of the injections and withdrawals of amounts of money . . . on the structure of relative prices and the consequent misallocation of resources and particularly the misdirection of investments which it causes." Following his arguments during the 1930s, Hayek believed that the fundamental problem increasing and decreasing the money supply causes is on the structure of production.

Interestingly, Hayek here criticized Friedman's proposals for indexing financial agreements on the grounds that this would do little to solve the underlying problem of inflation: the distortion of relative prices. This was a good point. Whether one agrees with all aspects of Hayek's monetary theory or not—particularly the extent to which it emphasizes changes in capital production as the underlying cause of economic fluctuations, and the primary problem that changes in money supply causes—there can be little doubt that among inflation's most pernicious aspects is that it distorts the information prices would otherwise convey.

Frank Johnson, a writer for the London *Daily Telegraph,* provided this profile of Hayek in 1975, the year after he won the Nobel Prize:

> He is tall and thin, aquiline of feature, with a clipped moustache and short, white hair. . . .
>
> Unlike other anti-socialist iconoclasts—such as the ebullient, knock-about Milton Friedman—Hayek, to a stranger, is distant and formal. There is a certain coldness. This, in a way, is emphasised by one of his great strengths—his precise, very rational way of thinking and speaking. Questions are answered exactly, and briefly. He is not easily drawn into random, unscientific speculation. Asked to account for the revival of Marxism among Western students in the Sixties, . . . he said he could not explain it. Just fashion, perhaps. Even an explanation of the underlying reasons why governments,

particularly in Britain, have become so inflationary was not something which he cared to attempt.

Many of Hayek's colleagues were in awe of him. His longtime friend, Arnold Plant, from the London School of Economics, concluded a 1970 article, "Homage to Hayek": "Contrary to ill-informed critics of his ideas, his contributions to academic discussion have been characterized by a sober attempt at rational persuasion. Those whose advocacy of social change is powered by strong emotion have often been repelled by the cold-blooded nature of his purely intellectual approach. They would do well to reflect that they would not wish a surgeon to operate upon them while his hands were trembling with emotion."

Hayek possessed a towering intellect. At the same time, his intelligence was as much brittle as it was powerful. He could construct strongly counterfactual views of reality that he maintained in the face of much evidence. His virtue was to be a highly evocative writer, whose words call forth in the minds of readers new ways of looking at the world and new ways of understanding.

18

"The Fatal Conceit"

AFTER HAYEK SUFFERED HIS PERIOD OF DEPRESSION FROM 1969 through the first half of 1974, he regained strength and completed *Law, Legislation and Liberty* during the middle 1970s. As he did so, he began to look at the world in a new way. He wrote in the preface to the third volume that he "found it necessary" to add an epilogue that expressed "more directly the general view of moral and political evolution which has guided me in the whole enterprise." This epilogue was "The Three Sources of Human Values." He was reluctant to publish what he thought would be his final systematic work without indicating in what direction his ideas were heading. Over the long period that had transpired since he discontinued work on the manuscript in 1969, his ideas "developed further."

Hayek gave the L. T. Hobhouse Lecture, "The Three Sources of Human Values," at the London School of Economics on May 17, 1978. In it he identified these sources as the genetic determination of human values, the rational construction of human values, and the "process of selective evolution to which is due the formation of complex cultural structures," stating "the decisively important selective evolution of rules and practices."

Interposition of William Warren Bartley, III, into Hayek's life was a decidedly mixed blessing. Bartley made possible publication of Hayek's final work, *The Fatal Conceit: The Errors of Socialism,* while Hayek still lived. He also began Hayek's collected works. At the same time, Bartley did an exceptionally poor job editing "The Fatal Conceit" and launched Hayek's collected works on the wrong foot, contrary to the plan in which Hayek participated. Bartley was also to be Hayek's official biographer, a charge he did not complete.

Bartley was born in 1934. After receiving degrees at Harvard, he earned a doctorate in logic and scientific method as a student of Karl Popper at the London School of Economics. He died in 1990.

In describing Popper in his own posthumously published *Unfathomed Knowledge, Unmeasured Wealth: On Universities and the Wealth of Nations,* Bartley provided this description of their first meeting in 1958, a description that also provided information on his own essential character. Popper "began the interview by telling me that he disagreed utterly with the philosophical views of my teachers at Harvard.... He then decreed ... I wrote very badly (I had been asked to submit an essay and had turned in one for which I had been awarded a prize), and that I would need to learn to write better.... He went on to explain exactly what was wrong with my essay: it was pretentious and in places was unclear, masking confusion, uncertainty, or ignorance with a brilliant, or at least eye-catching, style. I was, he told me, more interested in the effect I was producing than in reaching toward the truth."

Hayek's contact with Bartley began with Bartley's biography of Ludwig Wittgenstein. Hayek was among those with whom Bartley exchanged correspondence for the in-progress study, which was published in 1973. Interestingly, given the controversy the biography raised, in a 1974 letter to Oxford philosopher and later Wittgenstein biographer Brian McGuinness, Hayek rejected as highly improbable Bartley's depiction of Wittgenstein as a promiscuous homosexual, or a homosexual at all—Hayek had no knowledge of it, and he thought that had Wittgenstein engaged in such behavior, he would have been blackmailed, as the Wittgensteins were among the wealthiest families in Vienna. In addition, Hayek did not agree with Bartley's contention that Wittgenstein attempted to hide his Jewish ancestry. In his biography, Bartley had written that Wittgenstein "pleaded with a cousin living in England not under any circumstances to reveal his descent." Hayek wrote McGuinness that this was not the position taken by the family in Vienna, and that since he and John Stonborough were the only cousins of Wittgenstein living in England of whom he was aware, Hayek could say assuredly that no such suggestion had been made to them.

Bartley did not enjoy high professional esteem among many of his colleagues in academic philosophy, who were not close to Popper. He enjoyed good repute among Popperians. He did not obtain a teaching position at a leading national or international university for an extended time as a mature scholar and bounced around as a younger academic before obtaining a post in the department of philosophy at

California State University, Hayward, during the 1970s. He asked Hayek to write several letters of recommendation for him for appointments, without success. Later in his career, he became affiliated with the Hoover Institution at Stanford University, as a result of his work on Popper and Hayek. In *Unfathomed Knowledge, Unmeasured Wealth,* Bartley expressed the view that Popperian philosophers are subject to academic prejudice.

Bartley was an extensive writer. His works included *The Retreat to Commitment* (1962), *Morality and Religion* (1971), *Wittgenstein* (1973, 1985), *Werner Erhard; The Transformation of a Man: The Founding of* est (1978), and *Unfathomed Knowledge, Unmeasured Wealth* (1990). His work as an editor included *Lewis Carroll's Symbolic Logic* (1977), Popper's *Postscript to the Logic of Scientific Discovery* (1982–83) (the first volume of which Popper dedicated "To my editor for his rescue of the *Postscript*"), and, with Gerard Radnitzky, *Evolutionary Epistemology, Rationality, and the Sociology of Knowledge* (1987).

Bartley believed his relationship with Hayek to be closer than Hayek considered it to be, especially before about 1984. In a November 7, 1983, letter to Glenn Campbell of the Hoover Institution, Hayek gave reasons why Bartley would be his biographer. His biography would be published after his death. Bartley would be an appropriate biographer because he was familiar with Wittgenstein, Popper, Vienna, and England. Also, because Bartley lived in the San Francisco area and would be at the Hoover Institution, this would assist in the donation of Hayek's papers there. However, Hayek told Campbell in this letter that he had known Bartley only slightly to this time. It was because Bartley was to be Hayek's biographer that he also became his literary executor and general editor of Hayek's collected works.

Bartley, by contrast, in 1988 provided this recollection of his relationship with Hayek:

> My interest in F. A. Hayek . . . begins with my relationship with Karl Popper, as one of his closest students and colleagues. This put me in touch with Hayek by correspondence some time in the 'sixties. But we hadn't met. . . . I later found out that he had acquired and read all my early books . . . as they had come out, and had corresponded with Popper about them. I did not meet Hayek until 1975, when he was in California at Mills College, Stanford, and IHS [Institute for Humane Studies], and came to visit me at my house.

I saw Hayek frequently in the years that followed. He helped gain foundation support for my editorship of Popper's *Postscript*. And when I began to prepare the basic work for my biography of Popper he granted me a number of interviews and, in the early summer of 1982, threw open his files on Popper to me. I first met him with Walter Morris . . . —who plays an important role in the story— in November 1982 . . . at a conference that I had arranged. In January 1983, when I was in Freiburg, Hayek asked me to write his biography. . . .

. . . I was [also] to be appointed literary executor of Hayek, not only to write the biography, but also to edit *The Collected Works*. . . . By the end of 1984 . . . the plan for *The Collected Works* had been drawn up in detail. . . .

Stephen Kresge, Bartley's successor as general editor of *The Collected Works of F. A. Hayek* and significant other, writes in the most recent volume published in the series that its "initial impulse came from Walter Morris, who attended the keynote address given by Hayek at the convocation of the Open Society and Its Friends . . . in November 1982. . . . In what was to be only the first of many acts of generosity, Morris then brought together, at a dinner party in honor of Hayek, W. W. Bartley III. . . . In the following year, Walter Morris supplied the enthusiasm, good will, and persistence that convinced Hayek . . . that a collected works must be produced."

Bartley did not begin to participate in writing what became *The Fatal Conceit: The Errors of Socialism* until after Hayek's health deteriorated in August 1985, which forced conclusion of Hayek's professional career. Bartley strongly encouraged Hayek to allow him to play a role with the work that was not foreseen when Bartley became Hayek's biographer and literary executor. Hayek had intended to write "The Fatal Conceit" entirely by himself, because he attached the greatest importance to it. Bartley's initial role with the work was to be minimal.

Bartley was a collector of Chinese art and owned five cats. He was very involved in the International Conference on the Unity of the Sciences affiliated with the Reverend Sun Myung Moon's Unification Church, serving as a member of the group's Board of Advisers. Although Bartley was apparently not a member of the Unification Church, he always defended his involvement with this Moon-affiliated organization, in which he succeeded in persuading a number of prominent academics and scholars, including Hayek and Popper, to participate. In 1986, Hayek received the second Founder's Award from the International Conference on the Unity of the Sciences, to the criticism of some students and faculty in Freiburg. Hayek could not be present to accept the award because of illness, but Bartley accepted the award (which carried a substantial cash prize) on his behalf and read a paper of Hayek's.

Bartley was also highly involved with *est,* an offshoot of the human potential movement. He wrote a biography of *est* founder Werner Erhard and served several years as philosophical consultant to *est* and on the *est* Advisory Board.

Hayek was initially very taken with Bartley. He found him well educated, interesting, and pleasant. Bartley also had a sense of humor and was a flatterer. In a December 3, 1984, letter to Glenn Campbell, Hayek said that he liked Bartley even more than he had the previous year.

During the six or seven years between about 1978 and the middle of 1985 that Hayek worked on "The Fatal Conceit," he foresaw a three-part work in which a part on the morals of the market would be sequentially followed by parts on the economics and politics of the market. The published *The Fatal Conceit: The Errors of Socialism* was basically the first part.

Bartley was a far too enthusiastic editor of "The Fatal Conceit," concealing the extent to which he stylized and rewrote the manuscript and incorporated ideas of his own into it. Nevertheless the essential ideas of the published work and a substantial portion of the thought flow and much of the expression were Hayek's. In part as a result of his death in 1990 at age fifty-five, Bartley never wrote his biography of Hayek, though he conducted many interviews with Hayek and others regarding the project, almost all of which have not been made accessible.

One interview that is available is Bartley's session with Ludwig Lachmann, which is in the archive of the London School of Economics together with interviews of various economists conducted by Nadim Shehadi. It reveals Bartley to have conducted an informative interview. Undoubtedly his interviews with Hayek and others would have much of interest to Hayek scholars and others. Yet it is unlikely that they will offer much essential information with respect to Hayek's intellectual evolution. Hayek gave so many interviews to others, and there are so many interviews with and other materials about others available, that Hayek's intellectual development can be traced without resort to Bartley's materials, though these would be helpful and should be made available (as Bartley's Popper materials should be made available).

Hayek concluded the text proper of *Law, Legislation and Liberty* on the thought that "we ought to have learnt enough to avoid destroying our civilization by smothering the spontaneous process of the interaction of the individuals by placing its direction in the hands of any authority. But to avoid this we must shed the illusion that we can deliberately 'create the future of mankind.' . . . This is the final conclusion of the forty years which I have now devoted to the study of these problems since I became aware of the process of the Abuse and Decline of Reason which has continued throughout that period." He significantly added as a footnote at this point of "The Abuse and Decline of Reason": "This was the title I had intended to give a work I had planned in 1939, in which a part on the 'Hubris of Reason' was to be followed by one on 'The Nemesis of the Planned Society.' Only a fragment of this plan was ever carried out and the parts . . . reprinted in . . . *The Counter-Revolution of Science* . . . *The Road to Serfdom* was an advance sketch of what I had intended to make the second part. But it has taken me forty years to think through the original idea." "The Fatal Conceit" should, thus, be seen as a new departure in Hayek's thought.

He had concluded the preface of the 1959 German edition of *The Counter-Revolution of Science:* "I should like to add that the work of which this is a part will not be continued in the form originally conceived. I now hope to present the body of thought in another volume that is less historical but more systematic"—*The Constitution of Liberty.* Hayek's work in both *The Constitution of Liberty* and *Law, Legislation and Liberty* should, therefore, be considered more the fulfillment of the first part of his intended "The Abuse and Decline of Reason," the "Hubris of Reason," rather than the second part, "The Nemesis of the Planned Society," of which *The Road to Serfdom* was the initial sketch.

Hayek wrote in a preliminary draft of the introduction to "The Fatal Conceit" that it was an "attempted final realization" of a project he had formulated much earlier. The essays in *The Counter-Revolution of Science* were merely a part of a much more extensive work, "The Abuse and Decline of Reason." The historical presentation in these essays, a "critique of contemporary thought," proceeded too slowly, however, as a result of "the immediate dangers that I saw in the current trends of opinion." He therefore wrote an advance outline of the work's conclusion, which became *The Road to Serfdom.*

As a result of writing *The Road to Serfdom,* Hayek became aware that the classical liberal tradition had ceased to be understood, and he wrote *The Constitution of Liberty* to present the classical liberal tradition in contemporary form. After he wrote that work, he came to the view that the classical liberal tradition "left some important questions unanswered," and he wrote *Law, Legislation and Liberty.* This, in turn, brought him to reconsider the "intellectual sources of socialism" that had "largely destroyed" the classical liberal tradition, which, after his period of inactivity and depression, he began to consider from a new perspective. The final product of his work, which he had started in the essays he edited in *Collectivist Economic Planning* a half century before, was "the evolutionary interpretation of the growth of human civilization"—the subject of "The Fatal Conceit."

In the published *The Fatal Conceit: The Errors of Socialism,* it was written (in words that were mostly Hayek's own) that "the main point of my argument is . . . that the conflict between, on one hand, advocates of the spontaneous extended human order created by a competitive market, and on the other hand those who demand a deliberate arrangement of human interaction by central authority based on collective command over available resources is due to a factual error by the latter about how knowledge of these resources is and can be generated and utilised." His essential argument here followed from his pioneering breakthrough in "Economics and Knowledge": that prices and profits transmit knowledge—not all of which is verbal or explicit, and much of which is tacit or nonverbal. Only market capitalism can deliver, he thought, the wealth of which classical socialists dreamed.

∽

Hayek intended "The Fatal Conceit" as a larger work than the published version, and it is valuable to have an idea of his original plan to understand *The Fatal Conceit* best. He scrawled on the following table of contents: "This is the plan of my intended work on which I worked until 1985 or so when I fell ill. May 1988 F.A.H." Hayek was at this time very ill and decrepit:

The Fatal Conceit

Preface

Introduction: Was Socialism a Mistake?

Part One: Morals: The Taming of the Savage
1. Between Instinct and Reason
2. Evolution of Rules and the Expansion of Society
3. From Common Concrete Purposes to the Rule-Governed Macro-Society
4. The Ethics of Property and Honesty

"The Fatal Conceit" had no subtitle when Hayek's work on it ended unexpectedly. Most of the published *The Fatal Conceit: The Errors of Socialism* came from the originally intended first part of the larger intended treatise. Hayek worked on this first part most, from about 1982 to 1985.

By way of comparison, the contents of the published version were:

The Fatal Conceit: The Errors of Socialism

Appendices

As late as January or February 1988, "The Fatal Conceit" was to have been published in two volumes, the first comprised essentially of part I (which basically became the published version) and the second volume of parts II and III. Though *The Fatal Conceit* was, at this time, to be the first work *published* in *The Collected Works of F.A. Hayek,* it was to be volumes 12 and 13 of the series, which was to commence with Hayek's previously published works. Shortly thereafter, however, the decisions were made instead to issue "The Fatal Conceit" as the first of the planned two volumes and to inaugurate Hayek's collected works with it as volume 1.

Some of the biggest changes in what became *The Fatal Conceit: The Errors of Socialism* (and *The Collected Works of F. A. Hayek*) were made between about February and May 1988. It may be that Hayek indicated in May 1988 what had been his final intentions for the work on the 1985 contents draft in order to attempt to preserve a true historical record.

The idea of "The Taming of the State" was similar to the final chapter proper of *Law, Legislation and Liberty,* "The Containment of Power and the Dethronement of Politics." Hayek thought that just as the savage was tamed and became moral through obeying rules, so should the state. "The Taming of the State" followed "The Taming of the Savage."

In the second part of the originally contemplated whole work, he intended to present the technical economic justification for free market order. He returned to some of the problems that had occupied him decades earlier at the London School of Economics. One chapter in particular, "The Flow of Goods and Services," restated his views from the 1930s, given as his last lecture at the London School of Economics on the fiftieth anniversary of his first lecture there, in the same lecture room, on January 27, 1981. As he had a half century before, Lionel Robbins chaired the session. Hayek said in prefacing the talk that his 1931 "Prices and Production" lectures were the first time he "made use of what became the leading theme of most of my later work, an analysis of the signal function of prices in guiding production, a conception which I first expounded systematically . . . in . . . 'Economics and Knowledge.'"

Part III of the originally intended "The Fatal Conceit" was the least complete when Hayek discontinued work in 1985; a good portion was merely handwritten. One of the more finished chapters was 20, "The Muddle of the Middle," a lecture he gave in March 1980 to the Monday Club, a Conservative Party caucus in London.

He remarked in this lecture that "when thirty-six years ago I inscribed *The Road to Serfdom* 'To the Socialists of All Parties,' I am afraid this was not least aimed at an influential wing of the Conservative Party." He always opposed a "middle way" between socialism and capitalism, and thought that this would lead eventually to full-fledged socialism: "One cannot create harmony out of conflicting principles, and socialism is not half right but all wrong. It must be resisted in principle if one is not to be dragged step by step into a system which is both totalitarian and ineffective. I am afraid in this the Conservative Party has failed, failed because it refused to be bound by principles, but has abandoned principles in the service of expediency." At the same time: "I have, of course, always stressed that there was, in a wealthy country, a strong case for government providing *outside the market* a minimum for those poorest victims of acts of God or the King's enemies who were unable to provide for themselves." He ended this talk saying that the battle for Britain's survival as a wealthy and important nation was being fought inside the Conservative Party, and that Britain's continued prominence would depend on eliminating trade unions' privileges, controlling inflation, and rejecting the notion of "social justice."

In what was to be the final chapter proper of the originally planned "Fatal Conceit," on environmentalism and underdevelopment, Hayek expressed the view that these popular movements were largely based on the same misconceptions as socialism. He expressed similar thoughts in a 1981 communication to Nobel laureates: "It may appear an obvious truth that the 'massive transfer of wealth' which the Brandt Report proposes will keep many people alive for some time who would otherwise die—and in some measure this is of course true. But even if it were true that by such measures we could save more than a small proportion of those threatened by death of starvation—which is by no means certain—it may well reduce our future capacity to place people who are not able to maintain themselves in a position where they will be able to do so. . . . The deliberate subsidisation of such an increase from the outside would in that not too distant future raise problems much more serious than any which we face now."

Hayek's discussion of population in chapter 8 of the published version of *The Fatal Conceit: The Errors of Socialism* has been perhaps the most criticized portion of the book; his argument here was little altered by Bartley. Hayek's views, titled "The Extended Order and Population Growth," have not proven persuasive. The primary difficulty with Hayek's perspective is contained in the quote from Adam Smith used as the epigraph of the chapter: "'The most decisive [*sic*] of the prosperity of any country is the increase of the number of its inhabitants.'" This is a difficult case to make, notwithstanding that population is a factor in the influence and affluence of nations. China and India are not the most prosperous or powerful nations in the world today, they are not likely to be in the near future, and they have not been for hundreds, if not thousands, of years.

Hayek appears to have undergone something of a change with respect to his views on population between the time he wrote *The Constitution of Liberty* and later in his career. In the earlier work, he wrote of the "frightening rate" of world population growth, a different sentiment from what he would enunciate in "The Fatal Conceit." Terence Hutchison and others observe that Hayek gave little consideration to potential environmental issues. Hayek approved of the work of Ronald Coase and Peter Bauer in the area of the environment.

Despite his protestations to the contrary, Hayek embraced utilitarian maximization in "The Fatal Conceit," as elsewhere during his career. He wrote, using utilitarian philosophical reasoning in *The Fatal Conceit: The Errors of Socialism,* that "even if we do not like to face the fact, we constantly have to make such decisions ['when it is a question of sacrificing a few lives in order to serve a larger number elsewhere']. . . . When the army surgeon after a battle engages in 'triage'— when he lets one die who might be saved, because in the time he would have to devote to saving him he could save three other lives . . . —he is acting on a calculus of lives." This was pure utilitarianism.

He emphasized capital in "The Fatal Conceit": "The size of the stock of capital of a people, together with its accumulated traditions and practices for extracting and communicating information, determine whether that people can maintain large numbers. People will be employed, and materials and tools produced to serve future needs of unknown persons, only if those who can invest capital to bridge the interval between present outlay and future return will gain an increment from doing this which is at least as great as what they could have obtained from other uses of that capital."

His emphasis on capital followed Menger, who emphasized capital in the section titled "The Causes of Progress in Human Welfare" in *Principles of Economics*. Menger took Adam Smith to task for Smith's position that the division of labor is the most important factor in economic progress. Rather, Menger argued, it is the development of capital—or in his terminology, "goods of higher orders" (goods not intended for final consumption but for the production of goods that are finally consumed)—that is crucial:

> The further mankind progresses . . . , the more varied become the kinds of goods, the more varied consequently the occupations, and the more necessary and economic also the progressive division of labor. But it is evident that the increase in the consumption goods is not the exclusive effect of the division of labor. Indeed, the division of labor cannot even be designated as the more important cause of the economic progress of mankind. . . .
>
> . . . Increasing understanding of the causal connections between things and human welfare, and increasing control of the less proximate conditions responsible for human welfare, have led mankind . . . from a state of barbarism and the deepest misery to its present stage of civilization and well-being. . . . Nothing is more certain than that the degree of economic progress of mankind will still, in future epochs, be commensurate with the degree of progress of human knowledge.

Knowledge is the ultimate form of capital and wealth, and knowledge is, in an important sense, the capacity to predict. The ability to predict causal connections in the physical realm of the senses is the essence of Menger's conception of economic activity.

∾

Bartley did not come into the picture with respect to "The Fatal Conceit" until well into 1985, when Hayek became unable to work further, though it was not immediately apparent that Hayek would not be able to resume work. Hayek fell ill while on vacation in the summer of 1985. He wrote in February 1986 that he had been ill for five months. He wrote two months later that he was recovering from a long illness, which proved wishful thinking. He spent most of the summer of 1986 in the hospital with a bronchial infection, and when he returned home he suffered a fractured pelvis. At one point, he sent a memo to a few associates saying he had suffered a nervous breakdown.

Hayek's primary physical and intellectual diminishment occurred between July 1985 and January 1986. After this time, he was never the same again. In a January 24, 1986, letter to Bartley, he noted the great fluctuations in his state.

Hayek had a tough last almost seven years of his life, from about age 86 on. The few photos of him after 1986 show a shrunken old man from whom much life force had obviously departed. During the last six or seven years of his life he repeatedly expressed the concern that he was losing his mind, though this appears to have been overstated. He was depressed and at times felt suicidal. From at least 1987 on, he experienced significant diminution of memory, not being able to remember individuals with whom he had, even recently, been in frequent correspondence.

Hayek was initially reluctant to allow Bartley to edit "The Fatal Conceit," and it was only after some months that he consented. Bartley began to work on it around the second half of 1985. In his January 1986 letter to Bartley, Hayek indicated that the drafts for chapters 1 to 5 and 7 were largely complete compared to chapter 6.

Hayek had considered "The Fatal Conceit" to be the great project of the end of his career, perhaps of his career. His Salzburg research assistant Kurt Leube wrote in 1984 that "when not lecturing throughout the world, Hayek devotes himself entirely to the completion of this great work, which will contain some of the most significant developments in his intellectual thought." In declining to participate in a conference, Hayek himself wrote several years earlier that he had committed himself to writing what he thought might be his most important work and that for at least the next year he would be unable to undertake any other literary activities.

The work took much longer than this to write, as Hayek wrote draft after draft chapter. One preliminary version of the whole manuscript was submitted in 1982 to about fifteen Mont Pelerin Society colleagues, including George Stigler, James Buchanan, Ronald Coase, and Peter Bauer. This group did not think the version worthy of publication. Hayek then drafted and redrafted primarily the first part's chapters until 1985 and wrote first drafts of chapters in the latter two parts, some of which were originally given as public lectures.

As Hayek's physical condition prevented him from working further, Bartley assumed a greater role with the manuscript. It was not that Bartley wrote a new work, for he did not. Hayek had a reasonably good manuscript of the first part; Bartley could have pulled together a work that would have almost exclusively reflected Hayek's word as well as thought. In a July 26, 1985, letter, just before he became unable to continue working, Hayek wrote Bartley that he had completed all but one chapter of the first part of "The Fatal Conceit," which he hoped to finish during the next few weeks.

Instead of bringing this final chapter to completion (chapter 6, of seven chapters in the first part, and for which good material existed that Hayek had written) and publishing Hayek's remaining six chapters and introduction of the first part, Bartley substantially massaged the first part's entire text, organizing and rearranging chapters, introducing much extraneous connective material, and rewriting, rearranging, and deleting paragraphs and sentences. He inserted paragraphs from various individuals who reviewed the text and his own. He added citations, including to his own work (Bartley was among the most cited writers in the published version). He changed terminology, emphasis, and chapter titles. He apparently composed the conclusion of the work on page 140, Hayek's "final word." Emphasis on Hayek's agnostic religious views was not as prominent in Hayek's own versions of "The Fatal Conceit."

There was little reason for most of these changes. Most of the essential published work was Hayek's, but the form of expression and organization were not as true to his intention. In a December 11, 1986, letter, Hayek told Bartley that Bartley's initially revised version should not be published during Hayek's lifetime and that when it did appear, it should be under both their names. Hayek also expressed regret here that individuals past their middle eighties no longer possess the capacity for clear exposition of difficult ideas and that he had missed the opportunity to say what he wished while there was still time. Hayek also wrote, in an early 1987 letter to Walter Morris, promoter of Hayek's collected works, that while Bartley had improved the text, it had become as much Bartley's as Hayek's.

As Bartley continued to revise the manuscript during 1987, he made more changes. He began to shift the order and titles of volumes in *The Collected Works of F. A. Hayek,* although some of these changes were due to requests from the publisher. Bartley also considered changing the name of the collected works to "The Hayek Library."

The subtitle of "The Fatal Conceit," in its first part-one volume version, was initially to be the title of the first part, "The Taming of the Savage," not what it became, *The Errors of Socialism*. Hayek, in the title of the introduction to "The Fatal Conceit," merely asked, "Was socialism a mistake?"

As with many writers, Hayek had a tendency to overemphasize ideas on first presentation. As he refined his work, statements became more precise. However, under Bartley's editorial direction, both "The Fatal Conceit" and *The Collected Works of F. A. Hayek* moved in a more showy and flashy direction. Originally, for example, *The Counter-Revolution of Science* was to be titled in Hayek's collected works *The Counter-Revolution of Science*. Hayek wished it to be titled as one of his already published works. Under Bartley's general editorship, this work was retitled *The Uses and Abuses of Reason,* and Bartley moved its position, together with that of Hayek's other already published works. More recently, this volume—moved yet again from where it was originally intended and from where Bartley then moved it—has been listed to appear in Hayek's collected works in yet other places under the titles *The Demands of Science* and, now, *The Demons of Science* in two volumes. Hayek would undoubtedly have preferred *The Counter-Revolution of Science* in one volume. In addition, Hayek preferred that the essays in *Individualism and Economic Order* remain together in one volume of this title, rather than being split up as is now planned.

Bartley interpreted Hayek from a Popperian perspective. This results in a Bartleyean Hayek who was more concerned with the evolution of knowledge than Hayek was. Hayek's major point was epistemological limitations rather than the epistemological evolution of Bartley, who followed Popper and Donald T. Campbell.

When Bartley remarked that Hayek was (in Popperian terminology) a "fallibilist" and characterized Hayek's approach as an "evolutionary epistemology"—Bartley's own favored term—it is likely that he overstated these elements in Hayek's thought. To an extent, this may show through in the Bartley-edited published version, *The Fatal Conceit: The Errors of Socialism*. When, in the last paragraph of the introduction, it is stated (purportedly by Hayek): "I suggest that we need . . . an evolutionary epistemology," it is hard to know who was doing the talking here, Hayek or Bartley.

Indeed, in Hayek's own final introduction of "The Fatal Conceit," he apparently did not close on this note. While the document history of Hayek's drafts of the work is fragmentary and separated, enough information is available, including from private Hayek archival collections, reasonably to reconstruct what Hayek meant and what Bartley said. Bartley's changes to Hayek's final introduction from approximately 1985 provide a case example.

Hayek was a much better writer than Bartley. He wrote with power, conviction, and style. By way of contrast, Bartley's prose in *The Fatal Conceit: The Errors of Socialism* was academic. Hayek began the introduction of his own final version of "The Fatal Conceit" in these florid words: "The subject of this book is the inescapable fact that our civilization depends . . ." By way of contrast, Bartley's opening line was tepid and flat: "This book argues that our civilisation depends . . ." Also, while Hayek utilized the American spelling "civilization," Bartley preferred the British "civilisation," though in his writings after he left the University of Chicago, Hayek's English was neither uniformly American nor British.

Moreover, not only did Bartley begin the introduction of the published *The Fatal Conceit: The Errors of Socialism* on a weak note, but with the subtitle of the work as "*The Errors of Socialism,*" he advertised it as tendentious and polemical. Hayek came to favor the more provocatively simple "The Fatal Conceit." Bartley talked big in the title, as it were, but was diminutive in the opening line; Hayek was more modest in the title (and thus in the work's advertising) and attempted to entice the reader's interest through the opening line.

In addition, in the introduction, Hayek in his own version talked a little bit about the evolution of "The Fatal Conceit" through his earlier intended "The Abuse and Decline of Reason." Bartley removed this historical background. In his editorial foreword, Bartley made relatively favorable mention of Freud—which was regrettable, given Hayek's distaste for Freud (indeed, that distaste was some of the starting point for Hayek's writing of "The Fatal Conceit" in its earlier "The Three Sources of Human Values" form). Hayek concluded his introduction on the thundering note: "Socialism gravely endangers not only our present civilization but also the very lives of a very large part of present mankind." Bartley's conclusion in the published version was the far more tentative: "Surprising and paradoxical as it may seem to some to say this, these moral traditions outstrip the capacities of reason"—a Hayekian point, but not the point on which Hayek concluded his introduction.

Also characteristic of Bartley's editorial method was the book's preface, attributed to Hayek, but which Bartley apparently at least substantially wrote or altered. It was originally dated July 1986 but in the published version was dated April 1988. Since the preface concludes with Hayek thanking "Professor W. W. Bartley, III, of the Hoover Institution, Stanford University, who—when I fell ill for a time, just prior to the completion of the final draft—took this volume in hand and prepared it for the publishers," readers were misinformed as to Hayek's general recent participation in the book and intellectual activity level. This misinterpretation was heightened by Bartley's remark in his editorial foreword that *The Fatal Conceit: The Errors of Socialism* "is fresh from Hayek's hand"—when in fact Bartley had substantially molded the manuscript and Hayek had not worked on it for almost three years.

Hayek concluded a February 1979 talk on "The Fatal Conceit," just after he had originally conceived it as a debate challenge, that "I believe we can now demonstrate . . . that socialism is altogether based on an intellectual failure to comprehend the conditions under which we are able to produce enough to satisfy our expectations. And that will be, in a more elaborate form, my justification for proposing an affirmative answer to the challenge I am going to issue on the question, Was Socialism a Mistake?" This was Hayek's message in "The Fatal Conceit," not Bartley's philosophizing ending: "Perhaps what many people mean in speaking of God is just a personification of that tradition of moral values that keeps their community alive . . ." That Bartley apparently presumed, among myriad other stylistic and material changes, additions, and deletions, to compose Hayek's final words in what was intended to be Hayek's final work would have been beyond reproach.

Many more examples could be adduced. While the record on which the presentation here is made is incomplete and fragmentary, we can conclude that Bartley's version of *The Fatal Conceit: The Errors of Socialism* should be discarded and a new version as close as possible to Hayek's final written version of the entire "The Fatal Conceit" should be prepared. Bartley's version has distorted Hayek's final work and, because of the uncertainty regarding what was Bartley's and what was Hayek's, is leading to its reduced consideration and use, which is exactly the opposite of what Hayek would have wished.

Hayek collected works general editor Bruce Caldwell notes "interpretive puzzles surrounding Hayek's last book" and that "comparison between the finished and earlier manuscript version of *The Fatal Conceit* might . . . help us to decipher what Hayek originally had in mind." Peter Boettke writes that "Bartley was an extremely active editor . . . , and scholars are just beginning to assess not only the extent of the revisions made by Bartley—perhaps with or without Hayek's approval—and the judgement of whether the editorial changes made improved the manuscript or decreased the value of the final product." Intellectual historian Jerry Muller writes of his own work on Hayek and *The Fatal Conceit: The Errors of Socialism* that "I have not made much use of this volume because the question of how much of it was actually written by Hayek and how much by his editor, W. W. Bartley III, remains an open question among scholars."

At the same time, in this writer's opinion—based on review of many of Hayek's own preliminary drafts, almost all of which have not been generally available—the essential body of even the published *The Fatal Conceit: The Errors of Socialism* was mostly Hayek's. Bartley's dross was a veneer, though it obscured the jewel beneath.

Caldwell also says that in "the addition of new material and the cutting out of material already written . . . Bartley's role as editor was not a passive one." Caldwell is "leery of putting too much emphasis on Hayek's apparent new enthusiasm for Popperian themes in *The Fatal Conceit*," due to Bartley's role with the work. He speculates that "*acquiescence* rather than *endorsement* might best describe Hayek's attitude towards the new additions to his original manuscript," as a result of Hayek's ill health. Caldwell recalls that when he first read *The Fatal Conceit: The Errors of Socialism,* he thought it was "more a product of his [Bartley's] pen than Hayek's." Caldwell also reports that computer analysis of *The Fatal Conceit: The Errors of Socialism* indicates that another hand than Hayek's may have played a considerable role in its composition.

Critical Review editor Jeffrey Friedman provided the following recollection of Bartley's editorial technique in 1998:

> In 1986 I served as research assistant to W. W. Bartley, III, Hayek's officially designated biographer and the "editor" of the book [*The Fatal Conceit*]. . . . [T]he products of Bartley's labors were allegedly reviewed by Hayek. . . . The extent of Hayek's supervision of the project, however, is called into question by the appearance in the book, verbatim, of passages I submitted to Bartley as suggestions for how Hayek might consider updating his critique of constructivist rationalism. Among these are . . . passages mentioning Marcuse, Habermas, and Foucault. Since Hayek had not previously referred

to these figures in print, I was surprised to learn, upon the appearance of the book, that he would have accepted without alteration discussions of their work written by someone he had never met.

Friedman was a graduate student when Bartley incorporated this material into Hayek's final work.

Friedman also writes that Bartley thought that ideas go into the world and often take unpredictable paths that may not have been their author's intentions. He speculates that Bartley may have felt that Hayek's sanction of the *The Fatal Conceit: The Errors of Socialism* was unimportant.

Milton Friedman offered these views on the Bartley-edited version in 1995:

> Q: On *The Fatal Conceit,* there's sort of two schools of thought as to the extent to which Hayek pulled that together. What's your view?
> A: I've always been troubled by what role he played in that. I don't have enough knowledge to give you an answer. I don't think it's one of Hayek's better works. It's awfully forced. It's put into this form of, "I'm going to show you once and for all, by God, and after you hear this you'll have no answer to me whatsoever." It's not up to Hayek at his best.

A piece of contemporaneous correspondence in the small Bartley archive at the Hoover Institution provides insight into Bartley's editorial and writing techniques. In a January 16, 1988, letter to Leif Wenar, who was to edit the latter two parts of "The Fatal Conceit," Bartley encouraged Wenar, a graduate student at the time, to make very extensive changes in Hayek's manuscript drafts. He directed Wenar to compose introductions, conclusions, connective material, and summaries—all on behalf of Hayek—and to link the book with the first part and to compose its conclusion. Bartley had followed these methods in his own work on the first part; he told Wenar that he had massively edited it.

Part of the difficulty in disentangling Hayek's and Bartley's versions of "The Fatal Conceit" is that, between about 1979 and 1982, Hayek himself prepared a preliminary version of "The Fatal Conceit," which he subsequently discarded. James Buchanan has described this earlier version twice, once in a contemporaneous review of the published version of *The Fatal Conceit: The Errors of Socialism* and once in a reminiscence of Hayek. In the review, Buchanan wrote: "In August

1982, a small group of economists from several countries made a journey to Obergurgl, high in the Austrian Alps, for a two-day conference with Professor Hayek at his long-time summer habitat. The ostensible purpose of the conference was to criticize and discuss early manuscript versions of what was then projected to be a treatise, to be entitled *The Fatal Conceit*. I reveal no secrets when I state that the participants were skeptical, even after two-days discussion, about prospects for the circulated material to be transformed into a publishable book." He continued, in the reminiscence: "The work was eventually published, in one volume, . . . and we were quite pleased that the book had been markedly improved, due not only to Hayek's diligence in responding to our criticisms, but, probably, also to the help of William Bartley, who took over as editorial assistant in the final stages of preparation."

What Buchanan and others have apparently not been aware of is that Hayek largely discarded his first version of "The Fatal Conceit" after the Obergurgl meeting. Hayek then worked on a new version for about three years, from 1982 to 1985, completely without Bartley. Thus, "The Fatal Conceit" was largely improved from what Hayek presented to the Obergurgl conference in 1982, and Bartley diminished Hayek's final work product from 1985. Hayek's own, second version of "The Fatal Conceit" was not a casually written document, but one on which he worked for years and that he anticipated would be his last word and perhaps his most important work.

~

When *The Fatal Conceit: The Errors of Socialism* was published in late 1988, it received respectful and admiring, though not uncritical, reviews. At this point Hayek had not really been heard from for several years. He continued to be reasonably prominent throughout the first half of the 1980s and the question in the minds of many was whether he was working on another book, but after about 1985 the number of stories on his activities declined. He was not interviewed as frequently by the media, if at all.

The review in the *Economist* was perhaps the most favorable: "Friedrich Hayek, author of *The Road to Serfdom* and *The Constitution of Liberty,* will be ninety this year. Remarkably, his new book is as passionate and disputatious as anything he has written. . . . [I]t is a fully accessible account of many of the main strands of Mr. Hayek's thinking. . . . Despite its brevity, the book ranges over economics, political philosophy, religion, ethics and evolution."

Other reviews were more mixed. Oxford political philosopher David Miller's review was among the most critical. *The Fatal Conceit: The Errors of Socialism,* Miller held, is "repetitive, poorly organized, and above all fails to display that clarity of thought and expression which has in the past been such a distinguished feature of Hayek's work. I believe that many of Hayek's admirers will wish privately that the book had not been published, his reputation in political thought left to rest instead on his major works *The Constitution of Liberty* and *Law, Legislation and Liberty.*"

Arthur Seldon wrote that Hayek "*was* [emphasis added] careful with precise language"—that is, this was not the case in *The Fatal Conceit: The Errors of Socialism*—and also observed "words in the book that strike a former editor of Hayek's IEA texts as unHayekian." He concluded his review on the more positive note: "Hayek has shed light on many facets of human activity by his critical insights into the origins and development of co-operation, in the 'extended order' of the market, between individuals who know nothing of one another but yet who serve one another. . . ."

Terence Hutchison, writing in the *Economic Journal,* enunciated these favorable sentiments: "Hayek develops an intellectually wide-ranging thesis, involving law, psychology, economics, and cultural evolution, supported by an erudition stupendous in its breadth and depth." Other reviewers also complimented the interdisciplinary nature of the work. According to Lawrence Connin: "While some will contest many of his broad historical generalizations and will find his views on morality decidedly tilted toward commercial or market values, *The Fatal Conceit* is an important and original work in the classical liberal tradition."

A number, though, did not find much new in Hayek's final work. Christopher Nock, remarking on the introduction's title, "Was Socialism a Mistake?," commented that Hayek's answer, "which will come as no surprise to anyone familiar with his previous writings, is that it was." For Ian Steadman: "Although the book contains thought-provoking passages, it would seem unlikely that this first volume of Hayek's *Collected Works* will, in the long term, come to be seen as one of his most important contributions." This evaluation has proved correct of the Bartley-edited *The Fatal Conceit: The Errors of Socialism.*

Hayek expressed both pleasure and displeasure at Bartley's edition. On one hand, he wrote to Bartley more than once that he improved it. On the other, according to Hayek's secretary, Charlotte Cubitt, so extensive were Bartley's revisions that, when Hayek first saw the published version, he said he hardly recognized it.

Both of these remarks should be discounted as those of a very old man who was not always in control of his faculties. Hayek finally agreed to publication of Bartley's version of "The Fatal Conceit" after encouragement from Bartley because, according to Cubitt, "Bartley had spent so much time and effort on it."

The message of *The Fatal Conceit* could be obscured in the circumstances surrounding its writing, but this would be unfortunate. Hayek's idea was that through intellectually understanding the sources of socialism in human emotion, and through understanding the capitalist libertarian morals and values that allow the greatest economic production, humanity could produce the most and be happiest. If human empirical understanding of capitalism changed, then so would humanity's moral perspective of it, thereby allowing its greater realization.

This idea rests on the larger idea that there is a connection between the words a writer writes and future activity in the material world of the senses. One need not agree with Keynes or Hayek that the ideas of the political philosopher or economist have the import that they ascribed to them to recognize that their ideas have some influence and therefore that the activities of political philosophy and economic theorizing are worthwhile.

The idea that economists and political philosophers can influence human activity through their words is inspiring. Hayek thought that, by enlightening human understanding, he could help to pave the way for greater human cooperation and economic progress through "The Fatal Conceit."

Clearly, a new version of "The Fatal Conceit," comprised of Hayek's final drafts for all the chapters in the May 1985 table of contents, should be prepared and published. Fortunately, most, perhaps all, of these chapter drafts exist.

19

Sundown

AMONG THE FINAL PROJECTS ON WHICH HAYEK WAS WORKING WHEN HIS active career concluded in the summer of 1985 was an entry for *The New Palgrave: A Dictionary of Economics* on the Austrian school of economics. He had written on the Austrian school frequently during his career, and most of this essay covered earlier ground. However, he planned to add a section on developments in the Austrian tradition since the 1930s that he had not previously considered.

Hayek here wrote that, in contrast to Keynesianism and Mises's position, "the present writer, then largely unaware that he was merely developing a rather neglected part of the Mengerian tradition, contended that while it was true that the pure logic of choice by which the Austrian theory interpreted individual action was indeed purely deductive, as soon as the explanation moved to the interpersonal activities of the market, the crucial processes were those by which information was transmitted among individuals, and as such were purely empirical." He retained all of his faculties through the summer of 1985.

The final major award that Hayek received was the American Medal of Freedom from President George Bush on November 25, 1991, when he was ninety-two. He could not be present to accept this award, but his son did on his father's behalf. Larry Hayek read these dictated remarks from his father: "I have always been an admirer of the United States, and I have for many years been trying to teach the rest of the world what they could learn from that country." This was his last public word.

Hayek saw communism and the Berlin Wall fall. He wrote in a December 1990 letter to Ed Crane, president of the Washington D.C.–based

Cato Institute, that he could not be more pleased than to observe "the ultimate victory of our side in the long dispute of the principles of the free market, and will at the moment only say that I hardly expected to live to experience this."

In a question-and-answer session following a talk he gave, published by the Hoover Institution in 1983, he had this exchange:

> Q: Professor Hayek, you made a very optimistic statement with respect to the impending failure of communism. What is the basis of your optimism that communism is failing?
>
> A: I would not dare to make any predictions of what is going to happen in Russia. . . . But I will confess that my remark was inspired by one particular experience, not very long ago.
>
> I think it was last May, that in my London club I happened to sit on the same table as a Russian scientist, who had come to Western Europe for the first time to attend a scientific conference. He spoke quite good English, so I could ask him what surprised him most on visiting Western Europe. His answer was: "You still have so many Marxists. We haven't any!"

In a November 1, 1983, address at the Hoover Institution, Hayek said that "planned evolution would be the end of evolution itself." The problem he identified was that mankind does not understand the beneficial role that manners, ethics, rules, and law play in a free society. His object was to instruct others in this truth. If humanity understood the positive role that capitalist or libertarian rules play, we should embrace them. He placed his hope for the future of humanity ultimately in the expansion of knowledge, including the knowledge of which we are not, or are not now, verbally aware.

Through following the rules of libertarian order, humanity can, Hayek thought, "build better than it knows." In his later work, he began to emphasize the family more. "The two crucial groups of rules of conduct," he said in his 1983 Hoover Institution talk, are those of private property "and those concerning the family."

The diminution and eventual elimination of much scarcity—which is the economic problem—should be, he believed, a question of knowledge on which reasonable people ought to be able to agree. Once intellectual understanding of the virtues of a free market existed, much societal peace would follow. In this case, humanity's natural inclinations for solidarity, communality, and sociality would be met through the intellectual appreciation that market rules and capitalist morals lead to the most abundant and flourishing life for all.

Hayek died in Freiburg, Germany, on March 23, 1992, less than two months shy of his ninety-third birthday. After 1985, he was unable to work and lost contact with almost all friends and associates. In his last years, almost the only people with whom he had regular contact were his wife, Helene; secretary Charlotte Cubitt, whom he always called "Mrs. Cubitt"; children Larry and Christine Hayek; and Bartley. Hayek was grateful to Cubitt for her assistance from 1977 to 1992. He inscribed in her copy of *The Fatal Conceit* in 1990: "In gratitude for all her help over so many years F. A. Hayek."

During his last years, he had periods of more and less lucidity, as well as being ill and depressed. Lord Harris of the Institute of Economic Affairs wrote in his obituary of Hayek that "by 1989 the great man had lost touch with affairs." He was buried in Vienna, the place of his birth.

John Maynard Keynes wrote: "The ideas of economists and political philosophers, both when they are right and when they are wrong, are more powerful than is commonly understood. Indeed the world is ruled by little else. Practical men, who believe themselves to be quite exempt from any intellectual influences, are usually the slave of some defunct economist. Madmen in authority, who hear voices in the air, are distilling their frenzy from some academic scribbler of a few years back." Friedrich Hayek was the greatest political philosopher of liberty during the twentieth century.

Conclusion

HAYEK'S ARGUMENT IN *THE FATAL CONCEIT* WAS HISTORICAL and factual. Classical socialism defined as government ownership of the means of economic production literally cannot deliver the goods (and services) because the division of knowledge renders central economic control highly inefficient. He maintained a scientific view of his calling to the end. His goal was in largest part to put forward factual understandings of the world—of the way the world is and could be.

Hayek became less able to express his new ideas as he grew older—he saw the insights and connections but could not articulate them in words. At the same time, what he said could be of the highest quality. In the *Festschrift* for Arthur Seldon, *The Unfinished Agenda,* in which some of Hayek's final writing is contained, he wrote of his conception of economic activity. Explaining the role of prices in overcoming the division of knowledge was perhaps his greatest achievement:

> In 1936 . . . I suddenly saw, as I prepared my Presidential Address to the London Economic Club, that my previous work in different branches of economics had a common root. This insight was that the price system was really an instrument which enabled millions of people to adjust their efforts to events, demands and conditions, of which they had no concrete, direct knowledge. . . . The problem I had first identified in studying industrial fluctuations—that false price signals misdirected human efforts—I then followed up in various other branches of the discipline. . . .
>
> Here my thinking was inspired largely by Ludwig von Mises' conception of the problem of ordering a planned economy. . . .
>
> I gradually found that the basic function of economics was to explain the process of how human activity adapted itself to data about which it had no information. Thus the whole economic order rested on the fact that by using prices as a guide, or as signals, we were led to serve the demands and enlist the powers and capacities of people of whom we knew nothing. . . . [T]he insight that prices were signals

> bringing about ... unforeseen co-ordination ... became the leading idea behind my work.
>
> ... [I]t has taken me something like fifty years to be able to put it as briefly and in as few words as I have just attempted; even ten years ago I could not have put it as succinctly.

To convince the leaders of public opinion of "this truth" became Hayek's major project, and in considerable part he succeeded in this task. He wrote in the published version of *The Fatal Conceit,* in sentiments that were largely his alone: "The dispute between the market order and socialism is no less than a matter of survival. To follow socialist morality would destroy much of present [man]kind and impoverish much of the rest." Classical socialism is dead.

The division of knowledge is the factual premise on which economic systems and societies should be based. The fragmentation of knowledge renders central government control of an economy impossible, he argued. The best societies and economies are those that recognize and accommodate divided knowledge.

He emphasized that as a result of inevitable imperfections in human knowledge and communication, free market order is the most productive. It overcomes the division of knowledge and the absence of verbal knowledge. The great insight toward the end of his career that he attempted to enunciate in "The Fatal Conceit" is that humanity's instinctive emotions are often at war with the morals, rules, and laws necessary to sustain free market order. Through understanding this conflict, humanity may resolve it.

The struggle between the advocates of free market order and of classical socialism is not, Hayek concluded, a moral but an intellectual one: "The main point of my argument is ... that the conflict between ... advocates of the spontaneous extended human order created by a competitive market ... [and] those who demand a deliberate arrangement of human interaction by central authority based on collective command over available resources is due to a factual error by the latter about how knowledge of these resources is and can be generated and utilised. As a question of fact, this conflict must be settled by scientific study." "I am now profoundly convinced," he believed, "of what I had only hinted at before, namely, that the struggle between the advocates of a free society and the advocates of the socialist system is not a moral but an *intellectual* conflict." "What I am trying to do in *The Fatal Conceit* is to show that their [classical socialists'] argument is wholly based on factual mistakes." The division of knowledge, Hayek thought, precludes classical socialism. Ignorance of this truth, he believed, was the greatest obstacle to increased and improved economic production.

Now, of course, through the Internet and other improvements in communication technology, it is possible to centralize knowledge and decision making as never before. To the extent that Hayek's arguments for free market order rest on the inability to centralize knowledge and decision making, circumstances are likely to change—perhaps dramatically—in the years ahead.

John Stuart Mill wrote 150 years ago in his great work *Utilitarianism:* "No one whose opinion deserves a moment's consideration can doubt that most of the great . . . evils of the world are in themselves removable, and will, if human affairs continue to improve, be in the end reduced within narrow limits. Poverty, in any sense implying suffering, may be completely extinguished by the wisdom of society. . . . Even that most intractable of enemies, disease, may be indefinitely reduced in dimensions. . . . All the grand sources . . . of human suffering are in a great degree, many of them almost entirely, conquerable by human care and effort."

The economic problem for much of the world is close to being solved. While, particularly in sub-Saharan Africa, extreme privation regularly occurs, almost every other major population area on earth is now in better shape. There is no reason that this trend of improvement should not continue. In short, as Mill had it, almost all the main sources of human suffering may be conquered by "human care and effort." The greatest human population combined with the highest standard of living is both the utilitarian and the libertarian vision.

It is impossible to say what institutions, laws, policies, and ideas are most likely to guide humanity in the future. In his later years, Hayek gave some consideration to the work of John Rawls, who would perhaps be considered, together with Hayek and Leo Strauss, one of the three greatest political philosophers of the twentieth century. Rawls had a highly liberal (in a twentieth-century sense) perspective. His idea of a "difference principle" (sometimes also referred to as "maximin"—maximizing the status of the minimum class) may prove lasting.

This Rawlsian idea is that society's laws and rules should be structured so that those who are least well off in the society in question would have the highest standard of living as in any other possible society at the point in time. While Rawls thought that this would, empirically, result in societies in which material rewards would be quite evenly possessed, there is no reason that this should necessarily be the case.

As human knowledge of genetics increases, it becomes clearer that environmental explanations for many human abilities, capacities, and talents are not as strong as they appeared even two decades ago. The idea that, for example, being good at math or language or art is strictly or even mostly an environmental outcome is increasingly becoming considered not to be the case.

If individual humanity's talents are inherently diverse, it is likely that this diversity would manifest itself in social diversity. Diversity of social outcomes would be unexpected and would be especially unjust in a society in which everyone were innately identical.

The largely natalocracy that existed everywhere until a century ago—whereby those in positions of authority and wealth did not necessarily have ability, and those with ability did not necessarily have authority and wealth; economic position was largely a matter of birth—was especially unjust to able individuals of the lower classes. Intellectuals were a larger part of the working-class movement early in the twentieth century than is the case sixty to one hundred years later. Moreover, the injustice of not being able to rise to positions justified by their merits must have been particularly galling to truly intelligent and able individuals, when many positions of authority and wealth were held by persons almost exclusively on the basis of birth, and when genuine poverty existed among large numbers of intact families with no government safety net and a much lower standard of living than is today the case.

Democratic capitalist societies have become more meritocratic than any societies and economies in history, and their economic productivity demonstrates this reality. The freedom to exchange goods and services that capitalism allows has resulted in the greatest economic production ever. While democratic and capitalist meritocracy is by no means perfect, it is more effective than any previous system. There is no reason to assume that a society in which the living standard of the minimum class is maximized would be egalitarian. In fact, the opposite may be true.

Once the basics of food, clothing, shelter, education, and healthcare are guaranteed to every person in a society, as is more or less the case in every developed economy in the world today, the issues of social minima assume different character. Prime Minister Margaret Thatcher once argued in the House of Commons that the Conservative Party favored a society in which everyone at every step on the economic ladder would have the most, even if this resulted in more inequality, while the Labour Party preferred a society in which there would be more equality, even though everyone at every step on the economic ladder would have less.

Socialism and communism are no more dead today than capitalism was during the 1930s and 1940s. The ideas behind the words of socialism and communism—of greater equality in the possession of the fruits of collective effort and of the abolition of private property—will undoubtedly find support again, though perhaps not for decades. Now is the time of the entrepreneur. One of the great contributions of Austrian economists from Joseph Schumpeter to Israel Kirzner is to emphasize entrepreneurs, who typically possess tacit or implicit, as opposed to verbal or explicit, knowledge. They cannot necessarily say how they do what they do, but their works speak for themselves.

The relationship between the tacit knowledge of entrepreneurs and profits is vital to capitalistic production. In a capitalist system, the ability of entrepreneurs to make profits is what allows them to direct continually greater amounts of resources. When Hayek referred to competition as a discovery procedure, he meant in part that through competition, the individuals who are best at utilizing resources receive more profits and thus the ability to continue their trade. Those who are not as effective at using resources do not. Collected works general editor Bruce Caldwell describes Hayek's conception of tacit knowledge: " . . . the skills of craftsmen or athletes, the 'knowledge how' to perform certain 'hard to do' tasks. People who possess such skills typically cannot state how they do what they do." Not all knowledge is verbal.

Hayek early considered that the subtitle for the whole three-part *The Fatal Conceit* should have been *The Intellectual Error of Socialism*. He disagreed with socialists primarily about facts, not values, which is why the subtitle (apparently reinserted and modified by Bartley) of the published version of the work, *The Errors of Socialism,* was misleading. Hayek's point was the narrower, intellectual one.

∽

"Life has no purpose but itself," Hayek wrote in *The Fatal Conceit* (in words that apparently were his own)—to be abundant, overflowing, joyous. Classical socialists and present-day libertarians do not necessarily disagree about values. They disagree about facts. They disagree about the best way to produce the most goods and the most services for the most people. There is no necessary division among socialists, libertarians, and communists in values. Indeed, libertarianism might be said to emanate from socialism (just as socialism emanated from classical liberalism) and to be consistent with communism, to the extent that all seek the greatest material wealth or happiness for the greatest number.

The explosion of communicative technology, particularly and especially of the written word, and of other technological knowledge render greater centralization of societies, hierarchicalization of decision-making, and expansion of multinational police power to patrol the world for potential weapons of mass destruction all but inevitable in the immediate future. The world of 2013 may bear little resemblance to that of 2003. While classical socialism in the form of government ownership and management of the means of economic production proved unsuccessful during the twentieth century, this does not imply that the idea of socialism—as greater equality in the possession of the fruits of collective effort—is dead. Indeed, it likely will rise again with renewed vigor, both domestically and throughout the world.

Those days should not come too soon. John Stuart Mill, again, held as long ago as the middle of the nineteenth century that it would be better for the efforts of mankind to be employed in economic pursuits than in those of war and violence. Capitalism is a peaceful creed.

Focus on increased wealth for all is typically positive because the only way that this can come about is through production of many more goods and services for billions of people. Classical twentieth-century socialism in the form of government ownership and management of the means of economic production exactly reversed the true socialist idea. The core idea of socialism is not greater equality in the production of wealth; it is greater equality in the *possession* of wealth.

In a growing economy, there is no reason why there cannot be both increasing absolute resources directed to government and a gradually reducing government role. There is no necessary correlation between an increasing absolute government role in a society and an increasing relative role, although, of course, the former makes the latter more likely. For the immediate future, however, much of the goal should be, as it was during the nineteenth century, to reduce the excrescences of government that result in so much material and economic waste and prevent people from living their lives as they please.

Hayek's view of the ethical good was not exclusively material. He acknowledged that there is great natural beauty, and he emphasized the virtues of the mind above all else. However, he concluded "The Moral Imperative of the Market": "At this critical juncture for the kind of civilisation that we have built up, the most important contribution an economist can make is to insist that we can fulfil our responsibility to sustain our existing population only by continuing to rely on the market system, which brought this enlarged population into existence in the first place." He wrote in *The Constitution of Liberty* a quarter of a century before: "At this moment, when the greater part of mankind has only just awakened to the possibility of abolishing starvation, filth, and disease; when it has just been touched by the expanding wave of modern technology after centuries or millennia of relative stability; . . . even a small decline in our rate of advance might be fatal to us."

Only continued material development may literally preserve the planet. Self-described "environmentalists" who, in the name of protecting the earth, attempt to stop progress in fact may condemn the earth to destruction. Only further technological development will allow billions of people to have the standard of living now enjoyed in western Europe and the United States.

Spiritual values are the highest values. The philosophical-moral view on which Hayek's proposals for optimal government, state, and societal order were based is that all people everywhere should have the highest standard of living possible. This was his moral intent. He did not believe in God, but he thought that individuals should do what they can to make the world as good a place as it can be for themselves and for others. This is what he sought to do.

The only answer to the higher standard of living for all that Hayek sought is the creation of much more wealth, not the redistribution of existing wealth. Capitalism will remain as long as it is the most productive economic system. When this day passes, so, too, will capitalism. Capitalists who insist on the necessity of capitalism themselves display the fatal conceit. The libertarian age—the age of peace and plenty—is here, a time of the highest quality of life for the most people around the world.

Bibliographical Essay

THIS BIBLIOGRAPHICAL ESSAY IS DIVIDED INTO THREE PARTS. IN THE FIRST, development of *The Collected Works of F. A. Hayek* is discussed. In the second, consideration is given to Hayek's relationship with Jews, as a result of Melvin Reder's recent "The Anti-Semitism of Some Eminent Economists." In the third, brief presentation is made of a number of books and articles, mostly by authors in the contemporary Austrian movement in academic economics, on Austrian economic and Hayekian topics. Finally, this essay concludes with an appeal that private archival collections of Hayek materials should be made generally accessible.

Before commencing these topics, it should be said that the Friedrich Hayek Scholars' Page website maintained by Greg Ransom is the best source to find out more about and to discuss Hayek (www.Hayekcenter.org). John Gray, in *Hayek on Liberty* (1984), has an excellent bibliography of works by and about Hayek (though the bibliography was deleted from the 1998 3rd edition). This writer's *Friedrich Hayek: A Biography* (2001) also provides bibliographical information (pp. 325–46).

DEVELOPMENT OF THE COLLECTED WORKS OF F. A. HAYEK

I remarked in chapter 18 that William Bartley, first general editor of *The Collected Works of F. A. Hayek,* launched the series on the wrong foot. This essay is an appropriate place to discuss development of *The Collected Works.*

Hayek was not enamored with the idea of Keynes's collected works as a whole. In his centennial recollection of Keynes, published by the *Economist* on June 11, 1983, and presumably written a few months before, he concluded: "Inspired geniuses possessing a great power of conviction are not necessarily a blessing for the society in which they spring up. John Maynard Keynes was undoubtedly one of the great men of his age, . . . but hardly the great scientist whose growing insight moves along a single path. His *Collected Writings,* 'chiefly in the field of economics' and now approaching the thirtieth volume, are certainly a most revealing documentation of the intellectual movements of his time. But an economist may feel some doubt whether this distinction, for which Newton, Darwin, and great British philosophers all still have to wait, is not rather a token of the idolatry he enjoyed among his personal admirers than proportionate to his contribution to the advance of scientific knowledge" (p. 41).

Hayek thus placed the distinction of a collected works in the highest company of scientific advance. According to Stephen Kresge, who became general editor of *The Collected Works* after Bartley's death in 1990, it was during 1983 that Walter Morris, an Arkansas businessman, persuaded Hayek that a collected works should appear.

The collected works foreseen and planned by Hayek and Bartley was substantially different from what it has become. Bruce Caldwell, Kresge's successor as general editor, writes of the "often brilliant but also sometimes idiosyncratic arrangement of pieces" (*The Independent Review* [Fall 2001], p. 263) by Bartley of

Hayek's works—which was the case as the volumes began to appear, starting with
The Fatal Conceit: The Errors of Socialism in 1988.

As of 1985, an approximately twenty-eight-volume Hayek collected works was
foreseen:

Part I: Books published by Hayek
1. *Money, Capital and Fluctuations: Early Essays*
2. *Monetary Theory and the Trade Cycle*
3. *Prices and Production*
4. *Monetary Nationalism and International Stability*
5. *Profits, Interest and Investment*
6. *The Pure Theory of Capital*
7. *The Road to Serfdom*
8. *Individualism and Economic Order*
9. *John Stuart Mill and Harriet Taylor*
10. *The Counter-Revolution of Science*
11. *The Sensory Order*
12. *The Constitution of Liberty*
13. *Studies in Philosophy, Politics and Economics*
14. *Law, Legislation and Liberty*
15. *New Studies in Philosophy, Politics, Economics and the History of Ideas*
16. *The Fatal Conceit* (in three parts)

Part II: New collections of previously published papers
17. Essays in the history of economics and biography
18. Essays in economics and politics
19. Essays in public policy
20. Essays in money (including *The Denationalisation of Money*)
21. Essays in political philosophy

Part III. Documents, correspondence, and unpublished manuscripts
22. Early letters and letters to the editor
23. *The Battle with Keynes and Cambridge;* correspondence, documents
24. *The Battle with Socialism;* correspondence, documents
25. *The Battle Turns;* correspondence, documents (this would include material on
    the Mont Pelerin Society)
26. Correspondence, documents; particularly with Karl Popper and regarding *The
    Sensory Order*
27. Interviews with Hayek
28. Index

("Prospectus: The Collected Works of Friedrich A. von Hayek" [1985])

By way of contrast, volume 6, the most recently published of *The Collected
Works of F. A. Hayek,* lists the following order (with year of publication following al-
ready-published volumes):

***The Collected Works of F. A. Hayek* (as of 1999)**
1. The Fatal Conceit: The Errors of Socialism (1988)
2. The Sensory Order and Other Essays
3. The Trend of Economic Thinking: Essays on Political Economists and
   Economic History (1991)

4. The Fortunes of Liberalism and the Austrian School: Essays on Austrian Economics and the Ideal of Freedom (1992)
5. Good Money, Part I: The New World (1999)
6. Good Money, Part II: The Standard (1999)
7. The Demons of Science: On the Uses and Abuses of Reason
8. The Demons of Science: Economics and Knowledge
9. Contra Keynes and Cambridge: Essays, Correspondence (1995)
10. Socialism and War: Essays, Documents, Reviews (1997)
11. Prices, Production and Monetary Theory
12. Investigations in Economics
13. *The Pure Theory of Capital*
14. *The Road to Serfdom*
15. *The Constitution of Liberty*
16. Philosophy, Politics, and Economics
17. *Law, Legislation and Liberty*
18. Essays on Liberty
19. *John Stuart Mill and Harriet Taylor*
Supplement: Hayek on Hayek: An Autobiographical Dialogue (1994)

Bartley thought that he knew better than Hayek how Hayek's collected works should be titled and structured. He used the authority that Hayek gave him to the utmost to implant his vision on the series as Hayek became ill and decrepit. Of the sixteen titles of published works that Hayek intended to be volumes in his collected works, Bartley and Kresge's version of the series would retain only seven. Where Hayek intended his sixteen major works to form the body and start of the series, they are relegated to a secondary and subsidiary role in *The Collected Works*. Moreover, the titles of other volumes have been completely changed and moved. It is a positive sign that Caldwell foresees as many as ten additional volumes in the series than now planned.

Karl Popper had significant, inadvertent influence on Hayek's collected works, as not just Bartley, but Bartley's close friend, Stephen Kresge, became their general editor as a result of Bartley's original selection. Also, Popper recommended Kresge to Hayek in 1990 to succeed Bartley. Popper's correspondence with Hayek, in 1990 about Bartley's successor, was briefer and more distant in tone than had previously been the case. Popper remained uncommonly loyal to Bartley after the latter edited his *Postscript to the Logic of Scientific Discovery*. It is unknown to what extent Bartley may have encouraged Popper to write to Hayek on Kresge's behalf. Another influence on Hayek was his son, Larry, who thought well of Kresge.

According to David Theroux, who organized several conferences, talks, and publications by Hayek during the later 1970s and early 1980s and is now president of the Oakland-based Independent Institute, the crucial factor in Bartley's selection as Hayek's biographer was his relationship with Popper. Theroux remembers Hayek telling him that he wished that he could have been as successful as Popper. Charlotte Cubitt, too, remembers that Hayek selected Bartley to be his biographer and literary executor largely due to his desire to achieve Popper's success.

Theroux remembers this interaction with Hayek at the 1984 Mont Pelerin Society meeting in Cambridge: "I had the chance to sit down and casually speak with Hayek in the lobby of the hotel in which he was staying and speaking with various people. I asked him how he was doing and what he was involved with currently. He mentioned to me the collected works project and how highly he thought of Bartley's work with Popper. He mentioned how he was flattered that people might wish to pursue such a project and that he was hoping that a possible series of his work might also get favorable treatment because of Bartley's work for Popper" (September 7, 2002, correspondence from Theroux to author).

Publishing constraints and commercial factors were two of the reasons for the changes from the original plan for Hayek's collected works. The University of Chicago Press would not publish certain volumes of Hayek's collected works until earlier copies of these volumes that were in stock were sold, for example. Also, fund raising affected the ability to issue as many as twenty-eight volumes in a series.

It is sometimes said that Bartley did not write his biography of Hayek (as of Popper) because of his premature death, but this is not the whole story. Bartley also did not complete this projects because, for the last four and a half years of his career, from about the middle of 1985 through the end of 1989, he was busy with other projects—rewiting "The Fatal Conceit" and his *Unfathomed Knowledge, Unmeasured Wealth,* as well as other activities of his own. He had the time to write Hayek's biography in the seven years he lived after being given its commission (and longer, for Popper's biography).

Bartley began to have intimations of his mortality as early as mid-1985, when he was fifty-one. In a July 22, 1985, letter to Antony Fisher, initiator of the Institute of Economic Affair and someone who helped to start several other free market think tanks and institutes around the world, Bartley suggested that a committee be established to act as Hayek's literary executor, in part in case of his own premature death. This was a different sentiment from the one he enunciated just a few months earlier in the February 1985 preface to the revised edition of *Wittgenstein.* He wrote then that this work was "a small part of a larger work, as yet unfinished, which I hope one day to publish. This larger work, in several volumes, contains biographies and critical studies of the work of Sir Karl Popper and of F. A. von Hayek, as well as a longer study of Wittgenstein" (*Wittgenstein,* 2nd ed. [La Salle, Ill.: Open Court, 1994], 12). In addition, he hoped to write a biography of Keynes. All of these projects would have taken many years. Hayek's collected works was foreseen as at least a decade-long project.

It is inconceivable that a true scholar would have embarked on a major ten- to twelve-year project such as *The Collected Works of F. A. Hayek* plus Hayek's and Popper's biographies if he knew he only had a few years to live. Assuming, therefore, that Bartley learned of his fatal illness only after he became Popper's and Hayek's biographer, Hayek's literary editor, and general editor of *The Collected Works of F. A. Hayek* (to assume otherwise of him would make his actions completely reprehensible), it cannot be said that he left any of these in good shape, as, indeed, Bartley wrote in late correspondence to Hayek and Popper. Bartley began to experience serious health difficulties as early as 1984, when he was in Freiburg and had to go to the hospital. Earlier in his life, he suffered from insomnia.

Bartley was ill from about July 1989 until his death in February 1990, though he gave a paper on Popper's early life, a chapter from his intended "Karl Popper: A Life," at a Mont Pelerin Society conference in New Zealand in November. Bartley had been very concerned about his health, and thought that he might die, in July 1989, he wrote in a letter to Hayek at this time, but only sent months later. Bartley, who at one time was not to publish his biography of Hayek until after Hayek died, died before Hayek.

Kresge—Bartley's close friend, intellectual interlocutor, traveling companion, and significant other—became general editor of *The Collected Works of F. A. Hayek* following Bartley's death in 1990. During Bartley's last illness and subsequent death, there was a certain amount of jockeying about and concern expressed by various people interested in Hayek's legacy. Not a great deal about these machinations is known at this time. Kresge appears to have emerged as general editor in part because of Popper's recommendation. Hayek was close to ninety-one, and incapacitated, when Bartley died. At one point, Hayek may have reconsidered the appointment of Kresge as general editor;

however, Kresge disputes that this was the case. Kresge was not and had not been affiliated with an academic institution in a professional capacity, and had little to no publishing record, when he became general editor of *The Collected Works of F. A. Hayek*.

As with Bartley's general editorship, not all academics and scholars were pleased with Kresge's effects on *The Collected Works of F. A. Hayek*. Peter Boettke, editor of the *Review of Austrian Economics,* wrote on the transition of the general editorship from Kresge to Caldwell: "I always considered it a huge 'mistake' that accidents of history landed the project in his [Kresge's] hands. For that matter, I consider Bartley's involvement a mistake" (July 20, 2002 Hayek-List communication).

In his 1988 recollection of interaction with Hayek, Bartley wrote that when Hayek asked him to write his biography, he "made three firm conditions to insure my independence: I was to have a completely free hand and access to all materials; the book, however, was not only not to be published during his lifetime, but I also must pledge not even to show him a draft" ("Hayek's *Collected Works:* Background," *Institute Scholar* [Winter 1988], p. 1). This same standard of accessibility to all materials, was not practiced by *The Collected Works of F. A. Hayek* during the tenure of its first two general editors.

Popper scholars also have not had access to Popper materials now in the Bartley Institute. According to one prominent Popper scholar, there is likely considerable material of interest in that archive, based on the paper Bartley gave in 1989 on Popper's early life. This paper, a chapter from Bartley's intended Popper biography, reflected extensive interviewing and research, according to the scholar, though it was not always accurate.

During Kresge's general editorship, from 1990 to 2002, *The Collected Works of F. A. Hayek* continued to move farther afield from the original plan drafted with Hayek's participation. Kresge continued progression of the series away from the provisional plan.

During his dozen years, Kresge coedited (with Bartley) the second volume to appear in Hayek's collected works, volume 3, *The Trend of Economic Thinking: Essays on Political Economists and Economic History* (1991); oversaw publication of three volumes by others: vol. 4, *The Fortunes of Liberalism and the Austrian School: Essays on Austrian Economics and the Ideal of Freedom* (Peter Klein, ed., 1992), vol. 9, *Contra Keynes and Cambridge: Essays, Correspondence* (Bruce Caldwell, ed., 1995), and vol. 10, *Socialism and War: Essays, Documents, Reviews* (Bruce Caldwell, ed., 1997); coedited, with Leif Wenar, the supplement *Hayek on Hayek: An Autobiographical Dialogue* (1994); and edited two volumes himself in the collected works, vol. 5, *Good Money, Part I: The New World* (1999), and vol. 6, *Good Money, Part II: The Standard* (1999). Kresge stepped down as general editor of *The Collected Works of F. A. Hayek* in May 2002, and Caldwell then became general editor.

Ronald Hamowy, in a review of *Hayek on Hayek* in *Philosophy of the Social Sciences* (September 1996), criticizes Kresge's presentation in its introduction of John Nef's remark that Hayek did not receive a position in the economics department at the University of Chicago because *The Road to Serfdom* was too popular a book for a respectable scholar to publish. "What is left out," Hamowy writes, "is the fact that the leading members of the Economics Department were unalterably opposed to Hayek's joining the department in large part because of his connection with the Austrian school, which they viewed as somewhat disreputable" (p. 420). Hamowy was a student of Hayek's on the Committee on Social Thought at Chicago.

Milton Friedman provides these thoughts on *Hayek on Hayek* in a December 28, 1993, letter to Alex Philipson of the the University of Chicago Press: "I found Hayek's own comments on himself extremely interesting. However, I found the comments of the editors on the whole superficial. They do not do justice to Hayek and they contain statements that I think are simply wrong" (December 28, 1993 letter from Friedman to A. Philipson, copy in the possession of author); in conversation, Friedman was even sharper regarding Kresge's introduction (Friedman-Ebenstein interview, 1995).

Of the over eighty interview exchanges attributed to the "W. W. Bartley III audiotape archive, 1984–88" (p. xi) in *Hayek on Hayek,* about half—over forty—are not from interviews between Hayek and Bartley, but from a 1985 interview between Hayek and Gary North and Mark Skousen. Yet this interview is not identified as a source of *Hayek on Hayek,* despite the fact that seven other non-Bartley interviews, with less material than from the Hayek-North/Skousen interview, are separately identified. As a result, *Hayek on Hayek* appears to derive substantially more from Bartley's interviews with Hayek than is the case.

After the Hayek-North/Skousen material is excluded, only about one-ninth or so, at most, of *Hayek on Hayek* consists of Bartley interview exchanges. (It is not known to what extent other interview exchanges identified as from the Bartley audiotape archive might be from interviews other than those Bartley conducted.) This misperception is heightened by the front matter and foreword to *Hayek on Hayek,* which contain extensive reference to Bartley.

The editorial foreword cites two primary sources for the material in *Hayek on Hayek:* Hayek's autobiographical notes and the many interviews he gave over the years. The third paragraph begins: "Hayek later agreed to the publication of his notes. He had given them to W. W. Bartley III, who had undertaken Hayek's biography. Bartley realized that the notes should be published as they were." The next paragraph begins: "In reading through many interviews with Hayek, we found that he had provided the outline of an intellectual biography. This was, of course, his clear intention in his many talks with Bartley" (pp. ix-x).

Interview exchanges attributed to the "W. W. Bartley III audiotape archive" that are *not* between Hayek and Bartley occur on at least the following pages in *Hayek on Hayek:* 49, 51–57, 59–61, 67–68, 70–73, 76–78, 81–83, 96–97, 104–105, 126–128, 139–140, and 144–145. The entire book is 170 pages, and interview exchanges between Hayek and any interviewers occur only between pages 41 and 155. In all, close to one-third of all interview exchanges in *Hayek on Hayek* are misidentified.

Kresge appears to have considered his role as general editor of *The Collected Works of F. A. Hayek* as being largely to preserve Bartley's legacy. Subsequent volumes of *The Collected Works* have presented Bartley first as the "Founding Editor" of the series on the page near the front where the individuals and entities affiliated with the *The Collected Works of F. A. Hayek* are listed. Kresge wrote in the first volume, 4, of *The Collected Works* published after Bartley's death: "This volume was assembled under painful circumstances. The founding editor of the Collected Works of F. A. Hayek, W. W. Bartley III died . . . in February 1990. Nothing can prepare one for such a loss. But we were prepared to do the work that will remain as a testament to his foresight, perseverance, and intelligence" (p. xi).

HAYEK'S RELATIONSHIP WITH JEWS

The question of Hayek's relationship with Jews has taken on more significance as a result of an article, "The Anti-Semitism of Some Eminent Economists," published in the winter 2000 edition of *History of Political Economy* by former University of Chicago economic historian Melvin Reder. In this article, Reder puts forward the view that Keynes, Schumpeter, and Hayek were "ambivalent" anti-Semites.

As noted in chapter 8, Hayek's family in Austria was typical of many, perhaps most, Austrian Catholics. Hayek's mother became a strong supporter of Hitler, and

Hayek's children remember that she, to their parents' dismay, sent the family Aryan identification papers in England prior to World War II. One, or perhaps both, of Hayek's brothers became members of the Nazi Party, which caused at least one brother employment difficulties after the war.

Hayek's relationship with Jews was straightforward. The Viennese Catholic society in which he was born and grew to maturity was very anti-Semitic. Within this society, he was solidly on the liberal or progressive side in his relationships with Jews. As said in *Friedrich Hayek: A Biography:* "The Germanic world in 1899 was thoroughly prejudiced and anti-Semitism was rampant, particularly in Vienna," and: "Within contemporary Austro-Catholic culture, he [Hayek] was on the liberal or progressive side in his interaction with Jews once he entered the university. He had extensive relationships, both personal and professional, with a number of Jewish students and teachers" (pp. 8, 29).

Hayek's interaction with Jews grew apace during the 1920s at a time when prejudice and discrimination against Jews also grew swiftly. This was when Jews were becoming increasingly subject to popular, semiofficial, and official denunciation, discrimination, and segregation.

Hayek had extensive involvement, both academic and personal, with many Jewish students and teachers once he entered the University of Vienna. Mises, for whom he worked, was Jewish. Close to three-quarters of Mises's "private seminar" were Jewish, as was Hayek's *Geistkreis.* Among Hayek's longtime friends were Mises, Fritz Machlup, Karl Popper, and Milton Friedman—all were Jewish (at least, in Popper's case, by descent). Hayek had close relationships with many Jews throughout life. It may be true that not one of the many Jews who knew Hayek throughout life, whether they agreed with him politically or not, considered him anti-Semitic.

It is also the case, as said in *Friedrich Hayek: A Biography,* that "Hayek could be obtuse and insensitive of anti-Semitism. He wrote in a piece after World War II: 'It is scarcely easier to justify the prevention of a person from fiddling [playing in the Vienna Symphony] because he was a Nazi than the prevention because he is a Jew'" (p. 390). It was also said there that "Hayek could be culturally insensitive and stereotypical of particular nationalities" (p. 294).

In old age, Hayek apparently made mildly anti-Semitic remarks to his secretary, Charlotte Cubitt. She remembers him speaking words to the effect to her that he did not like Jews very much and felt uncomfortable with them, but also that one cannot dislike a nation, he liked individual Jews, and his feelings were a problem for him.

This writer is disinclined to put much stock in these comments, though he thinks it likely that Hayek made comments along these lines. To what extent they were an old man blowing off steam is not possible to establish. They do not appear characteristic of him over his life.

Hayek's situation might be considered comparable to someone who was born in the southern United States in 1899 and grew up in segregated southern society, was liberal or progressive in attitude and actions on racial issues in that society, and retained residual, anachronistic racial attitudes and outlooks that he occasionally expressed in private in old age. Hayek was not anti-Semitic for his time and place. When it truly mattered—when Jews were being killed for being Jews—he was a friend of and associated with many Jews.

Accordingly, to call Hayek an anti-Semite—when, in his time and place, he was among the more liberal and progressive with respect to Jews—would be inaccurate. The Austrian school of economics was, incidentally, sometimes called pejoratively the "Jewish" school during the 1920s and 1930s. During this time there were many anti-Semitic student protests at the University of Vienna against what was thought to be too large a proportion of Jewish professors and students.

It is hard to imagine today how anti-Semitic Vienna and the Germanic culture in which Hayek grew to maturity were. Steven Beller writes in his authoritative
Vienna and the Jews, 1867–1938 (1989) that Vienna was "anti-Jewish. There had always been hatred of the Jews in central European culture since the Middle Ages.
Until the enlightenment the Jews were a feared and despised people. While with the
triumph of liberalism the legal oppression of the Jews disappeared, the antipathy to
them did not. The Jew continued to be stereotyped as the evil instrument of Mam-
mon to the point where he became almost an archetype. When [financier and jour-
nalist] Richard Kola went to the Prater [in Vienna] in 1885, it was a matter of course
that the finale of the puppet show would be a Hanswurst beating 'den Juden' [the
Jews] to death" (p. 188).

After he received the Nobel Prize, Hayek signed a petition with other Nobel
laureates that denounced the United Nations for equating Zionism with racism. To
characterize Hayek as an anti-Semite would be a misunderstanding not only of Hayek,
but of anti-Semitism. In "A Note on Hayek and Anti-Semitism," in *History of Political
Economy* (Spring 2002), Ronald Hamowy considers further Reder's article. Hamowy
considers Hayek to have been "pro-Semitic" (p. 255).

BOOKS AND ARTICLES ON AUSTRIAN ECONOMIC AND HAYEKIAN TOPICS

Many good books have been written by authors in the contemporary Austrian academic economics movement recently, and it is possible to mention only a few here. Indeed, more works have been written about Austrian economics and Austrian
economists since 1990 than during any comparable period ever. This bodes well for the
future of contemporary Austrian economics.

Israel Kirzner is author of many diverse works in Austrian economics. He is
perhaps the most significant living exponent in the Austrian tradition and has enjoyed
considerable success as an author. His major works include *Competition and Entre-
preneurship* (1973) and, from a more historical perspective, *The Meaning of the Market Process: Essays in the Development of Modern Austrian Economics* (1992), *The
Driving Force of the Market: Essays in Austrian Economics* (2000), and *Ludwig von
Mises: The Man and His Economics* (2001).

With Kirzner's retirement, Richard Ebeling, Ludwig von Mises Professor of
Economics at Hillsdale College and incoming president of the Foundation for Economic Education, has become dean of the contemporary Austrian school. His leading works include a number of the volumes in the Hillsdale College Ludwig von
Mises Lecture Series, *Champions of Freedom,* which he has edited, including vol. 17,
Austrian Economics: Perspectives on the Past and Prospects for the Future (1991); vol.
18, *Austrian Economics: A Reader* (1991), which is an excellent resource of writings
on and in the history of Austrian economics; vol. 26, *The Age of the Economists: From
Adam Smith to Milton Friedman* (1999), a good collection; vol. 27, Human Action: *A
50-Year Tribute* (2000); vol. 28, *Competition or Compulsion* (2001); and vol. 29, *Glob-
alization* (2002), which contains Ebeling's excellent "The Economist as the Historian
of Decline: Ludwig von Mises and Austria Between the Two World Wars." Ebeling
also edits *Selected Writings of Ludwig von Mises,* a three-volume collection in the
process of being published by Liberty Fund, largely based on previously inaccessible
materials unearthed by Ebeling after the collapse of the Soviet Union. To all of
these, Ebeling provides extensive and scholarly introductions or chapters. Ebeling's
long-awaited intellectual biography of Mises will undoubtedly prove to be worth the
wait. In the meantime, the forthcoming *Austrian Economics and the Political Economy of Freedom,* a collection of essays, will appear.

Gerald Steele, one of the leading Hayek scholars, has written two books specifically on Hayek, *The Economics of Friedrich Hayek* (1993) and *Keynes and Hayek: The Money Economy* (2001). In addition, he has written an excellent article, "Hayek's *Sensory Order*," published in *Theory & Psychology* (2002). He writes in his new book that "[t]he 'vision thing' for Hayek undoubtedly derives from the one 'big thing' he claims to know: that is, the hugely limiting constraints upon human knowledge" (p. 22). Steele calls attention to the vital connection between tacit, unarticulated knowledge and societal progress. Institutions make societies. He writes in *The Economics of Friedrich Hayek:* "It is the inarticulated knowledge, captured by generally accepted institutional practices, which compensates for each individual's unique ignorance and uncertainty" (p. 15).

Roger Garrison is among the theoretical leaders of contemporary Austrian economists. Garrison seeks to weave greater congruence between modern Austrian and Keynesian, and between modern Austrian and Friedmanian, approaches, or is at least receptive to these directions. Garrison speaks a Keynesian language more than other contemporary Austrian economists in that he uses Keynesian macroeconomic terminology. He postulates a trade-off between the production of capital and consumer goods in the short run in *Time and Money: The Macroeconomics of Capital Structure* (2001). In the preface he remarks that "the reader will not fail to notice his [Hayek's] influence in virtually every chapter—and in virtually every graph—. . . . It is to Hayek . . . that I owe my greatest intellectual debt" (p. xiv).

Bruce Caldwell is one of the most prolific authors on Hayek, as well as general editor of *The Collected Works of F. A. Hayek*. In addition to the two volumes of *The Collected Works* that he has edited, he has written a number of articles on Hayek, including "Hayek and Socialism" *Journal of Economic Literature* (December 1997), and "The Emergence of Hayek's Ideas on Cultural Evolution," in the *Review of Austrian Economics* (February 2000). In the latter, he writes: "Hayek relates the growth of civilization to the growth of knowledge" (p. 8)—Caldwell does not, though, emphasize the foreknowledge aspect of knowledge. Caldwell also observes in this article of *The Fatal Conceit: The Errors of Socialism:* "It is not clear how much of the book should be attributed to Hayek, and how much to Bartley," and: "Nor is it likely that we will ever have an answer to that question, now that both of the principals are dead" (p. 18). Caldwell presented a paper, "Popper and Hayek: Who Influenced Whom?" at the 2002 Vienna Karl Popper conference, in which he said: "My own reading of the evidence is that neither Popper nor Hayek had much of an influence on the other." Caldwell's forthcoming *Hayek's Challenge: An Intellectual Biography* will focus on the development of Hayek's methodological thought, and is awaited by many Hayek scholars.

As observed in chapter 3, one of the surprising aspects about the Austrian school of economics is that there exists no really adequate history of the school from Menger to the present—nor even of its classical period from the 1870s through 1930s. This bibliographical essay merely skims the surface of recently published available resources. That there were probably more books and articles written during the 1990s on Austrian economics, Hayek, and related topics than during any previous decade indicates strong and growing interest in these fields. Enough information is now available in secondary sources to allow reconceptualizations and new hypotheses for further research.

As also mentioned in chapter 3, there is no satisfactory biography of Carl Menger or any of the other early main Austrian economists—Böhm-Bawerk, Wieser, or Mises. Menger merits a major biography, and the resources for one are gradually being collected. The document—if it becomes available—that would be of most value to Menger scholars and would-be biographers would be the biographical manuscript that was written by Carl Menger's son, Karl, the mathematician and logical positivist, which was in the hands of Albert Zlabinger, economist and formerly with the former

Carl Menger Institute, which was headquartered in Vienna. This would be an irreplaceable document, and its speedy translation and publication would be very useful.

David Theroux played a key role in getting Hayek and Karl Menger together for the first time in decades in 1977, which helped to prompt and spur Karl Menger's biography of his father and release of his father's papers for repository at a major university archive. In one of his last interviews, in 1985, Hayek mentioned the Menger biography: "On Menger's story, I ought not to anticipate too much, because I have now a great deal of information from what is still a confidential document. Menger's son . . . is producing a biography, which I have read in manuscript but which is not yet published. So I mustn't give away too much" (Hayek-North/Skousen interview, 1985).

Among the most valuable works on Menger published since 1990 include Hayek's own essays on Menger and the Austrian school of economics (included in volume 4 of *The Collected Works of F. A. Hayek, The Fortunes of Liberalism: Essays on Austrian Economics and the Ideal of Freedom* [Peter Klein, ed.; 1991]); the many articles and papers by Erich Streissler on historical Austrian economics, over the decades (a collection of Streissler's writings in this area would be beneficial); Streissler (ed., with Monika Streissler), *Carl Menger's Lectures to Crown Prince Rudolf of Austria* (1994); Bettina Bien Greaves (ed.), *Austrian Economics: An Anthology* (1996), which includes Mises's *The Historical Setting of the Austrian School* and Henry Seager's invaluable 1893 "Economics at Berlin and Vienna"; and Bruce Caldwell (ed.), *Carl Menger and His Legacy in Economics* (1990), a good collection.

Other noteworthy collections include Klaus Hennings and Warren Samuels, *Neoclassical Economic Theory, 1870 to 1930* (1990), which has valuable contributions by Streissler and Stephan Boehm; Bruce Caldwell and Stephan Boehm (eds.), *Austrian Economics: Tensions and New Directions* (1992), which includes an article by Boehm entitled "Austrian Economics Between the Wars"; Gerrit Meijer (ed.), *New Perspectives on Austrian Economics* (1995), which has several historical pieces; Peter J. Boettke (ed.), "The Elgar Companion to Austrian Economics" (1994), which is a compendium of pieces by authors connected with the Austrian movement in contemporary academic economics; and, among older works, Louis M. Spadaro (ed.), *New Directions in Austrian Economics* (1978), which contains a particularly good article by Mario Rizzo, "Praxeology and Econometrics: A Critique of Positivist Economics," which includes significant consideration of Milton Friedman.

William Jaffé's "Menger, Jevons and Walras De-Homogenized" in *Economic Inquiry* (December 1976) is an excellent older article discussing differences among the three economists usually considered to have launched the "marginalist revolution." Kiichiro Yagi's article, "Carl Menger's *Grundsätze* in the Making," in *History of Political Economy* (Winter 1993), provides information on Menger's early career. In *Carl Menger (1840–1921)* (1992), editor Mark Blaug provides a number of articles on Menger over the decades.

Klaus H. Hennings's *The Austrian Theory of Value and Capital: Studies in the Life and Work of Eugen von Böhm-Bawerk* (1997) is the most recent, extensive work on Böhm-Bawerk. Hennings's premature death was a blow to scholarship.

A number of partial histories of Austrian economics have been written, some of which are discussed in *Friedrich Hayek: A Biography*. Histories discussing Austrian economics and Hayek not found there include: A. M. Endres, *Neoclassical Microeconomic Theory: The Founding Austrian Version* (1997), which is an excellent historical summary presenting views of Menger, Wieser, and Böhm-Bawerk. Sandye Gloria-Palermo's *The Evolution of Austrian Economics: From Menger to Lachmann* (1999) is based on the author's dissertation and considers the Austrian founding trinity, emphasizing Menger, and also discusses Hayek, Mises, Kirzner, Rothbard, and Lachmann. It is possible from Gloria-Palermo's work (though she does not state it) to interpret the Austrian school as two branches—Menger, Böhm-Bawerk, Mises, and Kirzner; and Menger, Wieser, Hayek, and Lachmann—with much interpollination between the branches.

Raimondo Cubeddu's *The Philosophy of the Austrian School* (1993, translated from the Italian edition) is dense but deep. The effort of reading it is worthwhile. Cubeddu emphasizes Menger, Mises, and Hayek, and calls attention to the relationship between economic calculation and value, following Wieser's terminology. Cubeddu notes of Hayek's and Mises's influence after World War II through the 1960s that their "analysis rarely met with acclaim beyond the confines of the liberal tradition, and frequently exercised little influence even here. Objectively speaking, in those years the circulation of their ideas was quite limited, and they were remembered chiefly as figures from the past" (p. 148).

Randall G. Holcombe edited *15 Great Austrian Economists* (1999), a good but mistitled collection. Really only a third or so of the figures profiled can be considered to have been Austrian economists; the collection also omits others who surely are considered Austrian economists. However, these caveats noted, this collection includes interesting essays on several economists, including William Hutt and Wilhelm Röpke. For further information on Hutt, see Richard Ebeling, "William H. Hutt: A Centenary Appreciation," *The Freeman* (August 1999). Röpke is subject of a recent biography by John Zmirak, *Wilhelm Röpke: Swiss Localist, Global Economist* (2001). Also see Ebeling, "Wilhelm Röpke: A Centenary Appreciation," *The Freeman* (October 1999). Three of the essays in *15 Great Austrian Economists* are by or on Murray Rothbard.

In his chapter in *15 Great Austrian Economists*, Peter Klein makes this observation on the intellectual relationship between Hayek and Mises: "Recently, the relationship between Mises and Hayek has become a full-fledged 'dehomogenization' debate, with some seeing Hayek's emphasis on knowledge and discovery as substantially different from Mises's emphasis on purposeful human action. Indeed, it has been argued that there are two strands of modern Austrian economics, both descended from Menger. One, the Wieser-Hayek strand, focuses on dispersed knowledge and the price system as a device for communicating knowledge. Another, the Böhm-Bawerk-Mises strand, focuses on monetary calculation. . . . Thus, the dispute is whether the differences between Hayek and Mises are primarily matters of emphasis and language or matters of substance" (pp. 191–2). Klein's volume 4 in *The Collected Works of F. A. Hayek* is an excellent resource on the Austrian school of economics.

Allen Oakley's *The Revival of Modern Austrian Economics* (1999) is a comprehensive presentation of Austrian economics, emphasizing Hayek but also considering Lachmann as well as Menger and Mises. Oakley emphasizes subjectivism in Austrian thought. The predecessor volume to this work is *The Foundations of Austrian Economics from Menger to Mises* (1997), which provides considerable historical background, including discussion of the German historical school and Max Weber.

Austrian Economics: Historical and Philosophical Background (1986), edited by Wolfgang Grassl and Barry Smith, is an excellent collection of papers with contributions by Smith, Grassl, J. C. Nyiri, and Jeremy Shearmur. Smith's deep knowledge of Austrian philosophy makes his contributions especially informative. Also see Smith's outstanding *Austrian Philosophy: The Legacy of Franz Brenatano* (1994).

A three-volume collection, *Austrian Economics* (1990), edited by Stephen Littlechild, brings together many articles by Austrian economists, largely contemporary, as well as articles on Austrian economics. Parts I and II of the first volume include a number of older articles on the history of the Austrian school.

Alexander Shand's *Free Market Morality: The Political Economy of the Austrian School* (1990) is a largely philosophical and political examination of the Austrian position, as distinct from the more exclusively economic view presented in Shand's *The Capitalist Alternative: An Introduction to Neo-Austrian Economics* (1984).

Mark Skousen's *The Making of Modern Economics* (2001) is an exceptional new comprehensive history of economic thought. Three chapters contain extensive discussion of Menger, Mises, Hayek, and Schumpeter. Skousen's reading is deep and broad, and his style is entertaining.

Jeremy Shearmur's article, "Popper, Hayek, and the Poverty of Historicism Part I: A Largely Bibliographical Essay," in *Philosophy of the Social Sciences* (September 1998) is an interesting document in historical recovery. Shearmur presents the Hayek-edited portions of Popper's "The Poverty of Historicism" articles that appeared in *Economica* during World War II. Some of Hayek's cuts (which were for space reasons) seem as interesting as anything in the published essays, particularly with respect to "'[e]ffects of forecasts upon predicted happenings'" (p. 442), consideration of esoteric scientific circles, and Popper's comparison of historicism with astronomy. Shearmur's article is of interest for the light it gives to ideas and for indicating Hayek's editorial style and influence on Popper.

Hayek Revisited (2000), edited by Boudewijn Bouckaert and Annette Godart-van der Kroom, is a collection of essays almost entirely by European authors. Kurt Leube notes in his chapter that Hans Kelsen "became the first to introduce Hayek to legal philosophy" (p. 5), though Hayek soon turned away from Kelsen. The chapters by Paul Cliteur and Leonard Liggio discuss Hayek's legal theory.

A collection of essays by mostly British authors is Eamonn Butler and Madsen Pirie (eds.), *Hayek on the Fabric of Human Society* (1987). Kenneth Minogue perceptively observes that "Hayek finds himself in two minds on the question" of societal rules' justification. "On the one hand, he is tempted to make affirmations about the necessity for uncritically accepting rules whose point cannot be easily explicated. . . . On the other hand, he thinks that the real reason for these rules and practices has now emerged and it is a straightforwardly utilitarian one: private property, morality, and the family all conduce to prosperity, to the multiplication of people and to the displacement of those who do not live in terms of these practices" (p. 137). Pirie considers Hayek as a conservative.

The first part of Salvatore Rizzello's, *The Economics of the Mind* (1999) is titled "Hayek's Criticism of the Neoclassical Paradigm." Rizzello states: "The theory of knowledge is probably Hayek's most important contribution to economic theory" (p. 11). He emphasizes the idea that there is a tie between unarticulated or tacit knowledge and that not all institutions can be constructivistically or deliberately planned. Spontaneous order is in large part reliance on tacit or unarticulated as opposed to verbal or explicit knowledge. Furthermore, inadequacies in communication (either intrinsic or extrinsic) hinder planning. Rizzello also considers Hayek's *The Sensory Order.* Hayek's theory of mind leads to the conclusion that the physical brain may place limitations on individual understanding and interpersonal communication.

Howard Baetjer's "Capital as Embodied Knowledge: Some Implications for the Theory of Economic Growth" in *Review of Austrian Economics* (September 2000) is a good article. Baetjer emphasizes that classical Austrian economists, following in the Germanic tradition, defined capital as "the produced means of production," a different conception of capital than that put forward elsewhere at other times. Baetjer is completely correct when he states "Capital is embodied knowledge" and emphasizes that "knowledge is of the essence" (pp. 148–49).

What Do Economists Contribute? (1999), edited by Daniel B. Klein, is a provocative collection of ten essays written over the decades by critics of contemporary academic economic theory or its relevance. Essays by Coase, Hutt, Tullock, McCloskey, Kirzner, and Hayek are included.

Jerry Z. Muller's *The Mind and the Market: Capitalism in Modern European Thought* (2002) contains considerable discussion of Hayek in tracing the intellectual development of capitalism. Muller considers Hayek to have advocated a conservative liberalism and he notes Hayek's tendency to intellectual one-sidedness.

Leland B. Yeager's *Ethics as Social Science: The Moral Philosophy of Social Cooperation* (2001) is an exceptionally clear and well-written work in the utilitarian tradition that is one of the leading contributions to utilitarianism of the twentieth century. Yeager writes that "[a]dvantageous rules and social arrangements may arise without ever having been deliberately planned; . . . they can emerge as unforeseen results of individuals' strivings to achieve their own particular purposes. Social selection and transmission is a recurrent theme in the writings of . . . Hayek" (p. 72).

Libertarians and Liberalism: Essays in Honour of Gerard Radnitzky (1996), edited by Hardy Bouillon, is a superb collection by twenty European and North American authors, fifteen of whom are members of the Mont Pelerin Society. In his introduction, Bouillon says that an attempt after World War II to introduce "central planning after the Soviet model" in Sweden "failed largely thanks [to] the influence of Hayek's *The Road to Serfdom,* which had been translated in Swedish just in time before the decisive election" (p. 12). Radnitzky was a friend of Popper, Hayek, and Bartley, and European libertarian public figure as well. Bouillon quotes Radnitzky: "As he used to say: 'The trouble is not so much what people don't know, the trouble is what people know but know wrong'" (p. 14). Arthur Seldon calls for "a new laissez-faire" in his contribution and writes: "The rule of law is essential for organised human cooperation. . . . It now requires a new era of less government that is enforceable because it is confined to the very small part of life where it is indispensable. And it requires the liberal dream to become libertarian" (pp. 110–11).

The contribution of Vaclav Klaus, then prime minister of the Czech Republic, to the volume in honor of Radnitzky is of interest for Klaus's perspective, as a former East European dissident and current East European government leader, on the contribution of the Austrian school of economics:

> Examining the work of the economists of the Austrian School in the 20th century we clearly recognized that it was they who had undertaken the enormously important task of exposing the contradictions and the artificiality of socialist doctrines. This was shown with particular clarity in . . . the famous economic calculation debate. . . .
>
> . . . Socialists of all colors have in common the craving to suppress individual liberty and correspondingly to augment the role and the power of the state. . . . Hayek's exposure of their tendencies and striving as well as his warning against them is today as topical as ever. It is precisely this legacy of the Austrian School which we have kept in mind and which we will not forget. (pp. 255–56, 259)

George Selgin's essay, "Hayek versus Keynes on How the Price Level Ought to Behave," in *History of Political Economy* (Winter 1999) is a provocative interpretation. Selgin emphasizes that Keynes was, in contemporary parlance, a "stabiliser"—one who favored internal aggregate price stability—which today seems also to be an almost global national policy goal. Selgin observes that during the 1930s, Hayek "struggled to soften the deflationary tone of his arguments, moving closer to Keynes in the process." Selgin closes on the provocative thought that "Hayek came at last to accept a view of optimal price-level behavior [i.e., price stability] that was practically the same as the one he had found wanting in Keynes almost half a century before" (pp. 718–19).

Lawrence H. White's discussion, "Hayek's Monetary Theory and Policy: A Critical Reconstruction," in *Journal of Money, Credit, and Banking* (February 1999) is excellent. White notes, in agreement with Selgin, that "[a]t the end of his career, sur-prisingly switching from critic to advocate of consumer-price-level stabilization, Hayek (1978) was compelled to deny the practical relevance of his business-cycle theory" (p. 118).

Benjamin Cohen's "Electronic Money: New Day or False Dawn?" in *Review of International Political Economy* (Summer 2001) is a fascinating look at how techno-logical changes in commerce and, in particular, the emergence of "electronic money" may lead to Hayekian private currencies in the foreseeable future. If so, this would be a monumental paradigm and practical shift. In his concluding line, Cohen suggests that national governments may place greater reliance on fiscal policy compared to mone-tary policy than they have during recent decades. Gerald Steele concludes his *Keynes and Hayek: The Money Economy* (2001) on a similar but distinct thought:

> It is reasonable to expect that innovations in electronic communications and exchange will continue to shape the provision of financial services. In keep-ing with Hayek's theme of currency competition, those future developments might embrace registers of individuals' asset portfolios . . . with opportuni-ties to make virtually instantaneous withdrawals and deposits. . . . It is likely that advances in communications, information technology and financial ser-vices will raise the advantages and reduce the hazards of a money economy to the point where—in effect—arrangements would exist to allow the *barter* of assets and commodities alike. This poses an interesting question: would this constitute the practical achievement of a neutral money . . . ? It so, the problems of a money economy would have dissipated. (p. 204)

Peter Lewin's *Capital in Disequilibrium: The Role of Capital in a Changing World* (1999) is very clearly written. Lewin builds on the work of Ludwig Lachmann, who stressed the knowledgeable (as opposed to material) aspect of capital. Lewin also calls attention to the vital issue of "tacit," unarticulated, or nonverbal knowledge and provides historical perspective. When he states that "[c]apital accumulation thus nec-essarily involves knowledge accumulation" (p. 215), he is firmly in the tradition of Menger and Hayek. "The superior performance of capitalist economies rests . . . on the fact that they do not rely on central planners . . . knowing very much at all. It is, as Hayek realized . . . rather that capitalist economies are able to effect a division of knowledge that facilitates the accumulation and division of capital" (p. 216). Decen-tralized knowledge should lead to decentralized planning, which contemporary capi-talism allows but which classical socialism did not, calling instead for centralized planning. Lewin, a student of Gary Becker as well as of Lachmann, integrates aspects of Becker in his Austrian approach.

Microfoundations and Macroeconomics: An Austrian Perspective (2000), by Steven Horwitz, is at times almost brilliant in its historical scholarship, though this writer does not share all of Horwitz's, as Lewin's, perspectives. Horwitz appropriately calls attention to the work of Leland Yeager (perhaps "the most underappreciated monetary theorist of the twentieth century" [p. xi]) and William Hutt, emphasizes (fol-lowing Karen Vaughn) Hayek's intellectual role in the post-1970s Austrian renais-sance, and quotes, following Kirzner, this important passage from Hayek: "For Hayek, the notion of equilibrium could only be accurately understood if it was framed in terms of the knowledge held by the actors presumed to be in equilibrium. . . . Analogous to his understanding of individual equilibrium, Hayek defines social equilibrium as a state of affairs where each individual's plan could be successfully executed because each one's plan contains the plans of others as data. Social equilibrium is thus a perfect dovetailing of plans: 'Correct foresight is, then, not, as it has been sometimes understood, a precondition [of] equilibrium. It is rather the defining characteristic of a state of equilibrium'" (p. 24). Kirzner remarks of this passage of Hayek's on correct foresight as the defining characteristic of the state of equilibrium that "movement from disequilibrium to equilibrium is at once a movement from imperfect knowledge to perfect knowledge" (in *FH:AB,* p. 96). Kirzner also notes, of Hayek's 1933 Copenhagen lecture, that the "concept of equilibrium assumes . . . that everybody possesses correct foresight" (*The Driving Force of the Market,* p. 191).

Peter Boettke's 2001 presidential address to the Society for the Development of Austrian Economics is printed as "Information and Knowledge: Austrian Economics in Search of Its Uniqueness" in the *Review of Austrian Economics* (December 2002). "If you are looking for the unique Austrian research program," Boettke states, "it is to be found in this emphasis on these knowledge aspects of the economic process" (p. 267). "Liberty is essential in order to leave room for the unforeseeable and unpredictable" (p. 271), he also writes.

Juliet Williams's "On the Road Again: Hayek and the Rule of Law" in *Critical Review* (Winter 1997) is a provocative exploration of Hayek's thought in political philosophy. According to Williams, who offers telling criticisms of Hayek, Hayek is "a thinker whose position in the canon of liberal thought is, at best, precarious" (p. 105).

In *Hayek's Liberalism and Its Origins: His Idea of Spontaneous Order and the Scottish Enlightenment* (2001), Christina Petsoulas traces the development of Hayek's idea of spontaneous order in part through Hume and Smith. Also in this vein, see Ronald Hamowy, *The Scottish Enlightenment and the Theory of Spontaneous Order* (1987).

George Stigler wrote in his autobiography, *Memoirs of an Unregulated Economist* (1988), of Hayek:

> I believed much more in the central theme of *The Road to Serfdom* when it first appeared than I do now. The reason is that its main prediction, if true, lies in the uncertain future [when the work was written]. It is a fair reading of *The Road to Serfdom* to say that forty years more of the march toward socialism would lead to major losses of the political and economic freedom of individuals. Yet in those forty years we have seen that continuous expansion of the state in Sweden and England, even in Canada and the United States, without consequences for personal freedom so dire as those he predicted. . . .
>
> . . . Hayek denied that piecemeal regulations of a hundred different industries and callings could survive. The conflicts and inconsistencies would force the adoption of a single, centralized, comprehensive plan—and that plan could allow little individual choice. But that multitude of inconsistent, partial interventions by the state in economic life is exactly what we have. Hayek's orderly mind could not comprehend the survivability of our disorderly world. (pp. 146–47)

Charlotte Cubitt is working on a memoir of her years with Hayek. If she finishes it, it would provide a unique and intimate portrayal of his last years. Kenneth Hoover is working on a book that is to be published in 2003 on Hayek, Keynes, and Laski, tracing the connection between their ideologies and identities.

Works discussing Hayek and Popper's relationship mentioned in the main text here include Malachi Haim Hacohen's exceptional *Karl Popper—The Formative Years, 1902–1945; Politics and Philosophy in Interwar Vienna* (2000), which will no doubt be an authoritative work for at least decades; Jeremy Shearmur, "Popper, Hayek, and

Classical Liberalism," *Freeman* (February 1989); and Ian Jarvie and Sandra Pralong (eds.), *Popper's* Open Society *after Fifty Years: The Continuing Relevance of Karl Popper* (1999), which includes a chapter by Ernst Gombrich.

Hans Jörg Hennecke's *Friedrich August von Hayek: Die Tradition der Frieheit* (*The Tradition of Freedom*) (2000) is a German-language biography of Hayek, which, until its planned translation, will be inaccessible to virtually all non-German readers. Hennecke's work emphasizes Hayek's German-language life and work and extensively utilizes Hayek's archives and those of many of his colleagues and associates.

∽

Bruce Caldwell observes: "There is, particularly after a great person dies, a natural inclination for those who knew him . . . to want to keep back some mementos of the relationship. Although such sentiments are wholly understandable, it must also be understood that they inevitably hinder scholarship. To reconstruct a person's life and ideas is extremely difficult, and those who try to do so should be given access to all existing information" (*The Independent Review* [Fall 2001], p. 267). Private collections of Hayek material that should be deposited in the public realm through donation preferably to the Hoover Institution at Stanford University include the Sudha Shenoy collection of notes from talks with Hayek during the middle 1970s for an intended biography; Hayek's interview talks with Walter Morris, which are in the possession of the Morris Foundation; the files and correspondence and preliminary drafts of *The Fatal Conceit* in the possession of Charlotte Cubitt (or her son); the materials in the possession of the Bartley Institute that pertain to Bartley's work on Hayek; notebooks and scrapbooks in the possession of the Hayek family; and materials in the possession of this writer. Caldwell notes that some of these materials might "be of great use to Hayek scholars" (ibid.). Fortunately, the Cubitt materials appear headed to Hoover.

There are many good Hayek materials in the archives at the Hoover Institution (particularly the Popper archive) and elsewhere. It would be consistent with Bartley's intention that the Bartley Institute materials be placed at Hoover. Bartley wrote in his foreword to *The Fatal Conceit: The Errors of Socialism* of *The Collected Works of F. A. Hayek* that "[a]ll materials used in the creation of these volumes . . . will be available to scholars in the Hoover Institution Archives" (p. xii). More important, Hayek himself wished that all of his literary estate be located at the Hoover Institution and available to scholars and researchers. At least copies of materials in private collections should be made available. Not just Hayek scholars, but scholars of other figures should support this material being made available.

It has been mentioned to this writer that some holders of private collections of Hayek material (including sources other than those mentioned here) might retain those collections indefinitely if certain aspects of Hayek's legacy do not move in certain directions. These irreplaceable materials could become lost to history.

Hayek emphasized that "[i]f we are to advance, we must leave room for a continuous revision of our present conceptions and ideals which will be necessitated by further experience" (*CL*, p. 23). No one can say now what Hayek's legacy will be. The best course is for as many private collections to be placed in the public domain as possible.

While some of these materials might not be available for years (if ever), which would be unfortunate, there is enough information available now through the Hoover Institution and other resources—most especially, through Hayek's already published written words in their current published editions—to allow greater consideration of his work to move forward.

Notes

ABBREVIATIONS USED IN NOTES AND BIBLIOGRAPHICAL ESSAY

Hayek's Works

CEP	*Collectivist Economic Planning* (London: Routledge & Kegan Paul, 1950)
CH	*Capitalism and the Historians* (Chicago: University of Chicago Press, 1954) (editor)
CL	*The Constitution of Liberty* (Chicago: University of Chicago Press, 1960)
C-RS	*The Counter-Revolution of Science* (New York: Free Press, 1955)
CW	*The Collected Works of F. A. Hayek* (Chicago: University of Chicago Press, 1988–1999) (volume number follows *CW*)
DM	*Denationalisation of Money* (London: Institute of Economic Affairs, 1990)
EH	*The Essence of Hayek* (Chiaki Nishiyama and Kurt R. Leube, eds.) (Stanford, CA: Hoover Institution Press, 1984)
FC:E	*The Fatal Conceit: The Errors of Socialism* (Chicago: University of Chicago Press, 1988)
HH	*Hayek on Hayek* (Stephen Kresge and Leif Wenar, eds.) (Chicago: University of Chicago Press, 1994)
IEO	*Individualism and Economic Order* (Chicago: University of Chicago Press, 1948)
KES	*Knowledge, Evolution and Society* (London: Adam Smith Institute, 1983)
LLL	*Law, Legislation and Liberty* (Chicago: University of Chicago Press, 1973–79) (volume number follows *LLL*)
MCF	*Money, Capital, and Fluctuations: Early Essays* (Roy McCloughry, ed.) (Chicago: University of Chicago Press, 1984)
MNIS	*Monetary Nationalism and International Stability* (New York: Augustus M. Kelley, 1964)
MTTC	*Monetary Theory and the Trade Cycle* (New York: Augustus M. Kelley, 1966)
New Studies	*New Studies in Philosophy, Politics, Economics and the History of Ideas* (London: Routledge, 1978)
PII	*Profits, Interest and Investment* (Clifton, N.J.: Augustus M. Kelley, 1975)
PP	*Prices and Production* (New York: Augustus M. Kelley, 1967)
PTC	*The Pure Theory of Capital* (Chicago: University of Chicago Press, 1941)

262 HAYEK'S JOURNEY

RS   *The Road to Serfdom* (London: Routledge, 1944)
SO   *The Sensory Order* (London: Routledge, 1952)
Studies   *Studies in Philosophy, Politics and Economics* (Chicago: University of Chicago Press, 1967)

Other Sources

CCAC   Charlotte Cubitt Archival Collection
FH:AB   Alan Ebenstein, *Friedrich Hayek: A Biography* (New York: Palgrave, 2001)
HA   Hayek Archive, Hoover Institution, Stanford University (box and file number given)
UCLA   "Nobel Prize-Winning Economist Friedrich A. von Hayek," Oral History Program, University of California at Los Angeles (1983)

INTRODUCTION

xv   "to explain . . . talking." *Studies,* 92.
xviii "only by . . . society." *LLL* II, 144.

CHAPTER 1

1   "thoroughly imbued . . . sciences." *IEO,* 57.
1   "We have . . . importance." UCLA, 48.
2   "When August . . . forms." August von Hayek, *Prodomus Florae Peninsulae Balcanicae* (1970), i.
2   "I probably . . . immensely." UCLA, 22.
3   "It's very . . . over." Hayek-Shehadi interview.
3   "If we . . . mind." *IEO,* 68.
4   "since well . . . Spencer." Pat Shipman, *The Evolution of Racism* (New York: Simon & Schuster, 1994), 107.
4   "little doubt . . . skills." *CL,* 59.
4   "Darwin was . . . theory." *FC:E,* 24.
4–5 "Probably the . . . selection," *Studies,* 31.
5   "Hume may . . . unquestioned." Ibid., 111, 119.
5   "discussion of . . . evolution.'" *LLL* I, 23.
6   "characterized by . . . Paris." *C-RS,* 105.
6   "Darwin of society." Mark Skousen, *The Making of Modern Economics* (Armonk, N.Y.: M.E. Sharpe, 2001), 145.
6   "the foundation . . . struggle." In Richard P. Appelbaum, *Karl Marx* (Newbury Park, Calif.: Sage, 1988), 30.
6   "just as . . . history." Ibid., 36.
6   "have over . . . movement." Karl Marx and Friedrich Engels, *The Communist Manifesto* (1848), second chapter.
6   "It is . . . creator." *New Studies,* 265.
7   "The grand . . . diversity." John Stuart Mill, *On Liberty* (1859), epigraph.

CHAPTER 2

9   "Perhaps the . . . background." *CL,* vi.
11 "German philosophy . . . world." Barry Smith, *Austrian Philosophy: The Legacy of Franz Brentano* (Chicago: Open Court, 1994), 4.

11 "each monad . . . soul." Bertrand Russell, *A History of Western Philosophy* (New York: Simon and Schuster, 1972), 583.

12 "philosopers . . . concerned." *CL*, 79.

12 "conception of . . . framework." In *FH:AB*, 335.

12 "the relation . . . annihilated.'" Ibid., 150.

12 "on the . . . else." "Economics, Politics and Freedom," *Reason* (February 1975), 8.

12 "the fact . . . it." *SO*, 176.

12–3 "the British . . . categories." John Gray, "The Road from Freedom," *National Review* (April 27, 1992), 35.

13 "from a . . . theory' . . ." *SO*, xviii.

13 "'Empirical Data' . . . 'data.'" Greg Ransom e-mail communication to author (December 17, 2001).

13 "[i]n German . . . Marx . . ." William Ebenstein, *Great Political Thinkers*, 4th ed. (New York: Holt, Rinehart and Winston, 1969), 691–2.

15 "entirely in . . . lacking?'" *RS*, 105.

15–6 "take[s] to . . . practitioners." Thomas S. Kuhn, *The Structure of Scientific Revolutions*, 3rd ed. (Chicago: University of Chicago Press, 1996), x.

16 "The proud . . . gained." Barbara Tuchmann, *The Proud Tower* (New York: Macmillan, 1966), 118.

16–7 "He was . . . sort." *CW* IV, 125.

17 "the German . . . through." In Ray Monk, *Ludwig Wittgenstein: The Duty of Genius* (New York: The Free Press, 1990), 114.

17 "Seldom has . . . Mach." Allan Janik and Stephen Toulmin, *Wittgenstein's Vienna* (New York: Touchstone, 1973), 133.

17 "Mach's ideas . . . discussions." *CW* IV, 172.

17 "No accocunt . . . intelligentsia." Hilde Spiel, *Vienna's Golden Autumn, 1866–1938* (London: Weidenfeld and Nicolson, 1987), 133.

17 "My table . . . varies." Ernst Mach, *The Analysis of Sensations* (New York: Dover, 1959), 2.

17 "The table . . . senses." David Hume, *A Treatise of Human Nature* (Oxford: Clarendon Press, 1983), 34.

17 "stimulated by . . . senses," *CW* IV, 174.

18 "these two . . . viewpoint" Hayek-North/Skousen interview.

CHAPTER 3

19 "still saw . . . Russia": CW IV, 68.

19 "its fundamental . . . Menger." Ibid., 62.

20 "every economic . . . science." In *FH:AB*, 24.

20 "His fame . . . economics." In *CW* IV, 75.

20 "I was . . . know . . . satisfying." UCLA, 248, 174.

21 "All things . . . contrary." Carl Menger, *Principles of Economics* (Grove City, PA: Libertarian Press, 1994), 51.

21 "If a . . . need." Ibid., 52.

21 "the sterility . . . observation." Ibid., 46.

22 "In addition . . . order." In FH:AB, 24–25.

22 "time-consuming . . . Menger." Roger Garrison, *Time and Money* (London: Routledge, 2001), 4.

22 "The quantities . . . knowledge." Menger, *Principles*, 74.

22–3 "Knowledge of . . . foresight." Ibid., 89.

23 "all knowledge . . . predict." *IEO*, 51.

23 "To him . . . future." *CW* IV, 71.

23 "classical liberal . . . Smith." Erich Streissler and Monika Streissler, *Carl Menger's Lectures to Crown Prince Rudolf of Austria* (Hants, England:Edward Elgar, 1994), 4, 6, 14.

23 "Value is . . . men." Menger, *Principles,* 120–21.

23 "The concept . . . sense." *CW* IV, 70.

24 "groomed to . . . minister" Mark Skousen, *The Making of Modern Economics* (Armonk, N.Y.: M. E. Sharpe, 2001), 177.

24–5 "Economics in . . . nationalism." Ludwig von Mises, *The Historical Setting of the Austrian School of Economics* (New Rochelle, N.Y.: Arlington House, 1969), 23–24.

25 "vivid sketch . . . institutions." In Bettina Bien Greaves (ed.), *Austrian Economics: An Anthology* (Irvington-on-Hudson, N.Y.: FEE, 1996), 42.

25 "exists a . . . development." Carl Menger, *Investigations into the Method of the Social Sciences with Special Reference to Economics* (New York University Press, 1985), 129–30.

26 "social phenomena . . . mind." Ibid., 146, 149.

26 "He urged . . . markets." In Llewellyn Rockwell, (ed.), *The Gold Standard: An Austrian Perspective* (Lexington, Mass.: D.C. Heath, 1985), 29.

26 "Professor Menger . . . processes." Greaves, *Austrian Economics,* 42.

27 "From the . . . sterile." Mises, *Historical Setting,* 11, 14.

27 "civil liberties . . . trade" Ibid., 11.

28 "strict maintenance . . . bank." Ibid., 18.

29 "Menger, Böhm-Bawerk . . . it." J. R. Hicks and W. Weber (eds.), *Carl Menger and the Austrian School of Economics* (Oxford: Clarendon Press, 1973), 226.

29 "Menger exerted . . . standard." In Rockwell (ed.), *The Gold Standard,* 26.

29 "Hours devoted . . . thought." In Friedrich von Wieser, *Social Economics* (London: George Allen, 1927), xii.

29 "revered teacher . . . personality." *CW* IV, 108.

29–30 "uniquely . . . rationally." *The New Palgrave,* vol. 4 (London: Macmillan, 1987), 922.

30 "among the . . . subject." *CW* IV, 115.

30 "Even in . . . utility." Friedrich von Wieser, *Natural Value* (New York: Kelley & Millman, 1956), 60.

31 "As is . . . socialists." Ibid., 63–4.

31 "Socialist writers . . . serve." Ibid., 64.

31–2 "There are . . . place." In *CEP,* 87–8.

32 "knowledge of . . . hidden" Wieser, *Natural Value,* 212–13.

32 "the scientific . . . abstractness" *CW* IV, 114–15.

32 "the wealth . . . remade." In Wieser, *Natural Value,* xxii.

32 "when Professor . . . [Principles]." In Wieser, *Social Economics,* x.

33 "greatest names . . . revolution" Lionel Robbins, *A History of Economic Thought* (Princeton University Press, 1998), 317.

33 "Wieser as . . . Empire." Oscar Morgenstern, "Friedrich von Wieser 1851–1926," *American Economic Review,* vol. xvii (1927), 674.

33 "1890s the . . . factors." Fritz Machlup, in Douglas Greenwald (ed.), *The McGraw-Hill Encyclopedia of Economics,* 2nd ed. (New York: McGraw-Hill, 1994), 43.

33 "This probably . . . Lausanne." Ibid.

33 "[T]he eyes . . . years." Greaves, *Austrian Economics,* 35.

34 "although Hayek . . . all." In *FH:AB*, 388.

CHAPTER 4

35 "As a . . . parents." *CL*, 90.
35 "In a . . . child." *HH*, 46.
36 "Q: . . . I think . . . civilization." UCLA, 163–4. Transcript corrected from audio tape.
36 "I had . . . sciences." UCLA, 2.
36 "And I . . . ministries." Ibid.
36 "Behind the . . . professor." Ibid., 474.
37–8 "It was . . . distinguished." Ibid., 13–6.
38–9 "After Wieser's . . . lost." Ludwig von Mises, *Notes and Recollections* (South Holland, Ill.: Libertarian Press, 1978), 94–5.
39 "Q: Mises personally . . . be." UCLA, 42–3.
40 "There were . . . kind." Ibid., 52.
40 "the lowest . . . life" Murray Rothbard, in Randall G. Holcombe (ed.), *15 Great Austrian Economists* (Auburn, Ala.: Ludwig von Mises Institute, 1999), 160.
40 "bohemian . . . complete nonentity." Earlene Craver, "The Emigration of the Austrian Economists," *History of Political Economy* (Spring 1986), 12–3, 2.
40–1 "perhaps most . . . generation." *KES*, 18.
41 "many areas . . . sciences." In *FH:AB*, 352.
41 "what in . . . Germany." UCLA, 11.
41 "offered a . . . tax." Jeremy Shearmur, *Hayek and After* (London: Routledge, 1996), 26–7.
41 "In general . . . laissez-faire." Richard M. Ebeling. "Ludwig von Mises and the Gold Standard," *Austrian Economics and the Political Economy of Freedom* (London: Edward Elgar, 2003), 136.
42 "Q: In economics . . . school." UCLA, 49–55.
43 "contrary to . . . interested." Ibid., 180.
43 "I have . . . Seminar." In Margit von Mises, *My Years with Ludwig von Mises* (Cedar Falls, IA: Center for Futures Eduction, 1984), 207.
43 "I wonder . . . scholars." Ibid., 203.
43–4 "after some . . . economists." Ludwig von Mises, *The Historical Setting of the Austrian School of Economics,* (New Rochelle, N.Y.: Arlington House, 1969), 41.
44 "hardly any . . . success." *CW* IV, 52.
44 "Just when . . . Dispensation'" Raimondo Cubeddu, *The Philosophy of the Austrian School* (London: Routledge, 1993), 114.
44 "Not mythical . . . courage." Ludwig von Mises, *Socialism* (Indianapolis: LibertyClassics, 1981), 540.
45 "When Socialism . . . thesis." Ibid., xix, xxi.
45–6 "had the . . . form." UCLA, 13.
46 "the product . . . country." *RS*, 1–2.
47 "In the . . . capitalism." Henry Spiegel, *The Growth of Economic Thought*, 3rd ed. (Durham, NC: Duke University Press, 1991), 538–9.
47–8 "I came . . . happening." *CW* IV, 132.
48 "more and . . . development." *Austrian Economics Newsletter* (Spring 1996), 8.

48   "the studies . . . fluctuations." *MCF,* 2.
48   "The pursuit . . . prosperity." *CW* VI, 252.
49–50 "Probably the . . . cycle." *CW* IV, 36–37.
50   "for many . . . available." Ibid., 127.
50–1 "Forty years . . . money." Ludwig von Mises, *The Theory of Money and Credit*
        (Indianapolis: Liberty Classics, 1980), 17, 248.
51   "The central . . . equilibrium" *MTTC,* 128–29.
51   "came at . . . fall . . . ']." *PP,* 69–70.
51–2 "investigations of . . . so." *MTTC,* 116, 128–29, 118.
52   "monetary or . . . involved." Ludwig von Mises, *Human Action,* 4th ed. (San
        Francisco: Fox & Wilkes, 1996), 572.
53   "One episode . . . theory." *MCF,* 2–3.
53   "individual action . . . empirical." *CW* IV, 55–56.
53   "present work . . . States." *CW* V, 8.
54   "insisted that . . . view." In Hennecke, *Hayek,* 131.
54   "The nature . . . understood." *CW* IV, 13.
54   " . . . in most . . . construction." UCLA, 176–77.
55   "had great . . . it." Ibid., 241–42.
55   "Mises as . . . designed." Mises, *Socialism,* xxiv.
55   "instead of . . . this." UCLA, 186–87.
55   "That they . . . understood." *CW* IV, 159.

CHAPTER 5

57   "the organization . . . guise." *CW* V, 39.
57–8 "[d]uring the . . . phenomenon" *MCF,* 5–6.
58   "all economic . . . fluctuations." *MTTC,* 27, 30.
58   "[f]or Hayek . . . economy." *CW* IX, 15, 31.
58–9 "[a]ll economic activity . . . of time." *MCF,* 71.
59   "My *Prices* . . . times." *MTTC,* 17–18.
59–60 "*Prices and Production . . . Production.*" Gerald O'Driscoll, *Economics as a
        Coordination Problem* (Kansas City: Sheed Andrews and McMeel, 1977),
        10.
60   "the German . . . explanations." *Studies,* 268.
60   "refute certain . . . proportion." *MTTC,* 16, 18, 46, 117, 123.
61   "It is . . . contraction." Ibid., 18–19.
61–2 "The problem . . . latter." Ibid. 43–45.
62   "Hayek assumed . . . absent." *CW* IX, 38.
62   "Money by . . . working," *PTC,* 408.
62   "Money . . . equilibrium." *CL,* 325.
62   "Our money . . . better." *CW* VI, 252.
62–3 "Although Hayek's . . . consistency." *MCF,* viii.
63   "In this . . . money." *MTTC,* 114, 118–19.
63   "While my . . . life." *CW* V, 8.
63–4 "a continuation . . . phenomena" *PP,* ix, xiii.
64   "Everything depends . . . interest." *PP,* 11, 18.
64   "The cheapness . . . resources." Eamonn Butler, *Hayek* (New York: Universe
        Books, 1983), 58.
64   "the excessive . . . order." *MCF,* 7.
64   "Is the . . . power?" *CW* V, 5.
65   "Given what . . . system . . ." *MCF,* 97, 99.

65 "of course . . . one." *MTTC*, 19–20.

65 "There is . . . prosperity." Ibid.

65–6 "[f]rom 1927 . . . good." *CW* V, 1159, 164.

66 "in that . . . liquidation." *PP*, 162.

66 "is a . . . questions." *CW* IX, 66.

66 "If prices . . . ensues." In Alan Ebenstein, *Edwin Cannan* (London: Thoemmes, 1996), 96–97.

67 "there can . . . Cassel." *MTTC*, 41.

67 "famous . . . foresight." Israel Krizner, *The Driving Force of the Market* (London: Routledge, 2000), 192.

67 "disregarding the . . . correctly." *PII*, 139.

68 "will mean . . . former." *PP*, 89.

69 "Money is . . . factors." *PTC*, 407.

69 "the book . . . profession." Brian McCormick, *Hayek and the Keynesian Avalanche* (New York: St. Martin's, 1992), 122.

69 "improve and . . . Production." *PII*, vii.

69–70 "What amount . . . destruction." Ibid. 69–71.

70 "there is . . . freedom." *RS*, 90–91.

70–1 "might lead . . . sphere." Ibid., 91.

71 "contains important . . . answered." *DM*, 108.

71 "The immediate . . . future." *MNIS*, xi, xii, xiii, 94.

72 "sustained intensity . . . thought" G. L. S. Shackle, *Business, Time and Thought* (New York: New York University Press, 1988), 179.

72 "Hayek's economic . . . student." John Hicks, *Critical Essays in Monetary Theory* (Oxford: Clarendon Press, 1967), 203.

73 "present most . . . Sowell." *CW* IV, 55.

73 "He's a genius." Hayek-North/Skousen interview.

74 "F. A. Hayek . . . justice." Thomas Sowell, *A Conflict of Visions* (New York: William Morrow, 1987), 194.

75 "it is . . . falls." *CW* IX, 212.

CHAPTER 6

77 "Whatever one . . . routes." *Studies*, 345.

77–8 "man who . . . restaurant." Ibid.

78 "endowed with . . . factors." *New Studies*, 287.

78 "I would . . . met." Lionel Robbins, *Autobiography of an Economist* (London: Macmillan, 1971), 193.

78 "cannot be . . . advice," Joseph Schumpeter, *Ten Great Economists* (London: George Allen, 1956), 274.

78 "The forces . . . birth." John Maynard Keynes, *The Economic Consequences of the Peace* (New York: Penguin, 1988), 254.

78 "Though we . . . century." *RS*, 177–8.

78 "best book." *Economist*, June 4. 1983, 17.

79 "One of . . . Reform." *HH*, 88–89.

80 "stickiness of . . . arrangements." In Robert Skidelsky, *John Maynard Keynes: The Economist as Savior 1920–1937* (New York.: Allen Lane, 1994), 155.

80 "evils to . . . be shunned." Ibid., 156.

81 "probably true . . . again." Ibid.

83 "What an . . . improvement . . ." Keynes, *Economic Consequences*, 10–12.

84 "the forces . . . exhausted." Ibid., 254.

84 "Marxian socialism . . . history." In William Ebenstein, *Great Political Thinkers,* 4th ed. (New York: Holt, Rinehart and Winston, 1969), 884.

84 "How can . . . advancement?" In Skidelsky, *Economist as Savior,* 235.

85 "I've made . . . sure." Ibid., 521.

85 "believed that . . . it" "The Road from Serfdom," *Reason* (July 1992), 29.

85 "He wanted . . . capitalism": UCLA, 121.

85 "I think . . . qualifications." *The China News,* November 14, 1975.

86 "call[ing] such . . . Theory." *New Studies,* 287.

87 "The classical . . . unemployment." John Maynard Keynes, *The General Theory of Employment, Interest, and Money* (New York: Harcourt Brace Jovanovich, 1964), 6.

CHAPTER 7

90 "I had . . . time." *HH,* 90–91.

91 "the headlong . . . recognition." *RS,* 9.

91 "The great . . . world." Harold Macmillan, *The Middle Way* (New York: Macmillan, 1938), 7–8.

92 "about the . . . way," *New Studies,* 206.

93 "Once we . . . equilibrium." *MTTC,* 87.

93 "made use . . . production." Kirzner, *Driving Force,* 183.

93–4 "Q: . . . in retrospect . . . problem." Hayek-North/Skousen interview.

94 "expounded systematically" Kirzner, *Driving Force,* 183.

95 "invariably explain . . . place." *CEP,* 88.

95–6 "Q: I'd like . . . do." UCLA, 225–7.

96 "the majority . . . object." *CW* III, 19.

96 "the innocent . . . wishes" *New Studies,* 3.

96–7 "the time . . . organization." *CW* III, 26–7.

97 "the economist . . . common." Ibid., 34.

98 "the Soviet . . . thrive" Paul Samuelson and William Nordhaus, *Economics,* 13th ed. (New York: McGraw Hill, 1989), 837.

98 "the distribution . . . problem," *CEP,* 4.

99 "the end . . . spectacles." *CH,* 8.

99 "undoubtedly constitute . . . theory." *CW* III, 150.

99 "pleasure and profit." In Eamonn Butler, *Milton Friedman* (New York: Universe Books, 1985), 25.

99–100 "Hume's analysis . . . phases. . . ." *CW* III, 151–2.

101 "Gossen, contrary . . . lower." Ibid., 365.

101 "gem of . . . economics." *CW* III, 292, 246.

101 "It appears . . . relatives." Ibid., 297.

102 "banker and . . . interest." Spiegel, *Growth of Economic Thought,* 313–14.

102 "Thornton is . . . best." Hicks, *Critical Essays,* viii.

102 "one work . . . theory." *CW* III, 190–1.

102 "existence of . . . Thornton." *PP,* 12.

102 "not too . . . theory." Ibid., 321.

102 "part he . . . circle." *Studies,* 196.

103 "task to . . . Cannan." *CL,* 415.

103 "so happened . . . tradition." Hayek-Shehadi interview.

103 "fascinating book . . . Cantillon." *CW* III, 256.

103 "'the economists' . . . treatises." Edwin Cannan, *A Review of Economic Theory* (London: Routledge/Thoemmes, 1997), 19–20.

103 "wonderful way . . . success." Edwin Cannan, *The Economic Outlook* (London: Routledge/Thoemmes, 1997), 174–75.

104 "the aims . . . exist'" *CEP,* 26.

104 "this identification . . . areas." Cannan, *Economic Outlook,* 284–85.

104 "[a]ll those . . . lives" In Alan Ebenstein, *Edwin Cannan,* 4.

104 "the teacher . . . teacher" Ibid.

104 "the leading . . . thinker" In Randall Holcombe (ed.), *15 Great Austrian Economists* (Auburn, Ala.: Ludwig von Mises Institute, 1999), 196.

104–5 "one of . . . generation." *CW* IX, 64.

105 "many of . . . topical." *Studies,* 196.

105 "the leading . . . time." Spiegel, Growth *of Economic Thought,* 725.

105 "Cannan's strong . . . economists." Denis P. O'Brien, "Edwin Cannan: Economic Theory and the History of Economic Thought," *Research in the History of Economic Thought and Methodology* (Stamford, Conn.: JAI Press, 1999), 16.

CHAPTER 8

107 "together with . . . economics." *HH,* 79.

107–8 "Q: . . . Two things . . . print." UCLA, 424–26.

108 "exercised . . . concerning foresight." *IEO,* 34.

108–9 "It is . . . elsewhere." In Hans Jörg Hennecke, *Friedrich August von Hayek: Die Tradition der Frieheit* (Dusseldorf, Germany: Verlag Wirtschaft und Finanzen, 2001), 156.

109 "The link . . . cares." Friedrich Hayek, "Freedom and the Economic System," *Contemporary Review* (April 1938), 434

109–10 "What is . . . progress." Ibid., 441–42.

111–2 "'The generation . . . affairs.'" *RS,* 21.

112 "advance sketch" *LLL* III, 196.

112 "assembled in . . . bombs." Friedrich Hayek, *The Counter-Revolution of Science* (Indianapolis: Liberty Press, 1979), 9.

112 "preliminary results" Ibid., 10.

112–3 "first thing . . . comprehend." *IEO,* 6.

113 "False individualism . . . legislator.'" Ibid., 8.

114 "I propose . . . commands." Ibid., 1.

114 "True individualism . . . groups." Ibid., 23.

114 "In framing . . . itself." James Madison, *The Federalist,* no. 51.

CHAPTER 9

117 "light burden . . . before." *HH,* 99.

117 "political book . . . affairs," *RS,* v.

117–8 "spite of . . . work." Ibid., vii-ix.

118 "unexpectedly . . . proper." Ibid., vii.

119 "Nothing distinguishes . . . knowledge." Ibid., 54.

119 "under the . . . possible." Ibid.

119 "important question . . . plans." Ibid., 89.

120 "while it . . . action." *Studies,* 18.

120 "Arguments both . . . actions." *HH,* 28.

120 "most likely . . . them." *RS,* 83.

120 "overview of . . . Serfdom." Hayek, *Counter-Revolution of Science* (1979), 11.

120 "Friedrich A. . . . generation." In *FH:AB*, 134.

121 "really excellent . . . remarkable." Ibid., 353.

121 "has had . . . Britain." Ibid.

121 "news of . . . dicta." Ibid., 354.

123 "very intelligent" Friedman-Ebenstein interview.

123 "Now I . . . again," Larry Hayek-Ebenstein interview.

124 "behaved in . . . successor." In *FH:AB*, 155.

124–5 "Q: . . . I want . . . again." UCLA, 394–96.

125 "miserable business." Coase-Ebenstein interview.

126 "I am . . . husband." Helene Hayek statement to author.

CHAPTER 10

128 "Nearly sixty . . . *Sensations.*" In Walter Weimer and David Palermo (eds.), *Cognition and the Symbolic Processes* (Hillsdale, N.J.: Lawrence Erlbaum, 1982), 287.

128 "one and . . . science." Ernst Mach, *The Analysis of Sensations* (New York: Dover, 1959), xxxviii.

129 "Cf. L. Wittgenstein . . . it.'" *Studies,* 45.

130 "[t]he meaning . . . verification." In D. J. O'Connor, *A Critical History of Western Philosophy* (New York: The Free Press, 1964), 497.

130 "conclusive justification . . . statement." In *FH:AB*, 271.

130 "I do . . . true." *CL,* 64.

130 "What struck . . . himself." *CW* IV, 177.

131 "what can . . . silence." Ludwig Wittgenstein, *Tractatus Logico-Philosophicus* (London: Routledge, 1998), 3.

131 "account of . . . experience." *SO,* 165.

132 "In brief . . . phenomena." Ibid., xviii.

132 "While at . . . inside." *IEO,* 76.

132 "place where . . . synthetic." *C-RS,* 38–39.

132–3 "should not . . . all." *Studies,* 34.

133 "the Napoleonic . . . themselves," *C-RS,* 70.

133 "Q: . . . I think . . . essentially." UCLA, 256.

133–4 "Positivism, from . . . community." Mark Notturno, "Popper's Critique of Scientific Socialism . . . ," *Philosophy of the Social Sciences* (March 1999), 53, 51.

134 "the letter . . . Circle." Joseph Agassi, "To Salvage Neurath," *Philosophy of the Social Sciences* (March 1998), 99.

134–5 "A: . . . Vienna is . . . Yes." Hayek-North/Skousen interview.

135 "From the . . . justification." *SO,* 191.

137 "Basically, I . . . feeling." Weimer and Palermo, *Cognition,* 323.

138 "Friedrich Hayek . . . psychology." G. R. Steele, "Hayek's Sensory Order," *Theory & Psychology* (2002), 387.

138 "been tremendous . . . psychology." In Fritz Machlup (ed.), *Essays on Hayek* (New York: New York University Press, 1976), xxi.

138 "there is . . . philosophy." G. R. Steele, *The Economics of Friedrich Hayek* (London: Macmillan, 1996), xii.

CHAPTER 11

139–40 "Q: How would . . . position." Friedman-Ebenstein interview.

140–1 "big methodological . . . Chicago." Ibid.

141 "these twelve . . . me." Hayek 1962 talk on leaving Chicago, CCAC.
141 "I'm beginning . . . do." In Hennecke, *Hayek,* 255.
143 "In the . . . developments." *CL,* 112–13.
143 "impossible to . . . them.'" Ibid.
144 "known when . . . it." *LLL* I, 3.
144 "I then . . . person." Ibid.
144 "picture an . . . practice." *CL,* v.
144 "meant to . . . enthusiasm." Ibid., 6.
144 "my later . . . introduction." *RS,* viii.
144 "a man . . . forward . . ." *CL,* v-vi.
144–5 "Freedom . . . others." Ibid., 11–22.
145 "We are . . . coercion." Ibid., 11.
145 "Free society . . . others." Ibid., 21.
146 "The modern . . . nature," Leo Strauss, *Spinoza's Critique of Religion* (Chicago: University of Chicago Press, 1997), 15.
146 "Be fruitful . . . it . . ." Genesis 1:28.
146 "classical argument . . . action." *CL,* 220.
146 "permanent . . . possible." Ibid., 222.
146 "absolutely essential . . . line." UCLA, 457–58.
147 "'The end . . . own.'" *CL,* 162.
147 "Nothing distinguishes . . . Law," *RS,* 54.
147–8 "meaning of . . . 'freedom.'" *CL,* 12.
148 "There were . . . coercion." Ibid., 19–20.
148 "'three fundamental . . . promises.'" Ibid., 158.
148 "defining mark . . . autonomy." Robert Paul Wolff, *In Defense of Anarchism* (New York: Harper & Row, 1976), 18, 40.
149 "specificity and . . . abstractness." *CL,* 151.
149 "We are . . . others." Ibid., 140.
149 "recognition of . . . coercion." Ibid.
149 "'a people . . . freedom.'" Ibid.
149 "the conditions . . . sphere." Ibid.
151 " . . . sanitation or . . . effort . . ." Ibid., 141.
151 " . . . the non-coercive . . . infirm . . ." Ibid., 144.
151 " . . . activities which . . . education." Ibid., 223.
151 " . . . services which . . . cities." Ibid., 223.
151 "The effect . . . likes." Ibid., 229.
151 "the enforcement . . . buildings . . ." Ibid., 225.
151 "that the . . . disputed." Ibid., 217.
151 "So far . . . qualifications." Ibid., 227.
151–2 " . . . a free . . . legislation.'" Ibid., 224–25.
152 "The range . . . considerable." Ibid., 231.
152 "at all . . . own." Ibid., 395.
152–3 "a fear . . . nationalism," Ibid., 399–401, 405.
153 "In the . . . privilege." *Studies,* 222.
153–4 "Let me . . . move." *CL,* 398.
154 "I find . . . facts." Ibid., 404–5.
154 "characteristic conservative . . . it." Ibid., 404.
154 "used to . . . century." *EH,* lx.
155 "I have . . . discipline." *CL,* 3.
155 "a selection . . . answer." *Studies,* vii.
155 "nobody can . . . danger." Ibid., 123.

155 "I do . . . qualify." *CW* IX, 63.

CHAPTER 12

157 "magnificent wealth . . . economics." In *FH:AB,* 378.
157 "parts of . . . faultless." Ibid., 228.
157 "The central . . . Marx." *PP,* 101, 103.
158 "Capitalism . . . rest." *FC:E,* 124, 7.
158–9 "The object . . . others." Mill, *On Liberty,* Introduction.
159 "The only . . . others." Ibid.
159 "There is . . . others?" Lionel Robbins, "Hayek on Liberty," *Economica* (February 1961), 68.
159–60 "This is . . . liberty." *LLL* I, 170, 101.
160 "Q: . . . Let me . . . position." "Economics, Politics, and Freedom," *Reason* (February 1975), 9–10.
161 "Mrs. Hayek . . . scholars." HA 116.10.
161 "the culturally . . . Freud." *LLL* III, 174–76.
161–2 "permissiveness and . . . -culture" "The Fatal Conceit" draft, CCAC.

CHAPTER 13

163 "In the . . . 1990s." Daniel Yergin and Joseph Stanislaw, *The Commanding Heights* (New York: Simon and Schuster, 1998), 14–15.
164 "a sense . . . other." In *FH:AB,* 371–2.
164 "In the . . . socialist" George Stigler, *Memoirs of an Unregulated Economist* (New York: Basic Books, 1988), 148–49.
164–5 "not until . . . Chicago." In Don Patinkin, *Essays On and In the Chicago Tradition* (Durham, N.C.: Duke University Press, 1981), 266.
165 "writings and . . . 'school.'" In Henry Simons, *Economic Policy for a Free Society* (Chicago: University of Chicago Press, 1948), v.
165 "group . . . students." *Studies,* 198.
165 "always more . . . counterpart." Ross Emmett, preliminary draft of "Evolution and Human Beings: Frank H. Knight on Cultural Evolution and the Defense of a Free Enterprise Society" (2001), 7.
165 "If I . . . Cannan; . . ." *CL,* 415.
166 "introduced me . . . view," Milton and Rose Friedman, *Two Lucky People* (Chicago: University of Chicago Press, 1998), 32.
166 "There was . . . years." Stigler, *Memoirs,* 148.
166 "merely sketched . . . Friedman." George Stigler, "Comment," *Journal of Political Economy* (February 1962), 71.
167 "Hayek's influence . . . great." Friedman-Ebenstein interview.
167 "When the . . . campuses . . ." *New Individualist Review* (Indianapolis: Liberty Fund, 1981), ix-x; as modified by Friedman in February 18, 2003 letter to author.
167–8 "The *Review* . . . tradition." Ibid., xii-xiii.
168 "Two . . . War." Ibid., xiii.
168 "A second . . . it." *The Essence of Friedman* (Stanford, Calif.: Hoover Institution Press, 1987), 363.
168 "The crucial . . . Society.' . . ." Ibid., 22.
168 "made it . . . influence." In Friedrich Hayek, *The Road to Serfdom,* Fiftieth Anniversary Edition (Chicago: University of Chicago Press, 1994), ix-x.

168–9 "The thing . . . indeed." HA 114–13.
170 "Adam Smith . . . view." In Annelise Anderson and Dennis L. Bark (eds.), *Thinking About America* (Stanford, Calif.: Hoover Institution Press, 1988), 456, 459, 463.
170 "We are . . . gone." Milton Friedman, Hayek obituary, *National Review* (April 27, 1992), 35.

CHAPTER 14

171 "very great . . . world" Hayek 1962 Chicago event comments, CCAC.
171 "satisfactory execution . . . studies." Hayek, *Counter-Revolution of Science* (1979), 10.
171–2 "It was . . . scientific. . . ." UCLA, 18–19.
172 "*despite* Hayek's . . . Popper," Bruce Caldwell, "Reply to Hutchison," *Research in the History of Economic Thought and Methodology* (1992), 38.
172 "when his . . . matters." UCLA, 236, 20.
172–3 "Readers of . . . many. . . ." *Studies,* viii.
173 "The conception . . . points." Ibid., 4.
173 "connected variables . . . factors." Ibid., 3–4.
173–4 "Its basic . . . prediction.'" Ibid., 4, 9.
174 "not as . . . expect." Ibid., 9, 11.
174 "Economics tells . . . aims." Ibid., 17.
174 "we shall . . . control." Ibid., 18.
174 "individual . . . reach." Ibid., 34.
175 "Socratic maxim . . . society." *CL,* 22.
175 "correct method . . . one." Wittgenstein, *Tractatus,* 73–74.
176 "fundamental fact . . . attention." *CL,* 22.

CHAPTER 15

178 "he [i.e. . . . work." Michael T. Kaufman, *Soros* (New York: Alfred A. Knopf, 2002), 71.
178 "borrowed from . . . philosophy." Malachi Haim Hacohen, *Karl Popper* (Cambridge University Press, 2000), 276.
178 "Of course . . . non-science." Karl Popper, *Objective Knowledge* (Oxford: Clarendon Press, 1979), 1.
178 "You will . . . shall." In Hennecke, *Hayek,* 170; Hacohen, *Popper,* 501.
179 "Our intellectual . . . Karl" HA 2–6.
179 "I have . . . good." In Hacohen, *Popper,* 502.
179 "become a . . . philosophy." Ibid.
179 "By Hacohen's . . . view." David Papineau, *New York Times Book Review* (November 12, 2000), 28.
180 "Popper translated . . . propaganda." Hacohen, *Popper,* 405.
180 "very bad . . . positivism" In Ian Jarvie and Sandra Pralong (eds.), *Popper's Open Society after 50 Years* (London: Routledge, 1999), 7.
180–1 "impudent, dilettantish . . . scandal," Ibid.
181 "I thank . . . book." In Notturno, "Popper's Critique," 41.
181 "Just to . . . read'!" *RS,* vii
181–2 "I should . . . liberals." In Notturno, "Popper's Critique," 57.
182 "Hayek had . . . socialism." Ibid., 486.
182 "I do . . . reach." Ibid., 501.

182   "I think . . . Tarski," Ibid., 486.
183   "your remark . . . problems." Hennecke, *Hayek*, 172.
183   "a joke" Gombrich-Ebenstein interview.
183   "I am . . . School," Hacohen, *Popper*, 496.
184   "I regard . . . unnoticed." *Times Literary Supplement* (December 5, 1975), 1462.
184   "I may . . . book." In Hennecke, *Hayek*, 302.
184   "Although this . . . Serfdom." Karl Popper, *All Life is Problem Solving* (London: Routledge, 1999), 155.
184–5 "Hayek's openmindedness . . . was." Popper comments at September 23, 1992, memorial meeting in honor of Hayek at London School of Economics.

CHAPTER 16

187   "more original." *LLL* III, xiii.
188   "It is . . . gaps" Ibid., xii-xiii.
188–9 "preservation of . . . interests." Ibid., 2.
189   "I know . . . topic." LLL preliminary preface, CCAC.
189   "strong influence . . . live," Ibid.
189   "The reader . . . means." *LLL* III, xiii.
189   "Are you . . . direction." *HH*, 155.
190–1 "two ways . . . others." *LLL* I, 8–9.
191   "holds that . . . purposes." Ibid.
191   "the fragmentation . . . rests." Ibid., 14.
191–2 "All valid . . . it." *LLL* II, 24.
192   "although we . . . whole. . . ." *CL* 63, 69–70.
192   "Through contact . . . beings." Brian Barry, *Theories of Justice* (Berkeley: University of California Press, 1989), 3.
192   "Organization thinking . . . lines." *LLL* II, 105.
192   "worth of . . . banish." John Stuart Mill, *On Liberty* (1859), fifth chapter.
193   "the unalterable . . . mind." *LLL* I, 49.
194   "Look at . . . capacities." Ayn Rand, *The Fountainhead* (New York: Signet, 1971), 281–2.
195   "directed attention . . . State." In *FH:AB*, 202.
195–6 "strict limitation . . . taxation." *New Studies*, 144.
196   "sounds almost . . . admissible." In *FH:AB*, 381.
196   "Side by . . . action." Lionel Robbins, "Hayek on Liberty," *Economica* (February 1961), 78.
197   "Nobody . . . alter." *LLL* I, 73.
197   "body of . . . legislation." Ibid., 83.
197   "conception of . . . accepted." *CL*, 148, 162–63.
198   "even less . . . sacrilegious." *LLL* I, 82.
198   "Ideally the . . . amendment." *LLL* III, 123–24.
198   "'a rule . . . universal.'" *CL*, 173.
198   "Then [after . . . them." Plato (Thomas Pangle, trans.), *The Laws of Plato* (New York: Basic Books, 1980), 160.
199   "By calling . . . legislatures." *LLL* III 22, 4.
199   "The very . . . time." Leland Yeager, "Reason and Cultural Evolution," *Critical Review* (Spring 1989), 330.
199   "Hayek is . . . untenable?'" William Bartley, *Social Science Quarterly* (June 1990), 410.

199–200 "Reason undoubtedly . . . it." *CL,* 69.
   200 "not maintain . . . it." *LLL* II, 25.
   200 "the same . . . expression." *LLL* III, 204.
   201 "The only . . . engineering." Karl Popper, The Open Society, vol. II (London: Routledge, 1980), 222.
   201 "The term . . . sciences." Karl Popper, *The Poverty of Historicism* (London: Routledge, 1994), 58.
   201 "Francis Bacon . . . road." William Ebenstein and Alan Ebenstein, *Great Political Thinkers,* 5th ed. (Fort Worth, Tex.: Holt, Rinehart and Winston, 1990), 15.
   202 "[t]he constructivist . . . 'utilitarianism.'" *LLL* II, 17.
   202 "Which expectations . . . whole." *LLL* I, 103.
   202 "Every change . . . fulfilled." *LLL* II, 106.
   202 "Policy need . . . run." Ibid., 115.
   202 *"The Good . . . possible" LLL* II, 132.
   202 "What it . . . be." Ibid., 113.
   203 "It is . . . men." Ibid., 155.
   203 "A: I've become . . . answered." UCLA, 415–16.
203–4 "It can . . . borne." *LLL* III, 149.
   204 "Any governmental . . . money." Ibid., 147.

CHAPTER 17

   205 "proposal of . . . unmistakable. . . ." *LLL* III, xiii.
   205 "[t]ogether with . . . us." Ibid., xiii-xiv.
205–6 "lead to . . . institutions," *DM,* 84.
   206 "found in . . . activity." Vera Smith, *The Rationale of Central Banking* (Indianapolis: Liberty Press, 1990), 167.
   207 "It may . . . unstable." *New Studies,* 220.
   207 "somewhat startling suggestion" *DM,* 13.
   207 "happy reversal . . . law," In *FH:AB,* 282.
   207 "For years . . . reality." Benjamin Cohen, "Electronic Money: New Day or False Dawn?" *Review of International Political Economy* (Summer 2001), 221.
   207 "An august . . . tomorrow.'" *DM,* 12.
   208 "e-money's main . . . attenuated." Cohen, "Electronic Money," 215.
   208 "some of . . . do." CCAC.
   208 "foray into . . . terrain." *DM,* 13.
   208 "'an inflationary . . . circulation.'" Ibid., 79.
   209 "chief defect . . . causes." Ibid., 80.
209–10 "He is . . . attempt." Frank Johnson, "The Facts of Hayek," *Daily Telegraph Magazine* (September 26, 1975), 30.
   210 "Contrary to . . . emotion." Arnold Plant, *Selected Essays and Addresses* (London: Routledge and Kegan Paul, 1974), 173.

CHAPTER 18

   211 "found it . . . further." *LLL* III, xi.
   211 "process of . . . practices." Ibid., 154.
   212 "began the . . . truth." William Bartley, *Unfathomed Knowledge, Unmeasured Wealth* (La Salle, Ill.: Open Court, 1990), 154.

212 "pleaded with . . . descent." William Bartley, *Wittgenstein,* 2nd ed. (La Salle, Ill.: Open Court, 1994), 198.

213–4 "My interest . . . detail. . . ." William Bartley, "Hayek's Collected Works: Background," *Institute Scholar* (Winter 1988), 1–2.

214 "initial impulse . . . produced." *CW* VI, ix.

215–6 "we ought . . . idea." *LLL* III, 152, 196.

216 "I should . . . systematic" Hayek, *Counter-Revolution of Science* (1979), 12.

216 "attempted final . . . opinion." Friedrich Hayek, "The Fatal Conceit" introduction draft, CCAC.

216–7 "left some . . . civilization," Ibid.

217 "the main . . . utilised." *FC:E,* 7.

217–8 "This is . . . State" Contents draft in the possession of Larry Hayek.

219 "made use . . . Knowledge.'" In Kirzner, *Driving Force,* 183–84.

220 "when thirty-six . . . justice.'" CCAC.

220 "It may . . . now." 1981 Nobel laureate circular, CCAC.

221 "'The most . . . inhabitants.'" *FC,* 120.

221 "frightening rate" *CL,* 53.

221 "even if . . . lives." *FC:E,* 132.

221 "The size . . . capital." Ibid., 124.

222 "The further . . . knowledge." Menger, *Principles,* 73–74.

223 "when not . . . thought." *EH,* xxix.

225 "fallibilist" William Bartley, *Unfathomed Knowledge,* 28.

225 "evolutionary epistemology" Gerhard Radnitzky and William Bartley (eds.), *Evolutionary Epistemology, Rationality, and the Sociology of Knowledge* (La Salle, Ill.: Open Court, 1993), 433.

225 "I suggest . . . epistemology," *FC:E,* 10.

226 "The subject . . . depends . . ." "The Fatal Conceit" introduction draft, CCAC.

226 "This book . . . depends . . ." *FC:E,* 6.

226 "Socialism gravely . . . mankind." "The Fatal Conceit" introduction draft, CCAC.

226 "Surprising and . . . reason" *FC:E,* 10.

227 "Professor W. W. Bartley . . . pubishers," Ibid., 5.

227 "is fresh . . . hand" Ibid., xii.

227 "I believe . . . Mistake?" *KES,* 37.

227 "Perhaps what . . . alive. . . ." *FC:E,* 140.

227 "interpretive puzzles . . . book," Bruce Caldwell, "Popper and Hayek: Who Influenced Whom?," paper presented at Karl Popper 2002 conference (July 6, 2002), 4.

227–8 "comparison between . . . mind." Bruce Caldwell, "The Emergence of Hayek's Ideas on Cultural Evolution," *Review of Austrian Economics* (February 2000), 19.

228 "Bartley was . . . product." Peter Boettke, "Which Enlightenment, Whose Liberalism?: Hayek's Research Program for Understanding the Liberal Soceity," Internet article, 24.

228 "I have . . . scholars." Jerry Muller, "Chapter 12. The Untimely Liberalism of Friedrich Hayek," Internet version of Hayek chapter, 68.

228 "the addition . . . one." Caldwell, "Popper and Hayek," 16–7.

228–9 "In 1986 . . . met." Jeffrey Friedman, "What's Wrong with Libertarianism?" Critical Review (Summer 1998), 463.

229 "Q: On The . . . best." Friedman-Ebenstein interview.

229–30 "In August . . . book." In Caldwell, "The Emergence of Hayek's Ideas," 17.

230 "The work . . . preparation." James Buchanan, "I Did Not Call Him 'Fritz': Personal Recollections of Professor F. A. v. Hayek," *Constitutional Political Economy* (vol. 3, no. 2, 1992), 133.

230–1 "Friedrich Hayek . . . evolution." "Why Socialism Will Never Work," *Economist* (January 28, 1989), 85.

231 "repetitive, poorly . . . Liberty." David Miller, "The Fatalistic Conceit," *Critical Review* (Spring 1989), 310.

231 "*was* careful . . . another." Arthur Seldon, "Hayek on Capitalism and Socialism," *Economic Affairs* (June 1989), 42.

231 "Hayek develops . . . depth." Terence Hutchison, *Economic Journal* (September 1989), 893.

231 "While some . . . tradition." Lawrence Conlin, *American Political Science Review* (June 1990), 632.

231 "which will . . . was." Christopher Nock, *Canadian Journal of Political Science* (March 1990), 181.

231 "Although this . . . contributions." Ian Steadman, *Manchester School of Economic and Social Studies* (December 1990), 432.

232 "Bartley had spent so much time and effort on it." Charlotte Cubitt correspondence to author (July 8, 1996).

CHAPTER 19

233 "the present . . . empirical." *CW* IV, 55–56.
233 "I have . . . country." Larry Hayek-Ebenstein interview.
234 "the ultimate . . . this." In *FH:AB*, 316.
234 "Q: Professor Hayek . . . any!'" *KES*, 56–57.
234 "planned evolution . . . itself." *EH*, 318.
234 "The two . . . family." Ibid., 321.
235 "In gratitude . . . Hayek." CCAC
235 "by 1989 . . . affairs . . ." Lord Harris, "Obituary: Hayek's Life and Times," *Economic Affairs* (June 1992), 21.
235 "The ideas . . . back." Keynes, *General Theory*, 383.

CONCLUSION

237–8 "In 1936 . . . succinctly." Martin J. Anderson (ed.), *The Unfinished Agenda* (London: Institute of Economic Affairs, 1986), 143–44.
238 "The dispute . . . rest." *FC:E*, 7.
238 "The main . . . mistakes." Ibid.
239 "No one . . . effort." John Stuart Mill, *Utilitarianism* (1861), chapter 2.
241 " . . . the skills . . . do." Bruce Caldwell, "The Emergence of Hayek's Ideas on Cultural Evolution," *Review of Austrian Economics* (Feb. 2000), 13.
241 "Life has . . . itself," *FC:E*, 133.
243 "At this . . . place." Anderson, *Unfinished Agenda*, 149.
243 "At this . . . us." *CL*, 53.

Index

of Names in the Main Text and Bibliographical Essay